SKETCHES OF JEWISH SOCIAL LIFE

by
Alfred Edersheim

Sketches of
JEWISH SOCIAL LIFE

Updated Edition

ALFRED EDERSHEIM

HENDRICKSON
PUBLISHERS

Copyright © 1994 by Hendrickson Publishers, Inc.
P.O. Box 3473
Peabody, Massachusetts 01961-3473

Printed in the United States of America

Hardcover edition: ISBN 1-56563-138-2
Paperback edition: ISBN 1-56563-005-X

Second printing—May 1995

Scripture citations taken from the HOLY BIBLE, NEW INTERNATIONAL
VERSION. Copyright © 1973, 1978, 1994 International Bible Society. Used
by permission of Zondervan Bible Publishers.

CONTENTS

PREFACE

The object of this volume is kindred to that of my previous book on *The Temple, its Ministry and Services as they were at the Time of Jesus Christ.* In both I have wished to transport the reader into the land of Palestine at the time of our Lord and of His apostles, and to show him, so far as lay within the scope of each book, as it were, the scene on which, and the persons among whom the events recorded in New Testament history had taken place. For I believe, that in measure as we realise its surroundings—so to speak, see and hear for ourselves what passed at the time, enter into its ideas, become familiar with its habits, modes of thinking, its teaching and worship—shall we not only understand many of the expressions and allusions in the New Testament, but also gain fresh evidence of the truth of its history alike from its faithfulness to the picture of society, such as we know it to have been, and from the contrast of its teaching and aims to those of the contemporaries of our Lord.

For, a careful study of the period leaves this conviction on the mind: that—with reverence be it said—Jesus Christ was strictly of His time, and that the New Testament is, in its narratives, language, and allusions, strictly true to the period and circumstances in which its events are laid. But in another, and far more important, aspect there is no similarity between Christ and His period. "Never man"—of that, or any subsequent period—"spake like this man;" never man lived or died as He. Assuredly, if He was the Son of David, He also is the Son of God, the Saviour of the world.

In my book on *The Temple, its Ministry and Services,* I endeavoured to carry the reader with me into the Sanctuary, and to make him witness all connected with its institutions, its priesthood, and its solemnities. In this book I have sought to take him into ordinary civil society, and to make him mingle with the men and women of that period, see them in their homes and families, learn their habits and manners, and follow them in their ordinary life—all, as illustrative of New Testament history; at the same time endeavouring to present in a popular form the scenes witnessed.

Another, and perhaps the most important part in its bearing on Christianity, yet remains to be done: to trace the progress of religious thought—as regards the canon of Scripture, the Messiah, the law, sin, and salvation—to describe the character of theological literature, and to show the state of doctrinal belief at the time of our Lord. It is here especially that we should see alike the kinship in form and the almost contrast in substance between what Judaism was at the time of Christ, and the teaching and the kingdom of our Blessed Lord. But this lay quite outside the scope of the present volume, and belongs to a larger work for which this and my previous book may, in a sense, be regarded as forestudies. Accordingly, where civil society touched, as on so many points it does, on the theological and the doctrinal, it was only possible to "sketch" it, leaving the outlines to be filled up. To give a complete representation of the times of our Lord, in *all* their bearings—to show not only who they were among whom Jesus Christ moved, but what they knew, thought, and believed—and this as the frame, so to speak, in which to set as a picture the life of our Blessed Lord Himself, such must now be the work, to which, with all prayerful reverence and with most earnest study, I shall henceforth set myself.

It seemed needful to state this, in order to explain both the plan of this book and the manner of its treatment. I will only add, that it embodies the results of many years' study, in which I have availed myself of every help within my reach. It might seem affectation, were I to enumerate the names of all the authorities consulted or books read in the course of these studies. Those mentioned in the foot-notes constitute but a very small proportion of them.

Throughout, my constant object has been to illustrate the New Testament history and teaching. Even the "Scripture Index" at the close will show in how many instances this has been attempted. Most earnestly then do I hope, that these pages may be found to cast some additional light on the New Testament, and that they will convey fresh evidence—to my mind of the strongest kind—and in a new direction, of the truth "of those things which are most surely believed among us." And now it only remains at the close of these investigations once more to express my own full and joyous belief in that grand truth to which all leads up—that "CHRIST IS THE END OF THE LAW FOR RIGHTEOUSNESS TO EVERY ONE THAT BELIEVETH."

Alfred Edersheim.

The Vicarage, Loders, Bridport: November, 1876.

1

PALESTINE
EIGHTEEN CENTURIES AGO

Eighteen and a half centuries ago, and the land which now lies desolate—its bare, grey hills looking into ill-tilled or neglected valleys, its timber cut down, its olive- and vine-clad terraces crumbled into dust, its villages stricken with poverty and squalor, its thoroughfares insecure and deserted, its native population well-nigh gone, and with them its industry, wealth, and strength—presented a scene of beauty, richness, and busy life almost unsurpassed in the then known world. The Rabbis never weary of its praises, whether their theme be the physical or the moral pre-eminence of Palestine. It happened, so writes one of the oldest Hebrew commentaries,[1] that Rabbi Jonathan was sitting under a fig-tree, surrounded by his students. Of a sudden he noticed how the ripe fruit overhead, bursting for richness, dropped its luscious juice on the ground, while at a little distance the distended udder of a she-goat was no longer able to hold the milk. "Behold," exclaimed the Rabbi, as the two streams mingled, "the literal fulfilment of the promise: 'a land flowing with milk and honey.'" "The land of Israel is not lacking in any product whatever," argued Rabbi Meir, "as it is written (Deut. 8:9): 'Thou shalt not lack anything in it.'"[2] Nor were such statements unwarranted; for Palestine combined every variety of climate, from the snows of Hermon and the

For the LORD your God is bringing you into a good land—a land with streams and pools of water, with springs flowing in the valleys and hills; a land with wheat and barley, vines and fig trees, pomegranates, olive oil and honey; a land where bread will not be scarce and you will lack nothing (Deut. 8:7–9a).

---

[1] See Hamburger, *Real-Enc. d. Judenth.* i. p. 816, note 37.

[2] In discussing the lawfulness of a peppercorn on the Day of Atonement. *Yoma,* 91 *b,* towards the end.

The Mount of Olives

cool of Lebanon to the genial warmth of the Lake of Galilee and the tropical heat of the Jordan valley. Accordingly not only the fruit trees, the grain, and garden produce known in our colder latitudes were found in the land, along with those of sunnier climes, but also the rare spices and perfumes of the hottest zones. Similarly, it is said, every kind of fish teemed in its waters, while birds of most gorgeous plumage filled the air with their song.[3] Within such small compass the country must have been unequalled for charm and variety. On the eastern side of Jordan stretched wide plains, upland valleys, park-like forests, and almost boundless corn and pasture lands; on the western side were terraced hills, covered with olives and vines, delicious glens, in which sweet springs murmured, and fairy-like beauty and busy life, as around the Lake of Galilee. In the distance stretched the wide sea, dotted with spreading sails;

---

[3] Detailed references are here, of course, impossible; but compare, for example, the accounts of so careful and able a naturalist as Canon Tristram.

here was luxurious richness, as in the ancient possessions of Issachar, Manasseh, and Ephraim; and there,
beyond these plains and valleys, the highland scenery
of Judah, shelving down through the pasture tracts
of the Negev, or South country, into the great and
terrible wilderness. And over all, so long as God's
blessing lasted, were peace and plenty. Far as the eye
could reach, browsed "the cattle on a thousand hills;"
the pastures were "clothed with flocks, the valleys also
covered over with corn;" and the land, "greatly
enriched with the river of God," seemed to "shout for
joy," and "also to sing." Such a possession, heaven-
given at the first and heaven-guarded throughout,
might well kindle the deepest enthusiasm.

The grasslands of the desert overflow; the hills are clothed with gladness. The meadows are covered with flocks and the valleys are mantled with grain; they shout for joy and sing (Ps. 65:12–13).

"We find," writes one of the most learned
Rabbinical commentators, supporting each assertion
by a reference to Scripture,[4] "that thirteen things are
in the sole ownership of the Holy One, blessed be His
Name! and these are they: the silver, the gold, the
priesthood, Israel, the first-born, the altar, the first-
fruits, the anointing oil, the tabernacle of meeting,
the kingship of the house of David, the sacrifices, the
land of Israel, and the eldership." In truth, fair as the
land was, its conjunction with higher spiritual blessings gave it its real and highest value. "Only in
Palestine does the *Shechinah* manifest itself," taught
the Rabbis. Outside its sacred boundaries no such
revelation was possible.[5] It was there that rapt
prophets had seen their visions, and psalmists caught
strains of heavenly hymns. Palestine was the land that
had Jerusalem for its capital, and on its highest hill
that temple of snowy marble and glittering gold for a
sanctuary, around which clustered such precious
memories, hallowed thoughts, and glorious, wide-
reaching hopes. There is no religion so strictly local as
that of Israel. Heathenism was indeed the worship of
national deities, and Judaism that of Jehovah, the

---

[4] *R. Bechai.* The Scripture references are: Hagg. 2:8; Exod. 29:1; Num. 3:13; Lev. 25:55; Exod. 20:24; Exod. 25:2; Exod. 30:31; Exod. 25:8; Num. 28:2; 1 Sam. 16:1; Lev. 25:23. Comp. Relandi, *Palaest.* (ed. 1716), p. 14.

[5] See, for example, the discussion in *Mechilta* on Exod. 12:1.

They will know that I am the LORD, when I disperse them among the nations and scatter them through the countries (Ezek. 12:15).

Herod's Temple at Jerusalem

God of heaven and earth. But the national deities of the heathen might be transported, and their rites adapted to foreign manners. On the other hand, while Christianity was from the first *universal* in its character and design, the religious institutions and the worship of the Pentateuch, and even the prospects opened by the prophets were, *so far as they concerned Israel,* strictly *of* Palestine and *for* Palestine. They are wholly incompatible with the permanent loss of the land. An extra-Palestinian Judaism, without priesthood, altar, temple, sacrifices, tithes, first-fruits, Sabbatical and Jubilee years, must first set aside the Pentateuch, unless, as in Christianity, all these be regarded as blossoms designed to ripen into fruit, as types pointing to, and fulfilled in higher realities.[6] Outside the land even the people are no

---

[6] This is not the place to explain what substitution Rabbinism proposed for sacrifices, etc. I am well aware that modern Judaism tries to prove by such passages as 1 Sam. 15:22; Ps. 51:16, 17; Isa. 1:11–13; Hos. 6:6, that, in the view of the prophets, sacrifices, and with them all the ritual institutions of the Pentateuch, were of no permanent importance. To the unprejudiced reader it seems difficult to understand how even party-spirit could draw such sweeping conclusions from such premises, or how it could ever be imagined that the prophets had intended by their teaching, not to explain or apply, but to set aside the law so solemnly given on Sinai. However, the device is not new. A solitary voice ventured even in the second century on the suggestion that the sacrificial worship had been intended only by way of accommodation, to preserve Israel from lapsing into heathen rites!

longer Israel: in view of the Gentiles they are Jews; in their own view, "the dispersed abroad."

All this the Rabbis could not fail to perceive. Accordingly when, immediately after the destruction of Jerusalem by Titus, they set themselves to reconstruct their broken commonwealth, it was on a new basis indeed, but still within Palestine. Palestine was the Mount Sinai of Rabbinism. Here rose the spring of the *Halachah,* or traditional law, whence it flowed in ever-widening streams; here, for the first centuries, the learning, the influence, and the rule of Judaism centered; and there they would fain have perpetuated it. The first attempts at rivalry by the Babylonian schools of Jewish learning were keenly resented and sharply put down.[7] Only the force of circumstances drove the Rabbis afterwards voluntarily to seek safety and freedom in the ancient seats of their captivity, where, politically unmolested, they could give the final development to their system. It was this desire to preserve the nation and its learning in Palestine which inspired such sentiments as we are about to quote. "The very air of Palestine makes one wise," said the Rabbis. The Scriptural account of the borderland of Paradise, watered by the river Havilah, of which it is said that "the gold of that land is good," was applied to their earthly Eden, and paraphrased to mean, "there is no learning like that of Palestine." It was a saying, that "to live in Palestine was equal to the observance of all the commandments." "He that hath his permanent abode in Palestine," so taught the Talmud, "is sure of the life to come." "Three things," we read in another authority, "are Israel's through suffering: Palestine, traditional lore, and the world to come." Nor did this feeling abate with the desolation of their country. In the third and fourth centuries of our era they still taught, "He that dwelleth in Palestine is without sin."

Centuries of wandering and of changes have not torn the passionate love of this land from the heart of

Book of the Law

---

[7]See my *History of the Jewish Nation,* pp. 247, 248.

*Now the LORD was
gracious to Sarah as he
had said, and the LORD
did for Sarah what he
had promised...Sarah
said, "God has brought me
laughter, and everyone who
hears about this will laugh
with me" (Gen. 21:1, 6).*

the people. Even superstition becomes here pathetic. If the Talmud[8] had already expressed the principle, "Whoever is buried in the land of Israel, is as if he were buried under the altar," one of the most ancient Hebrew commentaries[9] goes much farther. From the injunction of Jacob and Joseph, and the desire of the fathers to be buried within the sacred soil, it is argued that those who lay there were to be the first "to walk before the Lord in the land of the living" (Ps. 116:9), the first to rise from the dead and to enjoy the days of the Messiah. Not to deprive of their reward the pious, who had not the privilege of residing in Palestine, it was added, that God would make subterranean roads and passages into the Holy Land, and that, when their dust reached it, the Spirit of the Lord would raise them to new life, as it is written (Ezek. 37:12–14): "O My people, I will open your graves, and cause you to come up out of your graves, and bring you into the land of Israel...and shall put My Spirit in you, and ye shall live; and I shall place you in your own land." Almost every prayer and hymn breathes the same love of Palestine. Indeed, it were impossible, by any extracts, to convey the pathos of some of those elegies in which the Synagogue still bewails the loss of Zion, or expresses the pent-up longing for its restoration.[10] Desolate, they cling to its ruins, and believe, hope, and pray—oh, how ardently! in almost every prayer—for the time that shall come, when the land, like Sarah of old, will, at the bidding of the Lord, have youth, beauty, and fruitfulness restored, and in Messiah the King "a horn of salvation shall be raised up"[11] to the house of David.

Yet it is most true, as noticed by a recent writer, that no place could have been more completely swept

---

[8]*Cheth.* iii. a.—the reference here being most curiously to Exod. 20:24: "An altar of earth shalt thou make to Me." Indeed, that whole page of the Talmud is very characteristic and interesting.

[9]*Ber. Rabba.*

[10]See especially the sublimest of these elegies, that by Judah ha-Levi.

[11]These are words of prayer taken from one of the most ancient fragments of the Jewish liturgy, and repeated, probably for two thousand years, every day by every Jew.

of relics than is Palestine. Where the most solemn transactions have taken place; where, if we only knew it, every footstep might be consecrated, and rocks, and caves, and mountain-tops be devoted to the holiest remembrances—we are almost in absolute ignorance of exact localities. In Jerusalem itself even the features of the soil, the valleys, depressions, and hills have changed, or at least lie buried deep under the accumulated ruins of centuries. It almost seems as if the Lord meant to do with the land what Hezekiah had done with that relic of Moses—the brazen serpent—when he stamped it to pieces, lest its sacred memories should convert it into an occasion for idolatry. The lie of land and water, of mountain and valley, are the same; Hebron, Bethlehem, the Mount of Olives, Nazareth, the Lake of Gennesaret, the land of Galilee, are still there, but all changed in form and appearance, and with no definite spot to which one could with absolute certainty attach the most sacred events. Events, then, not places; spiritual realities, not their outward surroundings, have been given to mankind by the land of Palestine.

[Hezekiah] removed the high places, smashed the sacred stones and cut down the Asherah poles. He broke into pieces the bronze snake Moses had made, for up to that time the Israelites had been burning incense to it (2 Kgs. 18:4a).

"So long as Israel inhabited Palestine," says the Babylonian Talmud, "the country was wide; but now it has become narrow." There is only too much historical truth underlying this somewhat curiously-worded statement. Each successive change left the boundaries of the Holy Land narrowed. Never as yet has it actually reached the extent indicated in the original promise to Abraham (Gen. 15:18), and afterwards confirmed to the children of Israel (Exod. 23:31). The nearest approach to it was during the reign of King David, when the power of Judah extended as far as the river Euphrates (2 Sam. 8:3–14). At present the country to which the name Palestine attaches is smaller than at any previous period. As of old, it still stretches north and south "from Dan to Beersheba;" in the east and west from Salcah (the modern Sulkhad) to "the great sea," the Mediterranean. Its superficial area is about 12,000 square miles, its length from 140 to 180, its breadth in the south about

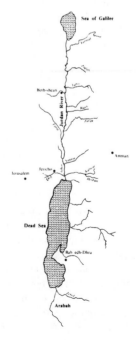

75, and in the north from 100 to 120 miles. To put it more pictorially, the modern Palestine is about twice as large as Wales; it is smaller than Holland, and about equal in size to Belgium. Moreover, from the highest mountain-peaks a glimpse of almost the whole country may be obtained. So small was the land which the Lord chose as the scene of the most marvellous events that ever happened on earth, and whence He appointed light and life to flow forth into all the world!

When our blessed Saviour trod the soil of Palestine, the country had already undergone many changes. The ancient division of tribes had given way; the two kingdoms of Judah and Israel existed no longer; and the varied foreign domination, and the brief period of absolute national independence, had alike ceased. Yet, with the characteristic tenacity of the East for the past, the names of the ancient tribes still attached to some of the districts formerly occupied by them (comp. Matt. 4:13, 15). A comparatively small number of the exiles had returned to Palestine with Ezra and Nehemiah, and the Jewish inhabitants of the country consisted either of those who had originally been left in the land, or of the tribes of Judah and Benjamin. The controversy about the ten tribes, which engages so much attention in our days, raged even at the time of our Lord.[12] "Will He go unto the dispersed among the Gentiles?" asked the Jews, when unable to fathom the meaning of Christ's prediction of His departure, using that mysterious vagueness of language in which we generally clothe things which we pretend to, but really do

To your descendants I give this land, from the river of Egypt to the great river, the Euphrates (Gen. 15:18b).

Leaving Nazareth, he [Jesus] went and lived in Capernaum, which was by the lake in the area of Zebulun and Naphtali...
Land of Zebulun and land of Naphtali,
  the way to the sea,
  along the Jordan,
  Galilee of the Gentiles
(Matt. 4:13, 15).

---

[12]This is not the place to discuss the question. There can be no reasonable doubt, that colonies from some of these tribes are scattered far and wide. Thus descendants of them are traced in the Crimea, where the dates on their gravestones are reckoned from "the *era of the exile,* in 696 B.C.; *i.e.,* the exile of the ten tribes; not 586 B.C., when Jerusalem was taken by Nebuchadnezzar" (Dr. S. Davidson, in Kitto's *Cycl. of Bibl. Lit.* iii. p. 1173). For notices of the wanderings of the ten tribes see my *Hist. of the Jewish Nation,* pp. 61–63; also the late Dr. Wolff's researches in his journeys. How prone even learned Talmudical Jews are to credulity in the matter of the ten tribes may be gathered from the Appendix to Rabbi Schwartz's (of Jerusalem) *Holy Land* (pp. 401–422 of the German ed.). The oldest Hebrew Crimean inscriptions date from the years 6, 30, and 89 of our era (Chwolson, *Mem. de l'Ac. de St. Petersb.* ix. 1866, No. 7).

not, know. "The ten tribes are beyond the Euphrates till now, and are an immense multitude, and not to be estimated by numbers," writes Josephus, with his usual grandiloquent self-complacency. But where—he informs us as little as any of his other contemporaries. We read in the earliest Jewish authority, the Mishnah (*Sanh.* x. 3): "The ten tribes shall never return again, as it is written (Deut. 29:28), 'And He cast them into another land, as this day.' As 'this day' goeth and does not return again, so they also go and do not return. This is the view of Rabbi Akiba. Rabbi Elieser says, 'As the day becomes dark and has light again, so the ten tribes, to whom darkness has come; but light shall also be restored to them.' "

At the time of Christ's birth Palestine was governed by Herod the Great; that is, it was nominally an independent kingdom, but under the suzerainty of Rome. On the death of Herod—that is, very close upon the opening of the gospel story—a fresh, though only temporary, division of his dominions took place. The events connected with it fully illustrate the parable of our Lord, recorded in Luke 19:12–15, 27. If they do not form its historical groundwork, they were at least so fresh in the memory of Christ's hearers, that their minds must have involuntarily reverted to them. Herod died, as he had lived, cruel and treacherous. A few days before his end, he had once more altered his will, and nominated Archelaus his successor in the kingdom; Herod Antipas (the Herod of the gospels), tetrarch of Galilee and Peraea; and Philip, tetrarch of Gaulonitis, Trachonitis, Batanaea, and Panias—districts to which, in the sequel, we may have further to refer. As soon after the death of Herod as circumstances would permit, and when he had quelled a rising in Jerusalem, Archelaus hastened to Rome to obtain the emperor's confirmation of his father's will. He was immediately followed by his brother Herod Antipas, who in a previous testament of Herod had been left what Archelaus now claimed. Nor were the two alone in Rome. They found there already a number of members of Herod's family, each clamorous for

Major Figures in the Herodian Family

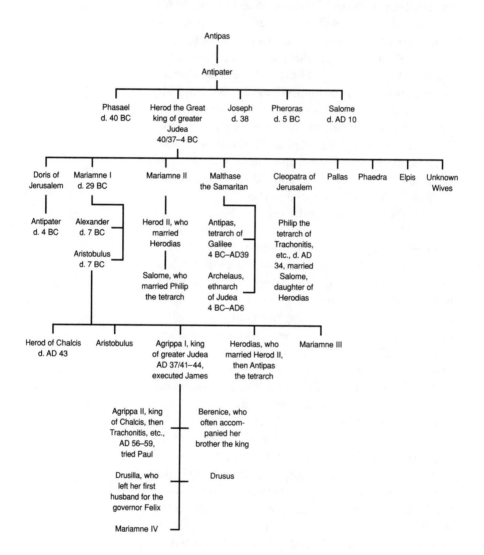

something, but all agreed that they would rather have none of their own kindred as king, and that the country should be put under Roman sway; if otherwise, they anyhow preferred Herod Antipas to Archelaus. Each of the brothers had, of course, his own party, intriguing, manoeuvring, and trying to influence the emperor. Augustus inclined from the first to Archelaus. The formal decision, however, was for a time postponed by a fresh insurrection in Judaea, which was quelled only with difficulty. Meanwhile, a Jewish deputation appeared in Rome, entreating that none of the Herodians might ever by appointed king, on the ground of their infamous deeds, which they related, and that they (the Jews) might be allowed to live according to their own laws, under the suzerainty of Rome. Augustus ultimately decided to carry out the will of Herod the Great, but gave Archelaus the title of ethnarch instead of king, promising him the higher grade if he proved deserving of it (Matt. 2:22). On his return to Judaea, Archelaus (according to the story in the parable) took bloody vengeance on "his citizens that hated him, and sent a message after him, saying, We will not have this man to reign over us." The reign of Archelaus did not last long. Fresh and stronger complaints came from Judaea. Archelaus was deposed, and Judaea joined to the Roman province of Syria, but with a procurator of its own. The revenues of Archelaus, so long as he reigned, amounted to very considerably over £240,000 a year; those of his brothers respectively to a third and sixth of that sum. But this was as nothing compared to the income of Herod the Great, which stood at the enormous sum of about £680,000; and that afterwards of Agrippa II, which is computed as high as half a million. In thinking of these figures, it is necessary to bear in mind the general cheapness of living in Palestine at the time, which may be gathered from the smallness of the coins in circulation, and from the lowness of the labour market. The smallest coin, a (Jewish) perutah, amounted to only the sixteenth of a penny. Again, readers of the New Testament will remember that a labourer was wont to receive for a day's work in field or vineyard a denarius (Matt. 20:2), or about 8d., while the Good Samaritan paid for the charge of the sick person whom he left in the inn only two denars, or about 1s. 4d. (Luke 10:35).

But we are anticipating. Our main object was to explain the division of Palestine in the time of our

But when he [Joseph] heard that Archelaus was reigning in Judea in place of his father Herod, he was afraid to go there. Having been warned in a dream, he withdrew to the district of Galilee (Matt. 2:22).

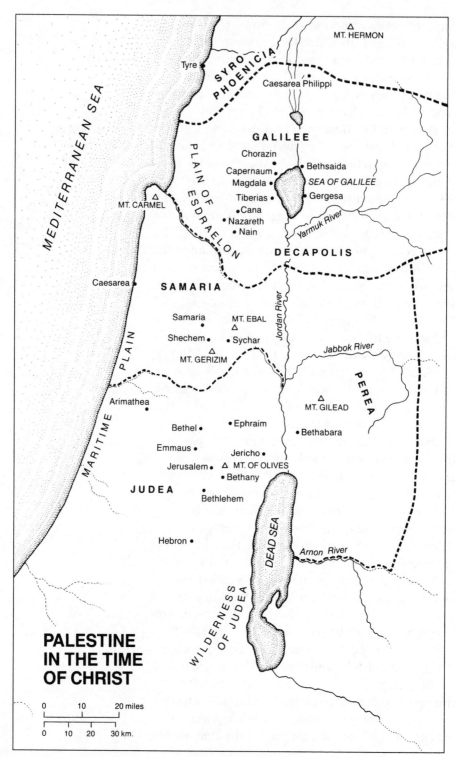

MT. HERMON

TYRE

SYRO PHOENICIA

Caesarea Philippi

MEDITERRANEAN SEA

GALILEE

Chorazin

Capernaum • Bethsaida

Magdala • SEA OF GALILEE

PLAIN OF ESDRAELON

MT. CARMEL

Tiberias • Gergesa

• Cana

Nazareth

• Nain

Yarmuk River

DECAPOLIS

Caesarea

SAMARIA

Jordan River

Samaria

MT. EBAL

Shechem • Sychar

Jabbok River

MT. GERIZIM

PEREA

MARITIME PLAIN

Arimathea

MT. GILEAD

Bethel • • Ephraim

• Bethabara

Emmaus •

Jericho •

Jerusalem • △ MT. OF OLIVES

• Bethany

JUDEA

Bethlehem

DEAD SEA

Hebron •

Arnon River

WILDERNESS OF JUDEA

**PALESTINE
IN THE TIME
OF CHRIST**

0   10   20 miles

0   10   20   30 km.

Palestine in the time of Christ

Lord. Politically speaking, it consisted of Judaea and
Samaria, under Roman procurators; Galilee and
Peraea (on the other side Jordan), subject to Herod
Antipas, the murderer of John the Baptist—"that
fox" full of cunning and cruelty, to whom the Lord,
when sent by Pilate, would give no answer; and
Batanaea, Trachonitis, and Auranitis, under the rule
of the tetrarch Philip. It would require too many
details to describe accurately those latter provinces.
Suffice, that they lay quite to the north-east, and that
one of their principal cities was Caesarea Philippi
(called after the Roman emperor, and after Philip
himself), where Peter made that noble confession,
which constituted the rock on which the Church was
to be built (Matt. 16:16; Mark 8:29). It was the wife of
this Philip, the best of all Herod's sons, whom her
brother-in-law, Herod Antipas, induced to leave her
husband, and for whose sake he beheaded John
(Matt. 14:3, etc.; Mark 6:17; Luke 3:19). It is well to
know that this adulterous and incestuous union
brought Herod immediate trouble and misery, and
that it ultimately cost him his kingdom, and sent him
into life-long banishment.

Such was the political division of Palestine.
Commonly it was arranged into Galilee, Samaria,
Judaea, and Peraea. It is scarcely necessary to say that
the Jews did not regard Samaria as belonging to the
Holy Land, but as a strip of foreign country—as the
Talmud designates it (*Chag.* 25 *a.*), "a Cuthite strip,"
or "tongue," intervening between Galilee and Judaea.
From the gospels we know that the Samaritans
were not only ranked with Gentiles and strangers
(Matt. 10:5; John 4:9, 20), but that the very term
Samaritan was one of reproach (John 8:48). "There
be two manner of nations," says the son of Sirach
(Ecclus. 1.25, 26), "which my heart abhorreth, and
the third is no nation; they that sit upon the mountain
of Samaria, and they that dwell among the Philistines,
and that foolish people that dwell in Sichem." And
Josephus has a story to account for the exclusion of
the Samaritans from the Temple, to the effect that in
the night of the Passover, when it was the custom to

*Simon Peter answered,
"You are the Christ, the
Son of the living God"
(Matt. 16:16).*

*Now Herod had arrested
John and bound him and
put him in prison because
of Herodias, his brother
Philip's wife (Matt. 14:3).*

*These twelve Jesus sent
out with the following
instructions: "Do not go
among the Gentiles or
enter any town of the
Samaritans" (Matt. 10:5).*

*The Samaritan woman
said to him, "You are a
Jew and I am a Samaritan
woman. How can you ask
me for a drink?" (For Jews
do not associate with
Samaritans) (John 4:9).*

open the Temple gates at midnight, a Samaritan had come and strewn bones in the porches and throughout the Temple to defile the Holy House. Most unlikely as this appears, at least in its details, it shows the feeling of the people. On the other hand, it must be admitted that the Samaritans fully retaliated by bitter hatred and contempt. For, at every period of sore national trial, the Jews had no more determined or relentless enemies than those who claimed to be the only true representatives of Israel's worship and hopes.

2
Jews and Gentiles in "the Land"

Coming down from Syria, it would have been difficult to fix the exact spot where, in the view of the Rabbis, "the land" itself began. The boundary lines, though mentioned in four different documents, are not marked in anything like geographical order, but as ritual questions connected with them came up for theological discussion.[1] For, to the Rabbis the precise limits of Palestine were chiefly interesting so far as they affected the religious obligations or privileges of a district. And in this respect the fact that a city was in heathen possession exercised a decisive influence. Thus the environs of Ascalon, the wall of Caesarea, and that of Acco, were reckoned within the boundaries of Palestine, though the cities themselves were

The LORD will inherit Judah as his portion in the holy land and will again choose Jerusalem (Zech. 2:12).

Caesarea

---

[1]Rappoport, *Er. Mill.* p. 208, in Neubauer's *Geogr. du Talmud,* p. 10.

not. Indeed, viewing the question from this point, Palestine was to the Rabbis simply "the land,"[2] all other countries being summed up under the designation of "outside the land." In the Talmud, even the expression "Holy Land," so common among later Jews and Christians,[3] does not once occur. It needed not that addition, which might have suggested a comparison with other countries; for to the Rabbinist Palestine was not only holy, but the only holy ground, to the utter exclusion of all other countries, although they marked within its boundaries an ascending scale of ten degrees of sanctity, rising from the bare soil of Palestine to the most holy place in the Temple (*Chel.* i. 6–9). But "outside the land" everything was darkness and death. The very dust of a heathen country was unclean, and it defiled by contact.[4] It was regarded like a grave, or like the putrescence of death. If a spot of heathen dust had touched an offering, it must at once be burnt. More than that, if by mischance any heathen dust had been brought into Palestine, it did not and could not mingle with that of "the land," but remained to the end what it had been—unclean, defiled, and defiling everything to which it adhered. This will cast light upon the meaning conveyed by the symbolical directions of our Lord to His disciples (Matt. 10:14), when He sent them forth to mark out the boundary lines of the true Israel—"the kingdom of heaven," that was at hand: "Whosoever shall not receive you, nor hear your words, when ye depart out of that house or city, shake off the dust of your feet." In other words, they were not only to leave such a city or household, but it was to be considered and treated as if it were heathen, just as in the similar case mentioned in Matt. 18:17. All contact with such must be avoided, all trace of it shaken off, and that, even though, like some of the cities in Palestine that were considered heathen, they

The land you are entering to possess is a land polluted by the corruption of its peoples. By their detestable practices they have filled it with their impurity from one end to the other (Ezra 9:11b).

If anyone will not welcome you or listen to your words, shake the dust off your feet when you leave that home or town (Matt. 10:14).

If he refuses to listen to them, tell it to the church; and if he refuses to listen even to the church, treat him as you would a pagan or a tax collector (Matt. 18:17).

---

[2] So mostly; the expression also occurs "the land of Israel."

[3] The only passage of Scripture in which the term is used is Zech. 2:12, or rather 2:16 of the Hebrew original.

[4] The references here are too numerous for special mention.

were surrounded on every side by what was reckoned as belonging to Israel.

The Mishnah[5] marks, in reference to certain ordinances, "three lands" which might equally be designated as Palestine, but to which different ritual regulations applied. The first comprised, "all which they who came up from Babylon took possession of in the land of Israel and unto Chezib" (about three hours north of Acre); the second, "all that they who came up from Egypt took possession of from Chezib and unto the river (Euphrates) eastward, and unto Amanah" (supposed to be a mountain near Antioch, in Syria); while the third, seemingly indicating certain ideal outlines, was probably intended to mark what "the land" would have been, according to the original promise of God, although it was never possessed to that extent by Israel.[6] For our present purpose, of course, only the first of these definitions must be applied to "the land." We read in *Menachoth* vii. 1: "Every offering,[7] whether of the congregation or of an individual (public or private), may come from 'the land,' or from 'outside the land, be of the new product (of the year) or of old product, except the *omer* (the wave-sheaf at the Passover) and the two loaves (at Pentecost), which may only be brought from new product (that of the current year), and from that (which grows) within 'the land.' " To these two, the Mishnah adds in another passage (*Chel.* i. 6) also the *Biccurim*, or first-fruits in their fresh state, although inaccurately, since the latter were likewise brought from what is called by the Rabbis Syria,[8] which seems

So I have come down to rescue them from the hand of the Egyptians and to bring them up out of that land into a good and spacious land, a land flowing with milk and honey—the home of the Canaanites, Hittites, Amorites, Perizzites, Hivites and Jebusites (Exod. 3:8).

There are ten degrees of holiness. The Land of Israel is holier than any other land. Wherein lies its holiness? In that from it they may bring the Omer, the Firstfruits, and the Two Loaves, which they may not bring from any other land (Mishnah, Kelim i.6).

---

[5] *Shev.* vi. 1; *Chall.* iv. 8.

[6] The expressions in the original are so obscure as to render it difficult to form a quite definite judgment. In the text we have followed the views expressed by M. Neubauer.

[7] Neither of the English words: "sacrifice," "offering," or "gift" quite corresponds to the Hebrew *Korban*, derived from a verb which in one mood means to be near, and in another to bring near. In the one case it would refer to the offerings themselves, in the other to the offerers, as brought near, the offerings bringing them near to God. The latter seems to me both etymologically and theologically the right explanation. Aberbanel combines both in his definition of *Korban*.

[8] Syria sent *Biccurim* to Jerusalem, but was not liable to second tithes, nor for the fourth year's product of plants (Lev. 19:24).

to have been regarded as, in a sense, intermediate between "the land" and "outside the land." The term *Soria*, or Syria, does not include that country alone, but all the lands which, according to the Rabbis, David had subdued, such as Mesopotamia, Syria, Zobah, Achlab, etc. It would be too lengthy to explain in detail the various ordinances in regard to which *Soria* was assimilated to, and those by which it was distinguished from, Palestine proper. The preponderance of duty and privilege was certainly in favour of Syria, so much so, that if one could have stepped from its soil straight to that of Palestine, or joined fields in the two countries, without the interposition of any Gentile strip, the land and the dust of Syria would have been considered clean, like that of Palestine itself (*Ohol.* xviii. 7). There was thus around "the land" a sort of inner band, consisting of those countries supposed to have been annexed by King David, and termed *Soria*. But besides this, there was also what may be called an outer band, towards the Gentile world, consisting of Egypt, Babylon, Ammon and Moab, the countries in which Israel had a special interest, and which were distinguished from the rest, "outside the land," by this, that they were liable to tithes and the *Therumoth*, or first-fruits in a prepared state. Of course neither of these contributions was actually brought into Palestine, but either employed by them for their sacred purposes, or else redeemed.

Maimonides arranges all countries into three classes, "so far as concerns the precepts connected with the soil"—"the land, Soria, and outside the land;" and he divides the land of Israel into territory possessed before and after the Exile, while he also distinguishes between Egypt, Babylon, Moab, and Ammon, and other lands.[9] In popular estimate other distinctions were likewise made. Thus Rabbi Jose of Galilee would have it,[10] that *Biccurim*[11] were not to be

If a man bought a field in Syria that lies close to the Land of Israel and he can enter it in cleanness, it is clean...
(Mishnah, Oholot xviii.7).

---

[9] *Hilch. Ther.* i. 6.
[10] *Bicc.* i. 10.
[11] For a full explanation of the distinction between *Biccurim* and *Therumoth* see my work on *The Temple: its Ministry and Services as they were at the Time of Jesus Christ.*

brought from the other side of Jordan, "because it was not a land flowing with milk and honey." But as the Rabbinical law in this respect differed from the view expressed by Rabbi Jose, his must have been an afterthought, probably intended to account for the fact that they beyond Jordan did not bring their first-fruits to the Temple. Another distinction claimed for the country west of the Jordan curiously reminds us of the fears expressed by the two and a half tribes on their return to their homes, after the first conquest of Palestine under Joshua (Joshua 22:24, 25), since it declared the land east of Jordan less sacred, on account of the absence of the Temple, of which it had not been worthy. Lastly, Judaea proper claimed pre-eminence over Galilee, as being the centre of Rabbinism. Perhaps it may be well here to state that, notwithstanding strict uniformity on all principal points, Galilee and Judaea had each its own peculiar legal customs and rights, which differed in many particulars one from the other.

The LORD has made the Jordan a boundary between us and you—you Reubenites and Gadites! You have no share in the LORD (Josh. 22:25a).

What has hitherto been explained from Rabbinical writings gains fresh interest when we bring it to bear on the study of the New Testament. For, we can now understand how those Zealots from Jerusalem, who would have bent the neck of the Church under the yoke of the law of Moses, sought out in preference the flourishing communities in Syria for the basis of their operations (Acts 15:1). There was a special significance in this, as Syria formed a kind of outer Palestine, holding an intermediate position between it and heathen lands. Again, it results from our inquiries, that, what the Rabbis considered as the land of Israel proper, may be regarded as commencing immediately south of Antioch. Thus the city where the first Gentile Church was formed (Acts 11:20, 21); where the disciples were first called Christians (Acts 11:26); where Paul so long exercised his ministry, and whence he started on his missionary journeys, was, significantly enough, just outside the land of Israel. Immediately beyond it lay the country over which the Rabbis claimed entire sway. Travelling southwards, the first district which

Some of them, however, men from Cyprus and Cyrene, went to Antioch and began to speak to Greeks also, telling them the good news about the Lord Jesus (Acts 11:20).

Antioch

one would reach would be what is known from the gospels as "the coasts (or tracts) of Tyre and Sidon." St. Mark describes the district more particularly (Mark 7:24) as "the borders of Tyre and Sidon." These stretched, according to Josephus (*Jewish War*, 3.35), at the time of our Lord, from the Mediterranean towards Jordan. It was to these extreme boundary tracts of "the land," that Jesus had withdrawn from the Pharisees, when they were offended at His opposition to their "blind" traditionalism; and there He healed by the word of His power the daughter of the "woman of Canaan," the intensity of whose faith drew from His lips words of precious commendation (Matt. 15:28; Mark 7:29). It was chiefly a heathen district where the Saviour spoke the word of healing, and where the woman would not let the Messiah of Israel go without an answer. She herself was a Gentile. Indeed, not only that district, but all around, and farther on, the territory of Philip, was almost entirely heathen. More than that, strange as it may sound, all around the districts inhabited by the Jews the country was, so to speak, fringed by foreign nationalities and by heathen worship, rites, and customs.

Properly to understand the history of the time and the circumstances indicated in the New Testament, a correct view of the state of parties in this respect is necessary. And here we must guard against a not unnatural mistake. If any one had expected to find within the boundaries of "the land" itself one nationality, one language, the same interests, or even one religion publicly professed, he would have been bitterly disappointed. It was not merely for the presence of the Romans and their followers, and of a more or less influential number of foreign settlers, but the Holy Land itself was a country of mixed and hostile races, of divided interests, where close by the side of the narrowest and most punctilious Pharisaism heathen temples rose, and heathen rites and customs openly prevailed. In a general way all this will be readily understood. For, those who returned from Babylon were comparatively few in number, and confessedly did not occupy the land in its former extent. During the troubled period which followed, there was a constant influx of heathen, and unceasing attempts were made to introduce and perpetuate foreign elements. Even the language of Israel had undergone a change. In the course of time the ancient Hebrew had wholly given place to the Aramaean dialect, except in public worship and in the learned academies of theological doctors. Such words and names in the gospels as Raka, Abba, Golgotha, Gabbatha, Akel-Dama, Bartholomaios, Barabbas, Bar-Jesus, and the various verbal quotations, are all Aramaean. It was probably in that language that Paul addressed the infuriated multitude, when standing on the top of the steps leading from the Temple into the fortress Antonia (Acts 21:40; 22:1ff.). But along with the Hebraic Aramaean—for so we would designate the language—the Greek had for some time been making its way among the people. The Mishnah itself contains a very large number of Greek and Latin

Babylonian Idols

words with Hebraic terminations, showing how
deeply Gentile life and customs around had affected
even those who hated them most, and, by inference,
how thoroughly they must have penetrated Jewish
society in general. But besides, it had been long the
policy of their rulers systematically to promote all
that was Grecian in thought and feeling. It needed the
obstinate determinateness, if not the bigotry, of
Pharisaism to prevent their success, and this may
perhaps partly explain the extreme of their antagonism against all that was Gentile. A brief notice of the
religious state of the outlying districts of the country
may place this in a clearer light.

Supposed site of Bethsaida

In the far north-east of the land, occupying at
least in part the ancient possession of Manasseh, were
the provinces belonging to the tetrarch Philip (Luke
3:1). Many spots there (Mark 8:22; Luke 9:10; Matt.
16:13) are dear to the Christian memory. After the
Exile these districts had been peopled by wild, preda-
tory nomads, like the Bedawin of our days. These
lived chiefly in immense caves, where they stored
their provisions, and in case of attack defended
themselves and their flocks. Herod the Great and his
successors had indeed subdued, and settled among
them, a large number of Jewish and Idumaean
colonists—the former brought from Babylon, under
the leadership of one Zamaris, and attracted, like the
modern German colonists in parts of Russia, by
immunity from taxation. But the vast majority of
the people were still Syrians and Grecians, rude,
barbarous, and heathens. Indeed, there the worship
of the old Syrian gods had scarcely given way to the
more refined rites of Greece. It was in this neighbourhood that Peter made that noble confession of
faith, on which, as on a rock, the Church is built. But
Caesarea Philippi was originally Paneas, the city
devoted to Pan; nor does its change of name indicate
a more Jewish direction on the part of its inhabitants.
Indeed, Herod the Great had built there a temple to
Augustus. But further particulars are scarcely necessary, for recent researches have everywhere brought
to light relics of the worship of the Phoenician

Astarte, of the ancient Syrian god of the sun, and even of the Egyptian Ammon, side by side with that of the well-known Grecian deities. The same may be said of the refined Damascus, the territory of which formed here the extreme boundary of Palestine. Passing from the eastern to the western bounds of Palestine, we find that in Tyre and Ptolemais Phrygian, Egyptian, Phoenician, and Greek rites contended for the mastery. In the centre of Palestine, notwithstanding the pretence of the Samaritans to be the only true representatives of the religion of Moses, the very name of their capital, Sebaste, for Samaria, showed how thoroughly Grecianised was that province. Herod had built in Samaria also a magnificent temple to Augustus; and there can be no doubt that, as the Greek language, so Grecian rites and idolatry prevailed. Another outlying district, the *Decapolis* (Matt. 4:25; Mark 5:20; 7:31), was almost entirely Grecian in constitution, language, and worship. It was, in fact, a federation of ten heathen cities within the territory of Israel, possessing a government of their own. Little is known of its character; indeed, the cities themselves are not always equally enumerated by different writers. We name those of most importance to readers of the New Testament. *Scythopolis,* the ancient *Beth-shean* (Josh. 17:11, 16; Judg. 1:27; 1 Sam. 31:10, 12, etc.), was the only one of those cities situated *west* of the Jordan. It lay about four hours south of Tiberias. *Gadara,* the capital of Peraea, is known to us from Matt. 8:28; Mark 5:1; Luke 8:26. Lastly, we mention as specially interesting, *Pella,* the place to which the Christians of Jerusalem fled in obedience to the warning of our Lord (Matt. 24:15–20), to escape the doom of the city, when finally beleaguered by the Romans. The situation of Pella has not been satisfactorily ascertained, but probably it lay at no great distance from the ancient Jabesh Gilead.[12]

But to return. From what has been said, it will appear that there remained only Galilee and Judaea proper, in which strictly Jewish views and manners

The god Ammon

Large crowds from Galilee, the Decapolis, Jerusalem, Judea and the region across the Jordan followed him (Matt. 4:25).

---

[12] Compare the full discussion in Caspari, *Chronol. Geogr. Einl. in d. Leben J. C.* pp. 87–90.

They sailed to the region of the Gerasenes, which is across the lake from Galilee (Luke 8:26).

Gadara

must be sought for. Each of these will be described in detail. For the present it will suffice to remark, that north-eastern or Upper Galilee was in great part inhabited by Gentiles—Phoenicians, Syrians, Arabs, and Greeks,[13] whence the name "Galilee of the Gentiles" (Matt. 4:15). It is strange in how many even of those cities, with which we are familiar from the

Tiberias

[13] Jos. *Jewish War* 3.419–427

New Testament, the heathen element prevailed. *Tiberias,* which gave its name to the lake, was at the time of Christ of quite recent origin, having been built by the tetrarch Herod Antipas (the Herod of the gospel history), and named in honour of the Emperor Tiberius. Although endowed by its founder with many privileges, such as houses and lands for its inhabitants, and freedom from taxation—the latter being continued by Vespasian after the Jewish war— Herod had to colonise it by main force, so far as its few Jewish inhabitants were concerned. For, the site on which the city stood had of old covered a place of burial, and the whole ground was therefore levitically unclean (Jos. *Ant.* 18.38). However celebrated, therefore, afterwards as the great and final seat of the Jewish Sanhedrim, it was originally chiefly un-Jewish. *Gaza* had its local deity; *Ascalon* worshipped Astarte; *Joppa* was the locality where, at the time when Peter had his vision there, they still showed on the rocks of the shore the marks of the chains, by which Andromeda was said to have been held, when Perseus came to set her free. *Caesarea* was an essentially heathen city, though inhabited by many Jews; and one of its most conspicuous ornaments was another temple to Augustus, built on a hill opposite the entrance to the harbour, so as to be visible far out at sea. But what could be expected, when in Jerusalem itself Herod had reared a magnificent theatre and amphitheatre, to which gladiators were brought from all parts of the world, and where games were held, thoroughly anti-Jewish and heathen in their spirit and tendency? (Jos. *Ant.* 15.274). The favourites and counsellors by whom that monarch surrounded himself were heathens; wherever he or his successors could, they reared heathen temples, and on all occasions they promoted the spread of Grecian views. Yet withal they professed to be Jews; they would not shock Jewish prejudices; indeed, as the building of the Temple, the frequent advocacy at Rome of the cause of Jews when oppressed, and many other facts show, the Herodians would fain have kept on good terms with the national party, or rather used it as their tool.

Astarte

...to make this place a habitation was to transgress the Jewish ancient laws, because many sepulchres were to be here taken away, in order to make room for the city Tiberias; whereas our law pronounces, that such inhabitants are unclean for seven days (Jos. Antiquities 18.38).

And truly foreigners were greatly surprised and delighted at the vastness of the expenses here exhibited, and at the great dangers that were here seen; but to natural Jews, this was no better than a dissolution of these customs for which they had so great a veneration (Jos. Antiquities 15.274).

Coin with Greek superscription

"Show me the coin used for paying the tax." They brought him a denarius, and he asked them, "Whose portrait is this? And whose inscription?" "Caesar's," they replied. Then he said to them, "Give to Caesar what is Caesar's, and to God what is God's" (Matt. 22:19–21).

And so Grecianism spread. Already Greek was spoken and understood by all the educated classes in the country; it was necessary for intercourse with the Roman authorities, with the many civil and military officials, and with strangers; the "superscription" on the coins was in Greek, even though, to humour the Jews, none of the earlier Herods had his own image impressed on them.[14] Significantly enough, it was Herod Agrippa I, the murderer of St. James, and the would-be murderer of St. Peter, who introduced the un-Jewish practice of images on coins. Thus everywhere the foreign element was advancing. A change or else a struggle was inevitable in the near future.

And what of Judaism itself at that period? It was miserably divided, even though no outward separation had taken place. The Pharisees and Sadducees held opposite principles, and hated each other; the Essenes looked down upon them both. Within Pharisaism the schools of Hillel and Shammai contradicted each other on almost every matter. But both united in their unbounded contempt of what they designated as "the country-people"—those who had no traditional learning, and hence were either unable or unwilling to share the discussions, and to bear the burdens of legal ordinances, which constituted the chief matter of traditionalism. There was only one feeling common to all—high and low, rich and poor,

---

[14] The coin mentioned in Matt. 22:20, which bore an "image," as well as a "superscription," must therefore have been either struck in Rome, or else one of the tetrarch Philip, who was the first to introduce the image of Caesar on strictly Jewish coins.

learned and unlettered: it was that of intense hatred of the foreigner. The rude Galileans were as "national" as the most punctilious Pharisees; indeed, in the war against Rome they furnished the most and the bravest soldiers. Everywhere the foreigner was in sight; his were the taxes levied, the soldiery, the courts of ultimate appeal, the government. In Jerusalem they hung over the Temple as a guard in the fortress of Antonia, and even kept in their custody the high-priest's garments,[15] so that, before officiating in the Temple, he had actually always to apply for them to the procurator or his representative! They were only just more tolerable as being downright heathens than the Herodians, who mingled Judaism with heathenism, and, having sprung from foreign slaves, had arrogated to themselves the kingdom of the Maccabees.

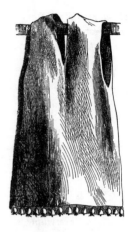

High-priest's garment

Readers of the New Testament know what separation Pharisaical Jews made between themselves and heathens. It will be readily understood, that every contact with heathenism and all aid to its rites should have been forbidden, and that in social intercourse any levitical defilement, arising from the use of what was "common or unclean," was avoided. But Pharisaism went a great deal further than this. Three days before a heathen festival all transactions with Gentiles were forbidden, so as to afford them neither direct nor indirect help towards their rites; and this prohibition extended even to private festivities, such as a birthday, the day of return from a journey, etc. On heathen festive occasions a pious Jew should avoid, if possible, passing through a heathen city, certainly all dealings in shops that were festively decorated. It was unlawful for Jewish workmen to

...the Romans...took possession of these vestments of the high priest, and had them reposited in a stone chamber, under the seal of the priests, and of the keepers of the temple the captain of the guard lighting a lamp there every day (Jos. Antiquities 18.93).

---

[15] The practice commenced innocently enough. The high-priest Hyrcanus, who built the Tower of Baris, kept his dress there, and his sons continued the practice. When Herod seized the government, he retained, for reasons readily understood, this custody, in the fortress of Antonia, which he had substituted for the ancient tower. On similar grounds the Romans followed the lead of Herod. Josephus (*Ant.* 18.93) describes "the stone chamber" in which these garments were kept, under seal of the priests, with a light continually burning there. Vitellius, the successor of Pilate, restored to the Jews the custody of the high-priestly garments, when they were kept in a special apartment in the Temple.

He said to them: "You are well aware that it is against our law for a Jew to associate with a Gentile or visit him. But God has shown me that I should not call any man impure or unclean" (Acts 10:28).

"Everything is permissible" —but not everything is beneficial. "Everything is permissible"—but not everything is constructive (1 Cor. 10:23).

So when Peter went up to Jerusalem, the circumcised believers criticized him and said, "You went into the house of uncircumcised men and ate with them" (Acts 11:2–3).

assist in anything that might be subservient either to heathen worship or heathen rule, including in the latter the erection of court-houses and similar buildings. It need not be explained to what lengths or into what details Pharisaical punctiliousness carried all these ordinances. From the New Testament we know, that to enter the house of a heathen defiled till the evening (John 18:28), and that all familiar intercourse with Gentiles was forbidden (Acts 10:28). So terrible was the intolerance, that a Jewess was actually forbidden to give help to her heathen neighbour, when about to become a mother (*Avod. S.* ii. 1)! It was not a new question to St. Paul, when the Corinthians inquired about the lawfulness of meat sold in the shambles or served up at a feast (1 Cor. 10:25, 27, 28). Evidently he had the Rabbinical law on the subject before his mind, while, on the one hand, he avoided the Pharisaical bondage of the letter, and, on the other, guarded against either injuring one's own conscience, or offending that of an on-looker. For, according to Rabbi Akiba, "Meat which is about to be brought in heathen worship is lawful, but that which comes out from it is forbidden, because it is like the sacrifices of the dead" (*Avod. S.* ii. 3). But the separation went much beyond what ordinary minds might be prepared for. Milk drawn from a cow by heathen hands, bread and oil prepared by them, might indeed be sold to strangers, but not used by Israelites. No pious Jew would of course have sat down at the table of a Gentile (Acts 11:3, Gal. 2:12). If a heathen were invited to a Jewish house, he might not be left alone in the room, else every article of food or drink on the table was henceforth to be regarded as unclean. If cooking utensils were bought of them, they had to be purified by fire or by water; knives to be ground anew, spits to be made red-hot before use, etc. It was not lawful to let either house or field, nor to sell cattle, to a heathen; any article, however distantly connected with heathenism, was to be destroyed. Thus, if a weaving-shuttle had been made of wood grown in a grove devoted to idols, every web of cloth made by it was to be destroyed; nay, if such pieces had been mixed with others, to the manufacture of which no possible objection could have been taken, these all became unclean, and had to be destroyed.[16]

These are only general statements to show the prevalent feeling. It was easy to prove how it pervaded every relationship of life. The heathens, though often tolerant, of course retorted. Circumcision, the Sabbath-rest, the worship of an invisible God, and Jewish abstinence from pork, formed a never-ending theme of merriment to the heathen.[17] Conquerors are not often chary in disguising their contempt for the conquered, especially when the latter presume to look down upon, and to hate them. In view of all this, what an almost incredible truth must it have seemed, when the Lord Jesus Christ proclaimed it among Israel as the object of His coming and kingdom, not to make of the Gentiles Jews, but of both alike children of one Heavenly Father; not to rivet upon the heathen the yoke of the law, but to deliver from it Jew and Gentile, or rather to fulfil its demands for all! The most unexpected and unprepared-for revelation, from the Jewish point of view, was that of the breaking down of the middle wall of partition between Jew and Gentile, the taking away of the enmity of the law, and the nailing it to His cross. There was nothing analogous to it; not a hint of it to be found, either in the teaching or the spirit of the times. Quite the opposite. Assuredly, the most unlike thing to Christ were His times; and the greatest wonder of all—"the mystery hidden from ages and generations"—the foundation of one universal Church.

I have become its servant by the commission God gave me to present to you the word of God in its fullness—the mystery that has been kept hidden for ages and generations, but is now disclosed to the saints. To them God has chosen to make known among the Gentiles the glorious riches of this mystery, which is Christ in you, the hope of glory (Col. 1:25–27).

---

[16]These particulars are gathered from the Mishnic tractate *Avodah Sarah* (idol-worship), although we have designedly given only a general outline.

[17]For details compare the well-known and valuable collection of Meier (*Judaica seu vet. scr. prof. de reb. Jud. frag.*).

3
IN GALILEE
AT THE TIME OF OUR LORD

"Land of Zebulun and
  land of Naphtali,
the way to the sea, along
  the Jordan,
Galilee of the Gentiles—
the people living in darkness
have seen a great light;
on those living in the land
  of the shadow of death
a light has dawned"
(Matt. 4:15–16).

"If any one wishes to be rich, let him go north; if he wants to be wise, let him come south." Such was the saying, by which Rabbinical pride distinguished between the material wealth of Galilee and the supremacy in traditional lore claimed for the academies of Judaea proper. Alas, it was not long before Judaea lost even this doubtful distinction, and its colleges wandered northwards, ending at last by the Lake of Gennesaret, and in that very city of Tiberias which at one time had been reputed unclean! Assuredly, the history of nations chronicles their judgment;[1] and it is strangely significant, that the authoritative collection of Jewish traditional law, known as the Mishnah, and the so-called Jerusalem Talmud, which is its Palestinian commentary,[2] should finally have issued from what was originally a heathen city, built upon the site of old forsaken graves. But so long as Jerusalem and Judaea were the centre of Jewish learning, no terms of contempt were too strong to express the supercilious *hauteur*, with which a regular Rabbinist regarded his northern co-religionists. The slighting speech of Nathanael (John 1:46), "Can there any good thing come out of Nazareth?" reads quite

---

[1]"The history of nations is the Nemesis of nations" ("Die Weltgeschichte ist das Weltgericht"), writes Schiller.

[2]There are two Talmuds—the Jerusalem and the Babylonian—to the text of the Mishnah. The Babylonian Talmud is considerably younger than that of Jerusalem, and its traditions far more deeply tinged with superstition and error of every kind. For historical purposes, also, the Jerusalem Talmud is of much greater value and authority than that of the Eastern Schools.

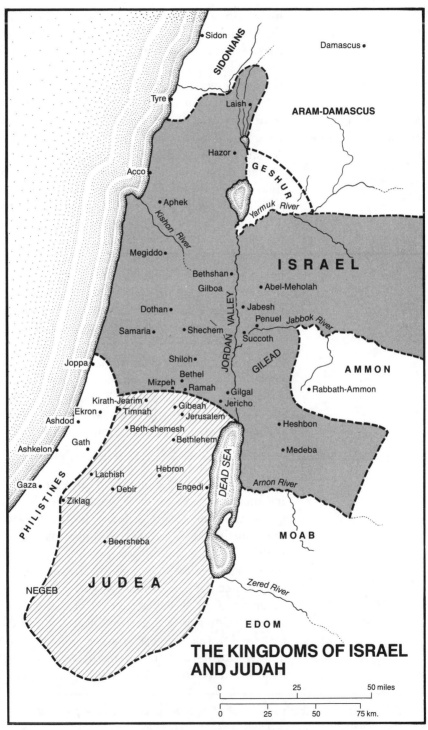

The kingdoms of Israel and Judah

"Cursed is the man who has sexual relations with any animal."
    Then all the people shall say, "Amen!"
(Deut. 27:21).

like a common saying of the period; and the rebuke of the Pharisees to Nicodemus (John 7:52), "Search, and look: for out of Galilee ariseth no prophet," was pointed by the mocking question, "Art thou also of Galilee?" It was not merely self-conscious superiority, such as the "towns-people," as the inhabitants of Jerusalem used to be called throughout Palestine, were said to have commonly displayed towards their "country cousins" and every one else, but offensive contempt, outspoken sometimes with almost incredible rudeness, want of delicacy and charity, but always with much pious self-assertion. The "God, I thank Thee that I am not as other men" (Luke 18:11) seems like the natural breath of Rabbinism in the company of the unlettered, and of all who were deemed intellectual or religious inferiors; and the parabolic history of the Pharisee and the publican in the gospel is not told for the special condemnation of that one prayer, but as characteristic of the whole spirit of Pharisaism, even in its approaches to God. "This people who knoweth not the law (that is, the traditional law) are cursed," was the curt summary of the Rabbinical estimate of popular opinion. To so terrible a length did it go that the Pharisees would fain have excluded them, not only from common intercourse, but from witness-bearing, and that they even applied to marriages with them such a passage as Deut. 27:21.[3]

But if these be regarded as extremes, two instances, chosen almost at random—one from religious, the other from ordinary life—will serve to illustrate their reality. A more complete parallel to the Pharisee's prayer could scarcely be imagined than the following. We read in the Talmud (*Jer. Ber.* iv. 2) that a celebrated Rabbi was wont every day, on leaving the academy, to pray in these terms: "I thank Thee, O Lord my God and God of my fathers, that Thou hast cast my lot among those who frequent the schools and synagogues, and not among those who attend the theatre and the circus. For, both I and they work and

---

[3]Every one who is curious to see the lengths to which Pharisaical pride could go in its contempt of the country people should read *Pes.* 49, *a* and *b*.

watch—I to inherit eternal life, they for their destruction." The other illustration, also taken from a Rabbinical work, is, if possible, even more offensive. It appears that Rabbi Jannai, while travelling by the way, formed acquaintance with a man, whom he thought his equal. Presently his new friend invited him to dinner, and liberally set before him meat and drink. But the suspicions of the Rabbi had been excited. He began to try his host successively by questions upon the text of Scripture, upon the Mishnah, allegorical interpretations, and lastly on Talmudical lore. Alas! on neither of these points could he satisfy the Rabbi. Dinner was over; and Rabbi Jannai, who by that time no doubt had displayed all the *hauteur* and contempt of a regular Rabbinist towards the unlettered, called upon his host, as customary, to take the cup of thanksgiving, and return thanks. But the latter was sufficiently humiliated to reply, with a mixture of Eastern deference and Jewish modesty, "Let Jannai himself give thanks in his own house." "At any rate," observed the Rabbi, "you can join with me;" and when the latter had agreed to this, Jannai said, "A dog has eaten of the bread of Jannai!"

Impartial history, however, must record a different judgment of the men of Galilee from that pronounced by the Rabbis, and that even wherein they were despised by those leaders in Israel. Some of their peculiarities, indeed, were due to territorial circumstances. The province of Galilee—of which the name might be rendered "circuit," being derived from a verb meaning "to move in a circle"—covered the ancient possessions of four tribes: Issachar, Zebulon, Naphtali, and Asher. The name occurs already in the Old Testament (compare Josh. 20:7; 1 Kings 9:11; 2 Kings 15:29; 1 Chron. 6:76; and especially Isa. 9:1). In the time of Christ it stretched northwards to the possessions of Tyre on the one side, and to Syria on the other; on the south it was bounded by Samaria—Mount Carmel on the western, and the district of Scythopolis (in the Decapolis) on the eastern side, being here landmarks; while the Jordan and the Lake of Gennesaret formed the general

Enjoying an elaborate meal

*I will lift up the cup of salvation
and call on the name
of the LORD
(Ps. 116:13).*

*Nevertheless, there will be no more gloom for those who were in distress. In the past he humbled the land of Zebulun and the land of Naphtali, but in the future he will honor Galilee of the Gentiles, by the way of the sea, along the Jordan
(Isa. 9:1).*

eastern boundary-line. Thus regarded, it would include names to which such reminiscences attach as "the mountains of Gilboa," where "Israel and Saul fell down slain;" little Hermon, Tabor, Carmel, and that great battle-field of Palestine, the plain of Jezreel. Alike the Talmud and Josephus divide it into Upper and Lower Galilee, between which the Rabbis insert the district of Tiberias, as Middle Galilee.[4] We are reminded of the history of Zaccheus (Luke 19:4) by the mark which the Rabbis give to distinguish between Upper and Lower Galilee—the former beginning "where sycomores cease to grow." The sycomore, which is a species of fig, must, of course, not be confounded with our sycamore, and was a very delicate evergreen, easily destroyed by cold (Ps. 78:47), and growing only in the Jordan valley, or in Lower Galilee up to the sea-coast. The mention of that tree may also help us to fix the locality where Luke 17:6 was spoken by the Saviour. The Rabbis mention Kefar Hananyah, probably the modern Kefr Anan, to the north-west of Safed, as the first place in Upper Galilee. Safed was truly "a city set on an hill;" and as such may have been in view of the Lord, when He spoke the Sermon on the Mount (Matt. 5:14). In the Talmud it is mentioned by the name of Zephath, and spoken of as one of the signal-stations, whence the proclamation of the new moon, made by the Sanhedrin in Jerusalem,[5] and with it the beginning of every month, was telegraphed by fire-signals from hill to hill throughout the land, and far away east of the Jordan, to those of the dispersion.

The mountainous part in the north of Upper Galilee presented magnificent scenery, with bracing air. Here the scene of the Song of Solomon is partly laid (Cant. 7:5). But its caves and fastnesses, as well as the marshy ground, covered with reeds, along Lake Merom, gave shelter to robbers, outlaws, and rebel chiefs. Some of the most dangerous characters came from the Galilean highlands. A little farther down,

Sycamore fig

He replied, "If you have faith as small as a mustard seed, you can say to this mulberry tree, 'Be uprooted and planted in the sea,' and it will obey you" (Luke 17:6).

---

[4] *Shev.* ix. 2.

[5] See my book on *The Temple: its Ministry and Services at the Time of Jesus Christ.*

Damascus

and the scenery changed. South of Lake Merom, where the so-called Jacob's bridge crosses the Jordan, we come upon the great caravan road, which connected Damascus in the east with the great mart of Ptolemais, on the shore of the Mediterranean. What a busy life did this road constantly present in the days of our Lord, and how many trades and occupations did it call into existence! All day long they passed— files of camels, mules, and asses, laden with the riches of the East, destined for the far West, or bringing the luxuries of the West to the far East. Travellers of every description—Jews, Greeks, Romans, dwellers in the East—were seen here. The constant intercourse with foreigners, and the settlement of so many strangers along one of the great highways of the world, must have rendered the narrow-minded bigotry of Judaea well-nigh impossible in Galilee.

About Asher he said: "Most blessed of sons is Asher; let him be favored by his brothers, and let him bathe his feet in oil" (Deut. 33:24).

We are now in Galilee proper, and a more fertile or beautiful region could scarcely be conceived.[6] It was truly the land where Asher dipped his foot in oil (Deut. 33:24). The Rabbis speak of the oil as flowing like a river, and they say that it was easier in Galilee to

[6] See also, generally, an interesting paper on "The Fertility of Ancient Palestine" in the *Quarterly Statement of the Palestine Exploration Fund* for July, 1876, pp. 120–132.

rear a forest of olive-trees than one child in Judaea!
The wine, although not so plentiful as the oil, was
generous and rich. Corn grew in abundance, especially
in the neighbourhood of Capernaum; flax also was
cultivated. The price of living was much lower than in
Judaea, where one measure was said to cost as much
as five in Galilee. Fruit also grew to perfection; and it
was probably a piece of jealousy on the part of the
inhabitants of Jerusalem, that they would not allow it
to be sold at the feasts in the city, lest people should
forsooth say, "We have only come up in order to taste
fruit from Galilee."[7] Josephus speaks of the country in
perfectly rapturous terms. He counts no fewer than
240 towns and villages, and speaks of the smallest as
containing not less than 15,000 inhabitants! This, of
course, must be gross exaggeration, as it would make
the country more than twice as thickly populated as
the densest districts in England or Belgium. Some one
has compared Galilee to the manufacturing districts
of this country. This comparison, of course, applies
only to the fact of its busy life, although various
industries were also carried on there—large potteries
of different kinds, and dyeworks. From the heights of
Galilee the eye would rest on harbours, filled with
merchant ships, and on the sea, dotted with white
sails. There, by the shore, and also inland, smoked
furnaces, where glass was made; along the great road
moved the caravans; in field, vineyard, and orchard
all was activity. The great road quite traversed Galilee,
entering it where the Jordan is crossed by the
so-called bridge of Jacob, then touching Capernaum,
going down to Nazareth, and passing on to the sea-
coast. This was one advantage that Nazareth had—
that it lay on the route of the world's traffic and intercourse. Another peculiarity is strangely unknown to
Christian writers. It appears from ancient Rabbinical
writings[8] that Nazareth was one of the stations of the
priests. All the priests were divided into twenty-four
courses, one of which was always on ministry in the

Laborers in a vineyard

*Fishing boat on the
Sea of Galilee*

[7] *Pes.* 8 *b.*
[8] See the reference in Neubauer, p. 190.

Some time after this, Jesus crossed to the far shore of the Sea of Galilee (that is, the Sea of Tiberias) (John 6:1).

Nazareth

Temple. Now, the priests of the course which was to be on duty always gathered in certain towns, whence they went up in company to the Temple; those who were unable to go spending the week in fasting and prayer for their brethren. Nazareth was one of these priestly centres; so that there, with symbolic significance, alike those passed who carried on the traffic of the world, and those who ministered in the Temple.

We have spoken of Nazareth; and a few brief notices of other places in Galilee, mentioned in the New Testament, may be of interest. Along the lake lay, north, Capernaum, a large city; and near it, Chorazin, so celebrated for its grain, that, if it had been closer to Jerusalem, it would have been used for the Temple;[9] also Bethsaida,[10] the name, "house of fishes," indicating its trade. Capernaum was the station where Matthew sat at the receipt of custom (Matt. 9:9). South of Capernaum was Magdala, the city of dyers, the home of Mary Magdalene (Mark 15:40; 16:1; Luke 8:2; John 20:1). The Talmud mentions its shops and its woolworks, speaks of its great wealth, but also of the corruption of its inhabitants. Tiberias, which had been built shortly before Christ, is only

---

[9]*Men.* 85 *a.*

[10]There were two places of that name, one east of the Jordan, Bethsaida Julias, referred to in Luke 9:10; Mark 8:22; the other on the western shore of the Lake of Galilee, the birthplace of Andrew and Peter (John 1:44). See also Mark 6:45; Matt. 11:21; Luke 10:13; John 12:21.

This, the first of his miraculous signs, Jesus performed at Cana in Galilee. He thus revealed his glory, and his disciples put their faith in him (John 2:11).

incidentally mentioned in the New Testament (John 6:1, 23; 21:1). At the time it was a splendid but chiefly heathen city, whose magnificent buildings contrasted with the more humble dwellings common in the country. Quite at the southern end of the lake was Tarichaea, the great fishing place, whence preserved fish was exported in casks (Strabo, 16.2). It was there that, in the great Roman war, a kind of naval battle was fought, which ended in terrible slaughter, no quarter being given by the Romans, so that the lake was dyed red with the blood of the victims, and the shore rendered pestilential by their bodies. Cana in Galilee was the birthplace of Nathanael (John 21:2), where Christ performed His first miracle (John 2:1–11); significant also in connection with the second miracle there witnessed, when the new wine of the kingdom was first tasted by Gentile lips (John 4:46, 47). Cana lay about three hours to the north-north-east of Nazareth. Lastly, Nain was one of the southernmost places in Galilee, not far from the ancient Endor.

It can scarcely surprise us, however interesting it may prove, that such Jewish recollections of the early Christians as the Rabbis have preserved, should linger chiefly around Galilee. Thus we have, in quite the apostolic age, mention of miraculous cures made, in the name of Jesus, by one Jacob of Chefar Sechanja (in Galilee), one of the Rabbis violently opposing on one occasion an attempt of the kind, the patient meanwhile dying during the dispute; repeated records of discussions with learned Christians, and other indications of contact with Hebrew believers. Some have gone farther,[11] and found traces of the general spread of such views in the fact that a Galilean teacher is introduced in Babylon as propounding the science of the *Merkabah,* or the mystical doctrines connected with Ezekiel's vision of the Divine chariot, which certainly contained elements closely approximating the Christian doctrines of the Logos, the

---

[11]See generally the learned volume of M. Neubauer, *La Géographie du Talmud,* p. 186, etc. Compare, also, Derenbourg, *L'Histoire et la Géographie de la Palestine,* pp. 347-365.

Trinity, etc. Trinitarian views have also been suspected in the significance attached to the number "three" by a Galilean teacher of the third century, in this wise: "Blessed be God, who has given the three laws (the Pentateuch, the Prophets, and the Hagiographa) to a people composed of three classes (Priests, Levites, and laity), through him who was the youngest of three (Miriam, Aaron, and Moses), on the third day (of their separation—Exod. 19:16), and in the third month." There is yet another saying of a Galilean Rabbi, referring to the resurrection, which, although far from clear, may bear a Christian application. Finally, the Midrash applies the expression, "The sinner shall be taken by her" (Eccl. 7:26), either to the above-named Christian Rabbi Jacob, or to Christians generally, or even to Capernaum, with evident reference to the spread of Christianity there. We cannot here pursue this very interesting subject farther than to say, that we find indications of Jewish Christians having endeavoured to introduce their views while leading the public devotions of the Synagogue, and even of contact with the immoral heretical sect of the Nicolaitans (Rev. 2:15).

Indeed, what we know of the Galileans would quite prepare us for expecting, that the gospel should have received at least a ready hearing among many of them. It was not only, that Galilee was the great scene of our Lord's working and teaching, and the home of His first disciples and apostles; nor yet that the frequent intercourse with strangers must have tended to remove narrow prejudices, while the contempt of the Rabbinists would loosen attachment to the strictest Pharisaism; but, as the character of the people is described to us by Josephus, and even by the Rabbis, they seem to have been a warm-hearted, impulsive, generous race—intensely national in the best sense, active, not given to idle speculations or wire-drawn logico-theological distinctions, but conscientious and earnest. The Rabbis detail certain theological differences between Galilee and Judaea. Without here mentioning them, we have no hesitation in saying, that they show more earnest practical

On the morning of the third day there was thunder and lightning, with a thick cloud over the mountain, and a very loud trumpet blast. Everyone in the camp trembled (Exod. 19:16).

*I find more bitter than death
   the woman who is a snare,
whose heart is a trap
   and whose hands are chains.
The man who pleases God
   will escape her,
   but the sinner she will ensnare
(Eccl. 7:26).*

But you have this in your favor: You hate the practices of the Nicolaitans, which I also hate (Rev. 2:6).

piety and strictness of life, and less adherence to those Pharisaical distinctions which so often made void the law. The Talmud, on the other hand, charges the Galileans with neglecting traditionalism; learning from one teacher, then from another (perhaps because they had only wandering Rabbis, not fixed academies); and with being accordingly unable to rise to the heights of Rabbinical distinctions and explanations. That their hot blood made them rather quarrelsome, and that they lived in a chronic state of rebellion against Rome, we gather not only from Josephus, but even from the New Testament (Luke 13:2; Acts 5:37). Their mal-pronunciation of Hebrew, or rather their inability properly to pronounce the gutturals, formed a constant subject of witticism and reproach, so current that even the servants in the High Priest's palace could turn round upon Peter, and say, "Surely thou also art one of them; for thy speech bewrayeth thee" (Matt. 26:73)—a remark this, by the way, which illustrates the fact that the language commonly used at the time of Christ in Palestine was Aramaean, not Greek. Josephus describes the Galileans as hard-working, manly, and brave; and even the Talmud admits (*Jer. Cheth.* iv. 14) that they cared more for honour than for money.

But the district in Galilee to which the mind ever reverts, is that around the shores of its lake.[12] Its beauty, its marvellous vegetation, its almost tropical products, its wealth and populousness, have been often described. The Rabbis derive the name of Gennesaret[13] either from a harp—because the fruits of its shores were as sweet as is the sound of a harp —or else explain it to mean "the gardens of the princes," from the beautiful villas and gardens

After him, Judas the Galilean appeared in the days of the census and led a band of people in revolt. He too was killed, and all his followers were scattered (Acts 5:37).

---

[12] The New Testament speaks so often of the occupation of fishers by the Lake of Galilee, that it is interesting to know that *fishing on the lake was free to all.* The Talmud mentions this as one of the ten ordinances given by Joshua of old (*Baba Kama,* 80 *b*).

[13] The Biblical name *Chinnereth* or *Chinneroth* (Num. 34:11, and in other places) is derived by the Rabbis from "harp" (*chinnor*); and its post-biblical form, *genessar,* is represented as extracted from *gener sarim,* gardens of the princes. The Biblical name is really "a basin," so that it can scarcely be derived from the town of *Genussar,* as M. Neubauer suggests (*ut supra,* p. 25, and in other places).

around. But we think chiefly not of those fertile fields and orchards, nor of the deep blue of the lake, enclosed between hills, nor of the busy towns, nor of the white sails spread on its waters—but of Him, Whose feet trod its shores; Who taught, and worked, and prayed there for us sinners; Who walked its waters and calmed its storms, and Who even after His resurrection held there sweet converse with His disciples; nay, Whose last words on earth, spoken from thence, come to us with peculiar significance and application, as in these days we look on the disturbing elements in the world around: "What is that to thee? Follow thou Me" (John 21:22).

4
TRAVELLING IN PALESTINE—
ROADS, INNS, HOSPITALITY, CUSTOM-HOUSE
OFFICERS, TAXATION, PUBLICANS

Then Levi held a great banquet for Jesus at his house, and a large crowd of tax collectors and others were eating with them (Luke 5:29).

It was the very busiest road in Palestine, on which the publican Levi Matthew sat at the receipt of "custom," when our Lord called him to the fellowship of the Gospel, and he then made that great feast to which he invited his fellow-publicans, that they also might see and hear Him in Whom he had found life and peace (Luke 5:29). For, it was the only truly international road of all those which passed through Palestine; indeed, it formed one of the great highways of the world's commerce. At the time of which we write, it may be said, in general, that six main arteries of commerce and intercourse traversed the country, the chief objective points being Caesarea, the military, and Jerusalem, the religious capital. *First,* there was the southern road, which led from Jerusalem, by Bethlehem, to Hebron, and thence westwards to Gaza, and eastwards into Arabia, whence also a direct road went northwards to Damascus. It is by this road we imagine St. Paul to have travelled, when retiring into the solitudes of Arabia, immediately after his conversion (Gal. 1:17, 18). The road to Hebron must have been much frequented by priestly and other pilgrims to the city, and by it the father of the Baptist and the parents of Jesus would pass. *Secondly,* there was the old highway along the sea-shore from Egypt up to Tyre, whence a straight, but not so much frequented, road struck, by Caesarea Philippi, to Damascus. But the sea-shore road itself, which successively touched Gaza, Ascalon, Jamnia, Lydda, Diospolis, and finally Caesarea and Ptolemais, was probably the most important military highway in the land, connecting the capital with the seat of the Roman procurator at Caesarea, and keeping the sea-board and its harbours free for communication. This road branched off for Jerusalem at Lydda, where it bifurcated, leading either by Beth-horon or by Emmaus, which was the longer way. It was probably by this road that the Roman escort hurried off St. Paul (Acts 23:31), the mounted soldiers leaving him at Antipatris, about twenty Roman miles from Lydda, and altogether from Jerusalem about fifty-two Roman miles (the Roman mile being 1,618 yards, the English mile 1,760). Thus the distance to Caesarea, still left to be traversed next morning by the cavalry would be about twenty-six Roman miles, or, the whole way, seventy-eight Roman miles from Jerusalem. This rate of travelling, though rapid, cannot be regarded as excessive, since an ordinary day's journey is computed in the Talmud (*Pes.* 93 *b*) as high as forty Roman miles. A *third* road led from Jerusalem, by Beth-horon and Lydda, to Joppa, whence it continued close by the sea-shore to Caesarea. This was the road which Peter and his companions would take when summoned to go and preach the gospel to Cornelius (Acts 10:23, 24). It was at Lydda, thirty-two Roman miles from Jerusalem, that Aeneas was miraculously healed, and "nigh" to it—within a few miles—was Joppa, where the raising of Tabitha, Dorcas, "the gazelle" (Acts 9:32–43), took place. Of the *fourth* great highway, which led from Galilee to Jerusalem, straight through Samaria, branching at Sichem eastwards to Damascus, and westwards to Caesarea, it is needless to say much, since, although much shorter, it was, if possible, eschewed by Jewish travellers; though, both in going to (Luke 9:53; 17:11), and returning from Jerusalem (John 4:4, 43), the Lord Jesus passed that way. The road from Jerusalem straight northwards also branched off at *Gophna*, whence it led across to Diospolis, and so on to Caesarea.[1] But ordinarily,

Peter sent them all out of the room; then he got down on his knees and prayed. Turning toward the dead woman, he said, "Tabitha, get up." She opened her eyes, and seeing Peter she sat up. He took her by the hand and helped her to her feet. Then he called the believers and the widows and presented her to them alive (Acts 9:40–41).

When the LORD learned of this, he left Judea and went back once more to Galilee. Now he had to go through Samaria (John 4:3–4).

---

[1]In Conybeare and Howson's *Life and Epistles of St. Paul* (ii. p. 331) this route is indicated as that taken by the Roman soldiery, when conducting St. Paul to Caesarea.

In reply Jesus said: "A man was going down from Jerusalem to Jericho, when he fell into the hands of robbers. They stripped him of his clothes, beat him and went away, leaving him half dead" (Luke 10:30).

Please let us pass through your country. We will not go through any field or vineyard, or drink water from any well. We will travel along the king's highway and not turn to the right or to the left until we have passed through your territory (Num. 20:17).

Jewish travellers would, rather than pass through Samaria, face the danger of robbers which awaited them (Luke 10:30) along the *fifth* great highway (comp. Luke 19:1, 28; Matt. 20:17, 29), that led from Jerusalem, by Bethany, to Jericho. Here the Jordan was forded, and the road led to Gilead, and thence either southwards, or else north to Peraea, whence the traveller could make his way into Galilee. It will be observed that all these roads, whether commercial or military, were, so to speak, Judaean, and radiated from or to Jerusalem. But the *sixth* and great road, which passed through Galilee, was not at all primarily Jewish, but connected the East with the West—Damascus with Rome. From Damascus it led across the Jordan to Capernaum, Tiberias, and Nain (where it fell in with a direct road from Samaria), to Nazareth, and thence to Ptolemais. Thus, from its position, Nazareth was on the world's great highway. What was spoken there might equally re-echo throughout Palestine, and be carried to the remotest lands of the East and of the West.

It need scarcely be said, that the roads which we have thus traced are only those along the principal lines of communication. But a large number of secondary roads also traversed the country in all directions. Indeed, from earliest times much attention seems to have been given to facility of intercourse throughout the land. Even in the days of Moses we read of "the king's highway" (Num. 20:17, 19; 21:22). In Hebrew we have, besides the two general terms (*derech* and *orach*), three expressions which respectively indicate a trodden or beaten-down path (*nathiv*, from *nathav*, to tread down), a made or cast-up road (*messillah*, from *salal*, to cast up), and "the king's highway"—the latter, evidently for national purposes, and kept up at the public expense. In the time of the kings (for example, 1 Kings 12:18), and even earlier, there were regular carriage roads, although we can scarcely credit the statement of Josephus (*Antiq.* 8.7.4) that Solomon had caused the principal roads to be paved with black stone—probably basalt. Toll was apparently levied in the time of Ezra (Ezra 4:13, 20); but the clergy were exempt from this as from all other taxation (7:24). The roads to the cities of refuge required to be always kept in good order (Deut. 19:3). According to the Talmud they were to be forty-eight feet wide, and provided with bridges, and with sign-posts where roads diverged.

Passing to later times, the Romans, as might have been expected, paid great attention to the modes of communication through the country. The military roads were paved, and provided with milestones. But the country roads were chiefly bridle-paths. The Talmud distinguishes between public and private roads. The former must be twenty-four, the latter six feet wide. It is added that, for the king's highway, and for the road taken by funerals, there is no measure (*Baba B.* vi. 7). Roads were annually repaired in spring, preparatory for going up to the great feasts. To prevent the possibility of danger, no subterranean structure, however protected, was allowed under a public road. Overhanging branches of trees had to be cut down, so as to allow a man on a camel to pass. A similar rule applied to balconies and projections; nor

Furthermore, the king should know that if this city is built and its walls are restored, no more taxes, tribute or duty will be paid, and the royal revenues will suffer...You are also to know that you have no authority to impose taxes, tribute or duty on any of the priests, Levites, singers, gatekeepers, temple servants or other workers at this house of God (Ezra 4:13; 7:24).

Roman road

were these permitted to darken a street. Any one allowing things to accumulate on the road, or dropping them from a cart, had to make good what damage might be incurred by travellers. Indeed, in towns and their neighbourhood the police regulations were even more strict; and such ordinances occur as for the removal within thirty days of rotten trees or dangerous walls; not to pour out water on the road; not to throw out anything on the street, nor to leave about building materials, or broken glass, or thorns, along with other regulations for the public safety and health.[2]

Egyptian cart

Along such roads passed the travellers; few at first, and mostly pilgrims, but gradually growing in number, as commerce and social or political intercourse increased. Journeys were performed on foot, upon asses, or in carriages (Acts 8:28), of which three kinds are mentioned—the round carriage, perhaps like our gig; the elongated, like a bed; and the cart, chiefly for the transport of goods. It will be understood that in those days travelling was neither comfortable nor easy. Generally, people journeyed in company, of which the festive bands going to Jerusalem are a well-known instance. If otherwise, one would prepare for a journey almost as for a change of residence, and provide tent, victuals, and all that was needful by the way. It was otherwise with the travelling hawker, who was welcomed as a friend in every district through which he passed, who carried the news of the day, exchanged the products of one for those of another district, and produced the latest articles of commerce or of luxury. Letters were only conveyed by special messengers, or through travellers.

In such circumstances, the command, "Be not forgetful to entertain strangers," had a special meaning. Israel was always distinguished for hospitality; and not only the Bible, but the Rabbis, enjoin this in the strongest terms. In Jerusalem no man was to account a house as only his own; and it was said, that

---

[2] Chiefly gathered from the juridical tractates *Baba Kama* and *Baba Bathra*.

during the pilgrim-feasts none ever wanted ready reception. The tractate *Aboth* (1. 5), mentions these as two out of the three sayings of Jose, the son of Jochanan, of Jerusalem: "Let thy house be wide open, and let the poor be the children of thy house." Readers of the New Testament will be specially interested to know, that, according to the Talmud (*Pes.* 53), Bethphage and Bethany, to which in this respect such loving memories cling, were specially celebrated for their hospitality towards the festive pilgrims. In Jerusalem it seems to have been the custom to hang a curtain in front of the door, to indicate that there was still room for guests. Some went so far as to suggest, there should be four doors to every house, to bid welcome to travellers from all directions. The host would go to meet an expected guest, and again accompany him part of the way (Acts 21:5). The Rabbis declared that hospitality involved as great, and greater merit than early morning attendance in an academy of learning. They could scarcely have gone farther, considering the value they attached to study. Of course, here also the Rabbinical order had the preference; and hospitably to entertain a sage, and to send him away with presents, was declared as meritorious as to have offered the daily sacrifices (*Ber.* 10, *b*).

But let there be no misunderstanding. So far as the duty of hospitality is concerned, or the loving care for poor and sick, it were impossible to take a higher tone than that of Rabbinism. Thus it was declared, that "the entertainment of travellers was as great a matter as the reception of the *Shechinah.*" This gives a fresh meaning to the admonition of the Epistle addressed specially to the Hebrews (13:2): "Be not forgetful to entertain strangers: for thereby some have entertained angels unawares." Bearing on this subject, one of the oldest Rabbinical commentaries has a very beautiful gloss on Ps. 109:31: "He shall stand at the right hand of the poor." "Whenever," we read, "a poor man stands at thy door, the Holy One, blessed be His Name, stands at his right hand. If thou givest him alms, know that thou shalt receive a reward from Him who standeth at his right hand." In

But when our time was up, we left and continued on our way. All the disciples and their wives and children accompanied us out of the city, and there on the beach we knelt to pray (Acts 21:5).

The LORD God made garments of skin for Adam and his wife and clothed them (Gen. 3:21).

The LORD appeared to Abraham near the great trees of Mamre while he was sitting at the entrance to his tent in the heat of the day (Gen. 18:1).

After Abraham's death, God blessed his son Isaac, who then lived near Beer Lahai Roi (Gen. 25:11).

When you enter a house, first say, "Peace to this house." If a man of peace is there, your peace will rest on him; if not, it will return to you (Luke 10:5–6).

another commentary God Himself and His angels are said to visit the sick. The Talmud itself counts hospitality among the things of which the reward is received alike in this life and in that which is to come (*Shab.* 127 *a*), while in another passage (*Sot.* 14 *a*) we are bidden imitate God in these four respects: He clothed the naked (Gen. 3:21); He visited the sick (Gen. 18:1); He comforted the mourners (Gen. 25:11); and He buried the dead (Deut. 34:6).

In treating of hospitality, the Rabbis display, as in so many relations of life, the utmost tenderness and delicacy, mixed with a delightful amount of shrewd knowledge of the world and quaint humour. As a rule, they enter here also into full details. Thus the very manner in which a host is to bear himself towards his guests is prescribed. He is to look pleased when entertaining his guests, to wait upon them himself, to promise little and to give much, etc. At the same time it was also caustically added: "Consider all men as if they were robbers, but treat them as if each were Rabbi Gamaliel himself!" On the other hand, rules of politeness and gratitude are equally laid down for the guests. "Do not throw a stone," it was said, "into the spring at which you have drunk" (*Baba K.* 92); or this, "A proper guest acknowledges all, and saith, 'At what trouble my host has been, and all for my sake!'—while an evil visitor remarks: 'Bah! what trouble has he taken?' Then, after enumerating how little he has had in the house, he concludes; 'And, after all, it was not done for me, but only for his wife and children!' " (*Ber.* 58 *a*).[3] Indeed, some of the sayings in this connection are remarkably parallel to the directions which our Lord gave to His disciples on going forth upon their mission (Luke 10:5–11, and parallels). Thus, one was to inquire for the welfare of the family; not to go from house to house; to eat of such things as were set before one; and, finally, to part with a blessing.

---

[3]Abbreviated from the Jer. and the Bab. Talmud. See also *Ber.* 63 *b*; 64 *a*, where Scriptural examples of the blessing attaching to hospitality are given.

Eastern Inn or Khan

...and she gave birth to her firstborn, a son. She wrapped him in cloths and placed him in a manger, because there was no room for them in the inn (Luke 2:7).

All this, of course, applied to entertainment in private families. On unfrequented roads, where villages were at great intervals, or even outside towns (Luke 2:7), there were regular khans, or places of lodgment for strangers. Like the modern khans, these places were open, and generally built in a square, the large court in the middle being intended for the beasts of burden or carriages, while rooms opened upon galleries all around. Of course these rooms were not furnished, nor was any payment expected from the wayfarer. At the same time, some one was generally attached to the khan—mostly a foreigner—who would for payment provide anything that might be needful, of which we have an instance in the parabolic history of the Good Samaritan (Luke 10:35). Such hostelries are mentioned so early as in the history of Moses (Gen. 42:27; 43:21). Jeremiah calls them "a place for strangers" (Jer. 41:17), wrongly rendered "habitation" in our Authorised Version. In the Talmud their designations are either Greek or Latin, in Aramaic form—one of them being the same as that used in Luke 10:34—proving that such places were chiefly provided by and for strangers.[4] In later times we also read of the *oshpisa*—evidently from *hospitium,* and showing its Roman origin—as a house of

The next day he took out two silver coins and gave them to the innkeeper. "Look after him," he said, "and when I return, I will reimburse you for any extra expense you may have" (Luke 10:35).

---

[4] In the ancient Latin Itineraries of Palestine, journeys are computed by *mansiones* (night-quarters) and *mutationes* (change of horses)—from five to eight such changes being computed for a day's journey.

public entertainment, where such food as locusts, pickled, or fried in flour or in honey, and Median or Babylonian beer, Egyptian drink, and home-made cider or wine, were sold; such proverbs circulating among the boon companions as "To eat without drinking is like devouring one's own blood" (*Shab.* 41 *a*), and where wild noise and games of chance were indulged in by those who wasted their substance by riotous living. In such places the secret police, whom Herod employed, would ferret out the opinions of the populace while over their cups.[5] That police must have been largely employed. According to Josephus (*Ant.* 15.366) spies beset the people, alike in town and country, watching their conversations in the unrestrained confidence of friendly intercourse. Herod himself is said to have acted in that capacity, and to have lurked about the streets at night-time in disguise to overhear or entrap unwary citizens. Indeed, at one time the city seems almost to have been under martial law, the citizens being forbidden "to meet together, to walk or eat together,"—presumably to hold public meetings, demonstrations, or banquets. History sufficiently records what terrible vengeance followed the slightest suspicion. The New Testament account of the murder of all the little children at Bethlehem (Matt. 2:16), in hope of destroying among them the royal scion of David, is thoroughly in character with all that we know of Herod and his reign. There is at least indirect confirmation of this narrative in Talmudical writings, as there is evidence that all the genealogical registers in the Temple were destroyed by order of Herod.[6] This is a most remarkable fact. The Jews retaliated by an intensity of hatred which went so far as to elevate the day of Herod's death (2 Shebet) into an annual feast-day, on which all mourning was prohibited.[7]

...nor did he permit the citizens either to meet together, or to walk, or eat together, but watched everything they did, and when any were caught, they were severely punished;...and there were spies set everywhere, both in the city and in the roads, who watched those that met together (Jos. Antiquities *15.366).*

When Herod realized that he had been outwitted by the Magi, he was furious, and he gave orders to kill all the boys in Bethlehem and its vicinity who were two years old and under, in accordance with the time he had learned from the Magi (Matt. 2:16).

[5] See a very graphic scene sketched in Delitzsch, *Handwerker-Leben zur Z. Jesu.*

[6] Hamburger, *Real Enc. P.* ii. p. 293; Jost, *Gesch. d. Jud.* i. p. 324.

[7] See the *Meg. Taan.* or roll of fasts, xi. 1. Compare on this date Derenbourg, *Hist. de Pal.* p. 164, 165; and Grätz, *Gesch. d. J.* iii. pp. 426, 427.

But whether passing through town or country, by quiet side-roads or along the great highway, there was one sight and scene which must constantly have forced itself upon the attention of the traveller, and, if he were of Jewish descent, would ever awaken afresh his indignation and hatred. Whithersoever he went, he encountered in city or country the well-known foreign tax-gatherer, and was met by his insolence, by his vexatious intrusion, and by his exactions. The fact that he was the symbol of Israel's subjection to foreign domination, galling though it was, had probably not so much to do with the bitter hatred of the Rabbinists towards the class of tax-farmers (*Moches*) and tax-collectors (*Gabbai*), both of whom were placed wholly outside the pale of Jewish society, as that they were so utterly shameless and regardless in their unconscientious dealings. For, ever since their return from Babylon, the Jews must, with a brief interval, have been accustomed to foreign taxation. At the time of Ezra (Ezra 4:13, 20; 7:24) they paid to the Persian monarch "toll, tribute, and custom"— *middah, belo,* and *halach*—or rather "ground-tax" (income and property-tax?), "custom" (levied on all that was for consumption, or imported), and "toll," or road-money. Under the reign of the Ptolemies the taxes seem to have been farmed to the highest bidder, the price varying from eight to sixteen talents—that is, from about £3,140 to about £6,280—a very small sum indeed, which enabled the Palestine tax-farmers to acquire immense wealth, and that although they had continually to purchase arms and court favour.[8] During the Syrian rule the taxes seem to have consisted of tribute, duty on salt, a third of the produce of all that was sown, and one-half of that from fruit-trees, besides poll-tax, custom duty, and an uncertain kind of tax, called "crown-money" (the *aurum coronarium* of the Romans), originally an annual gift of a crown of gold, but afterwards compounded for in money.[9] Under the Herodians the royal revenue seems to have

I issued an order and a search was made, and it was found that this city has a long history of revolt against kings and has been a place of rebellion and sedition. Jerusalem has had powerful kings ruling over the whole of Trans-Euphrates, and taxes, tribute and duty were paid to them (Ezra 4:19–20).

And when he was at Askelon, and demanded the taxes of the people of Askelon they refused to pay anything, and affronted him also: upon which he seized upon about twenty of the principal men, and slew them, and gathered what they had together, and sent it all to the king; and informed him what he had done (Jos. Antiquities 12.181).

---

[8] Jos. *Ant.* 12.154–185.
[9] *Ant.* 12.129–137.

Satan rose up against Israel and incited David to take a census of Israel. So David said to Joab and the commanders of the troops, "Go and count the Israelites from Beersheba to Dan. Then report back to me so that I may know how many there are" (1 Chron. 21:1–2).

been derived from crown lands, from a property and income-tax, from import and export duties, and from a duty on all that was publicly sold and bought, to which must be added a tax upon houses in Jerusalem.

Heavily as these exactions must have weighed upon a comparatively poor and chiefly agricultural population, they refer only to civil taxation, *not* to *religious dues.*[10] But, even so, we have not exhausted the list of contributions demanded of a Jew. For, every town and community levied its own taxes for the maintenance of synagogue, elementary schools, public baths, the support of the poor, the maintenance of public roads, city walls, and gates, and other general requirements.[11] It must, however, be admitted that the Jewish authorities distributed this burden of civic taxation both easily and kindly, and that they applied the revenues derived from it for the public welfare in a manner scarcely yet attained in the most civilized countries. The Rabbinical arrangements for public education, health, and charity were, in every respect, far in advance of modern legislation, although here also they took care themselves not to take the grievous burdens which they laid upon others, by expressly exempting from civic taxes all those who devoted themselves to the study of the law.

But the Roman taxation, which bore upon Israel with such crushing weight, was quite of its own kind—systematic, cruel, relentless, and utterly regardless. In general, the provinces of the Roman Empire, and what of Palestine belonged to them, were subject to two great taxes—poll-tax (or rather income-tax) and ground-tax. All property and income that fell not under the ground-tax was subject to poll-tax; which amounted, for Syria and Cilicia, to one per cent. The "poll-tax" was really twofold, consisting of income-tax and head-money, the latter, of course, the same in all cases, and levied on all persons (bond or free) up to the age of sixty-five—

---

[10] Comp. my *Temple: its Ministry and Services at the Time of Jesus Christ*, p. 334).
[11] For a brief general *aperçu* of these taxes, see Hamburger, *u.s.* p. 431.

women being liable from the age of twelve and men from that of fourteen. Landed property was subject to a tax of one-tenth of all grain, and one-fifth of the wine and fruit grown, partly paid in product and partly commuted into money.[12] Besides these, there was tax and duty on all imports and exports, levied on the great public highways and in the seaports. Then there was bridge-money and road-money, and duty on all that was bought and sold in the towns.[13] These, which may be called the regular taxes, were irrespective of any forced contributions, and of the support which had to be furnished to the Roman procurator and his household and court at Caesarea. To avoid all possible loss to the treasury, the proconsul of Syria, Quirinus (Cyrenius), had taken a regular census to show the number of the population and their means. This was a terrible crime in the eyes of the Rabbis, who remembered that, if numbering the people had been reckoned such great sin of old, the evil must be an hundredfold increased, if done by heathens and for their own purposes. Another offence lay in the thought, that tribute, hitherto only given to Jehovah, was now to be paid to a heathen emperor. "Is it lawful to pay tribute unto Caesar?" was a sore question, which many an Israelite put to himself as he placed the emperor's poll-tax beside the half-shekel of the sanctuary, and the tithe of his field, vineyard, and orchard, claimed by the tax-gatherer, along with that which he had hitherto only given unto the Lord. Even the purpose with which this inquiry was brought before Christ—to entrap Him in a political denunciation—shows, how much it was agitated among patriotic Jews; and it cost rivers of blood before it was not answered, but silenced.

The Romans had a peculiar way of levying these taxes—not directly, but indirectly—which kept the treasury quite safe, whatever harm it might inflict on

They came to him and said, "Teacher, we know you are a man of integrity. You aren't swayed by men, because you pay no attention to who they are; but you teach the way of God in accordance with the truth. Is it right to pay taxes to Caesar or not?" (Mark 12:14).

---

[12]Northern Africa alone (exclusive of Egypt) furnished Rome, by way of taxation, with sufficient corn to last eight months, and the city of Alexandria to last four months (*Jewish War*, 2.345–401).

[13]Compare, among others, Hausrath, *Neutest. Zeitg.* i. p. 167, etc.

As you are going with your adversary to the magistrate, try hard to be reconciled to him on the way, or he may drag you off to the judge, and the judge turn you over to the officer, and the officer throw you into prison. I tell you, you will not get out until you have paid the last penny (Luke 12:58–59).

the taxpayer, while at the same time it threw upon him the whole cost of the collection. Senators and magistrates were prohibited from engaging in business or trade; but the highest order, the equestrian, was largely composed of great capitalists. These Roman knights formed joint-stock companies, which bought at public auction the revenues of a province at a fixed price, generally for five years. The board had its chairman, or *magister,* and its offices at Rome. These were the real Publicani, or publicans, who often underlet certain of the taxes. The Publicani, or those who held from them, employed either slaves or some of the lower classes in the country as tax-gatherers —the publicans of the New Testament. Similarly, all other imposts were farmed and collected; some of them being very onerous, and amounting to an *ad valorem* duty of two and a half, of five, and in articles of luxury even of twelve and a half per cent. Harbour-dues were higher than ordinary tolls, and smuggling or a false declaration was punished by confiscation of the goods. Thus the publicans also levied import and export dues, bridge-toll, road-money, town-dues, etc.; and, if the peaceable inhabitant, the tiller of the soil, the tradesman, or manufacturer was constantly exposed to their exactions, the traveller, the caravan, or the pedlar encountered their vexatious presence at every bridge, along the road, and at the entrance to cities. Every bale had to be unloaded, and all its contents tumbled about and searched; even letters were opened; and it must have taken more than Eastern patience to bear their insolence and to submit to their "unjust accusations" in arbitrarily fixing the return from land or income, or the value of goods, etc. For there was no use appealing against them, although the law allowed this, since the judges themselves were the direct beneficiaries by the revenue; for they before whom accusations on this score would have to be laid, belonged to the order of knights, who were the very persons implicated in the farming of the revenue. Of course, the joint-stock company of Publicani at Rome expected its handsome dividends; so did the tax-gatherers in the provinces, and those to whom they on occasions sublet the imposts. All wanted to make money of the poor people; and the cost of the collection had of course to be added to the taxation. We can quite understand how Zaccheus, one of the supervisors of these tax-gatherers in the district of Jericho, which, from its growth and export of balsam, must have yielded a large revenue, should, in remembering his past life, have at once said: "If I have taken anything from any man by false accusation"—or, rather, "Whatever I have wrongfully exacted of any man."[14] For nothing was more common than for the publican to put a fictitious value on property or income. Another favourite trick of theirs was to advance the tax to those who were unable to pay, and then to charge usurious interest on what had thereby become a private debt. How summarily and harshly such debts were exacted, appears from the New Testament itself. In Matt. 18:28 we read of a creditor who, for the small debt of one hundred denars (about £3 6s. 8d.), seizes the debtor by the throat in the open street, and drags him to prison; the miserable man, in his fear of the consequences, in vain falling down at his feet, and beseeching him to have patience, in not exacting immediate full payment. What these consequences were, we learn from the same parable, where the king threatens not only to sell off all that his debtor has, but even himself, his wife, and children into slavery (ver. 25). And what short shrift such an unhappy man had to expect from "the magistrate," appears from the summary procedure, ending in imprisonment till "the last mite" had been paid, described in Luke 12:58.

However, therefore, in far-off Rome, Cicero might describe the Publicani as "the flower of knighthood, the ornament of the state, and the strength of the republic," or as "the most upright and respected men," the Rabbis in distant Palestine might be excused for their intense dislike of "the publicans," even although it went to the excess of declaring them incapable of bearing testimony in a Jewish court of

But Zacchaeus stood up and said to the LORD, "Look, LORD! Here and now I give half of my possessions to the poor, and if I have cheated anybody out of anything, I will pay back four times the amount" (Luke 19:8).

But when that servant went out, he found one of his fellow servants who owed him a hundred denarii. He grabbed him and began to choke him. "Pay back what you owe me!" he demanded (Matt. 18:28).

Since he was not able to pay, the master ordered that he and his wife and his children and all that he had be sold to repay the debt (Matt 18:25).

---

[14]Dean Alford's translation.

Men may vow to murderers, robbers, or tax-gatherers that what they have is Heave-offering even though it is not Heave-offering; or that they belong to the king's household even though they do no belong to the king's household (Mishnah, Nedarim iii. 4).

law, of forbidding to receive their charitable gifts, or even to change money out of their treasury (*Baba K. x.* 1), of ranking them not only with harlots and heathens, but with highwaymen and murderers (*Ned.* iii. 4), and of even declaring them excommunicate. Indeed, it was held lawful to make false returns, to speak untruth, or almost to use any means to avoid paying taxes (*Ned.* 27 *b.*; 28 *a*). And about the time of Christ the burden of such exactions must have been felt all the heavier on account of a great financial crisis in the Roman Empire (in the year 33 of our era), which involved so many in bankruptcy, and could not have been without its indirect influence even upon distant Palestine.

Of such men—despised Galileans, unlettered fishermen, excommunicated publicans—did the blessed Lord, in His self-humiliation, choose His closest followers, His special apostles! What a contrast to the Pharisaical notions of the Messiah and His kingdom! What a lesson to show, that it was not "by might nor by power," but by His Spirit, and that God had chosen the base things of this world, and things that were despised, to confound things that were mighty! Assuredly, this offers a new problem, and one harder of solution than many others, to those who would explain everything by natural causes. Whatever they may say of the superiority of Christ's teaching to account for its success, no religion could ever have been more weighted; no popular cause could ever have presented itself under more disadvantageous circumstances than did the Gospel of Christ to the Jews of Palestine. Even from this point of view, to the historical student familiar with the outer and inner life of that period, there is no other explanation of the establishment of Christ's kingdom than the power of the Holy Ghost.

So he said to me, "This is the word of the LORD to Zerubbabel: 'Not by might nor by power, but by my Spirit,' says the LORD Almighty" (Zech. 4:6).

As Jesus went on from there, he saw a man named Matthew sitting at the tax collector's booth. "Follow me," he told him, and Matthew got up and followed him (Matt. 9:9).

Such a custom-house officer was Matthew Levi, when the voice of our Lord, striking to the inmost depths of his heart, summoned him to far different work. It was a wonder that the Holy One should speak to such an one as he; and oh! in what different accents from what had ever fallen on his ears. But it was not merely condescension, kindness, sympathy, even familiar intercourse with one usually regarded as a social pariah; it was the closest fellowship; it was reception into the innermost circle; it was a call to the highest and holiest work which the Lord offered to Levi. And the busy road on which he sat to collect customs and dues would now no more know the familiar face of Levi, otherwise than as that of a messenger of peace, who brought glad tidings of great joy.

5
IN JUDAEA

So Rachel died and was buried on the way to Ephrath (that is, Bethlehem). Over her tomb Jacob set up a pillar, and to this day that pillar marks Rachel's tomb (Gen. 35:19–20).

If Galilee could boast of the beauty of its scenery and the fruitfulness of its soil; of being the mart of a busy life, and the highway of intercourse with the great world outside Palestine, Judaea would neither covet nor envy such advantages. Hers was quite another and a peculiar claim. Galilee might be the outer court, but Judaea was like the inner sanctuary of Israel. True, its landscapes were comparatively barren, its hills bare and rocky, its wilderness lonely; but around those grey limestone mountains gathered the sacred history—one might almost say, the romance and religion of Israel. Turning his back on the luxurious richness of Galilee, the pilgrim, even in the literal sense, constantly went up towards Jerusalem. Higher and higher rose the everlasting hills, till on the uppermost he beheld the sanctuary of his God, standing out from all around, majestic in the snowy pureness of its marble and glittering gold. As the hum of busy life gradually faded from his hearing, and he advanced into the solemn stillness and loneliness, the well-known sites which he successively passed must have seemed to wake the echoes of the history of his people. First, he approached *Shiloh,* Israel's earliest sanctuary, where, according to tradition, the Ark had rested for 370 years less one. Next came *Bethel,* with its sacred memorial of patriarchal history. There, as the Rabbis had it, even the angel of death was shorn of his power. Then he stood on the plateau of *Ramah,* with the neighbouring heights of Gibeon and Gibeah, round which so many events in

Jerusalem from the South

Jewish history had clustered. In Ramah Rachel died, and was buried.[1] We know that Jacob set up a pillar on her grave. Such is the reverence of Orientals for the resting-places of celebrated historical personages, that we may well believe it to have been the same pillar which, according to an eye-witness, still marked the site at the time of our Lord.[2] Opposite to it were the graves of Bilhah and of Dinah.[3] Only five miles from Jerusalem, this pillar was, no doubt, a well-known landmark. By this memorial of Jacob's sorrow and shame had been the sad meeting-place of the captives when about to be carried into Babylon (Jer. 40:1). There was bitter wailing at parting from those left

The word came to Jeremiah from the LORD after Nebuzaradan commander of the imperial guard had released him at Ramah. He had found Jeremiah bound in chains among all the captives from Jerusalem and Judah who were being carried into exile to Babylon (Jer. 40:1).

---

[1]This appears, to me at least, the inevitable inference from 1 Sam. 10:2, 3, and Jer. 31:15. Most writers have concluded from Gen. 35:16, 19, that Rachel was buried close by Bethlehem, but the passage does *not* necessarily imply this. The oldest Jewish Commentary (*Sifre*, ed. Vienna, p. 146) supports the view given above in the text. M. Neubauer suggests that Rachel had died in the possession of Ephraim, and been buried at Bethlehem. The hypothesis is ingenious but fanciful.

[2]*Book of Jubil.* cxxxii. *Apud Hausrath, Neutest. Zeitg.* p. 26.

[3]Ibid. c. p. 34.

behind, and in weary prospect of hopeless bondage, and still bitterer lamentation, as in the sight of friends, relations and countrymen, the old and the sick, the weakly, and women and children were pitilessly slaughtered, not to encumber the conqueror's homeward march. Yet a third time was Rachel's pillar, twice before the memorial of Israel's sorrow and shame, to re-echo her lamentation over yet sorer captivity and slaughter, when the Idumaean Herod massacred her innocent children, in the hope of destroying with them Israel's King and Israel's kingdom. Thus was her cup of former bondage and slaughter filled, and the words of Jeremy the prophet fulfilled, in which he had depicted Rachel's sorrow over her children (Matt. 2:17, 18).

Then what was said through the prophet Jeremiah was fulfilled: "A voice is heard in Ramah, weeping and great mourning, Rachel weeping for her children and refusing to be comforted, because they are no more" (Matt. 2:17–18).

But westward from those scenes, where the mountains shelved down, or more abruptly descended towards the *Shephelah,* or wolds by the sea, were the scenes of former triumphs. Here Joshua had pursued the kings of the south; there Samson had come down upon the Philistines, and here for long years had war been waged against the arch-enemy of Israel, Philistia. Turning thence to the south, beyond the capital was royal Bethlehem, and still farther the priest-city Hebron, with its caves holding Israel's most precious dust. That highland plateau was the wilderness of Judaea, variously named from the villages which at long distances dotted it;[4] desolate, lonely, tenanted only by the solitary shepherd, or the great proprietor, like Nabal, whose sheep pastured along its heights and in its glens. This had long been the home of outlaws, or of those who, in disgust with the world, had retired from its fellowship. These limestone caves had been the hiding-place of David and his followers; and many a band had since found shelter in these wilds. Here also John the Baptist prepared for his work, and there, at the time of which we write, was the retreat of the Essenes, whom a vain hope of finding purity in separation from the world

David left Gath and escaped to the cave of Adullam. When his brothers and his father's household heard about it, they went down to him there (1 Sam. 22:1).

---

[4]Such as Tekoah, Engedi, Ziph, Maon, and Beersheba, which gave their names to districts in the wilderness of Judaea.

Jericho

and its contact had brought to these solitudes. Beyond, deep down in a mysterious hollow, stretched the smooth surface of the Dead Sea, a perpetual memorial of God and of judgment. On its western shore rose the castle which Herod had named after himself, and farther south that almost inaccessible fastness of Masada, the scene of the last tragedy in the great Jewish war. Yet from the wild desolateness of the Dead Sea it was but a few hours to what seemed almost an earthly paradise. Flanked and defended by four surrounding forts, lay the important city of Jericho. Herod had built its walls, its theatre and amphitheatre; Archelaus its new palace, surrounded by splendid gardens. Through Jericho led the pilgrim way from Galilee, followed by our Lord Himself (Luke 19:1); and there also passed the great caravan-road, which connected Arabia with Damascus. The fertility of its soil, and its tropical produce, were almost proverbial. Its palm-groves and gardens of roses, but especially its balsam-plantations, of which the largest was behind the royal palace, were the fairy land of the old world. But this also was only a source of gain to the hated foreigner. Rome had made it a central station for the collection of tax and custom, known to us from Gospel history as that by which the chief publican Zaccheus had gotten his wealth. Jericho, with its general trade and its traffic in balsam —not only reputed the sweetest perfume, but also a cherished medicine in antiquity—was a coveted prize to all around. A strange setting for such a gem were its surroundings. There was the deep depression of the *Arabah,* through which the Jordan wound, first with tortuous impetuosity, and then, as it neared the Dead Sea, seemingly almost reluctant to lose its waters in that slimy mass.[5] Pilgrims, priests, traders, robbers, anchorites, wild fanatics, such were the figures to be met on that strange scene; and almost within hearing were the sacred sounds from the Temple-mount in the distance.[6]

It might be so, as the heathen historian put it in regard to Judaea, that no one could have wished for its own sake to wage serious warfare for its possession.[7] The Jew would readily concede this. It was not material wealth which attracted him hither, although the riches brought into the Temple from all quarters of the world ever attracted the cupidity of the Gentiles. To the Jew this was the true home of his soul, the centre of his inmost life, the longing of his heart. "If I forget thee, O Jerusalem, let my right hand forget her cunning," sang they who sat by the rivers of Babylon, weeping as they remembered Zion. "If I do not remember thee, let my tongue cleave to the roof of my mouth; if I prefer not Jerusalem above my chief joy" (Ps. 137:5, 6). It is from such pilgrim-psalms by the way as Ps. 84 or from the Songs of Ascent to the Holy City,[8] that we learn the feelings of Israel, culminating in this mingled outpouring of prayer and

Balsam

---

[5] Plin. *Hist. Nat.* vi. 5, 2.

[6] According to the Jerus. Talmud (*Succ.* v. 3) six different acts of ministry in the Temple were heard as far as Jericho, and the smell of the burning incense also could be perceived there. We need scarcely say that this was a gross exaggeration.

[7] Strabo, *Geogr.* xvi. 2.

[8] Commonly known as the Psalms of Degrees.

praise, with which they greeted the city of their longings as first it burst on their view:

> *Jehovah hath chosen Zion;*
> *He hath desired it for His habitation.*
> *This is my rest for ever:*
> *Here will I dwell, for I desire after it!*
> *I will abundantly bless her provision:*
> *I will satisfy her poor with bread.*
> *I will also clothe her priests with salvation:*
> *And her saints shall shout aloud for joy.*
> *There will I make the horn of David to bud:*
> *I ordain a lamp for Mine anointed.*
> *His enemies will I clothe with shame:*
> *But upon himself shall his crown flourish.*
> *(Ps. 132:13–18)*

Words these, true alike in their literal and spiritual applications; highest hopes which, for nigh two thousand years, have formed and still form part of Israel's daily prayer, when they plead: "Speedily cause Thou 'the Branch of David,' Thy servant, to shoot forth, and exalt Thou his horn through Thy salvation."[9] Alas, that Israel knows not the fulfilment of these hopes already granted and expressed in the thanksgiving of the father of the Baptist: "Blessed be the Lord God of Israel; for He hath visited and redeemed His people, and hath raised up an horn of salvation for us in the house of His servant David; as He spake by the mouth of His holy prophets, which have been since the world began" (Luke 1:68–70).[10]

Such blessings, and much more, were not only objects of hope, but realities alike to the Rabbinist and the unlettered Jew. They determined him willingly to bend the neck under a yoke of ordinances otherwise unbearable; submit to claims and treatment against which his nature would otherwise have rebelled, endure scorn and persecutions which would have broken any other nationality and crushed any other religion. To the far exiles of the Dispersion, this was the one fold, with its promise of good shepherding, of green pastures, and quiet waters. Judaea was,

> *Blessed are those whose strength is in you,*
> *who have set their hearts on pilgrimage.*
> *As they pass through the Valley of Baca,*
> *they make it a place of springs;*
> *the autumn rains also cover it with pools.*
> *They go from strength to strength,*
> *till each appears before God in Zion*
> *(Ps. 84:5–7).*

---

[9] This is the fifteenth of the eighteen "benedictions" in the daily prayers.

[10] Compare Delitzsch, *Comm. ü. d.* Ps. 2, p. 269.

And indeed it so came to pass, that our nation suffered these things under Antiochus Epiphanes, according to Daniel's vision, and what he wrote many years before they came to pass. In the very same manner Daniel also wrote concerning the Roman government, and that our country should be made desolate by them (Jos. Antiquities 10.276).

so to speak, their *Campo Santo,* with the Temple in the midst of it, as the symbol and prophecy of Israel's resurrection. To stand, if it were but once, within its sacred courts, to mingle with its worshippers, to bring offerings, to see the white-robed throng of ministering priests, to hear the chant of Levites, to watch the smoke of sacrifices uprising to heaven—to be there, to take part in it was the delicious dream of life, a very heaven upon earth, the earnest of fulfilling prophecy. No wonder, that on the great feasts the population of Jerusalem and of its neighbourhood, so far as reckoned within its sacred girdle, swelled to millions, among whom were "devout men, out of every nation under heaven" (Acts 2:5), or that treasure poured in from all parts of the inhabited world.[11] And this increasingly, as sign after sign seemed to indicate that "the End" was nearing. Surely the sands of the times of the Gentiles must have nearly run out. The promised Messiah might at any moment appear and "restore the kingdom to Israel." From the statements of Josephus[12] we know that the prophecies of Daniel were specially resorted to, and a mass of the most interesting, though tangled, apocalyptic literature, dating from that period, shows what had been the popular interpretation of unfulfilled prophecy.[13] The oldest Jewish paraphrases of Scripture, or *Targumim,* breathe the same spirit. Even the great heathen historians note this general expectancy of an impending Jewish world-empire, and trace to it the origin of the rebellions against Rome.[14] Not even the allegorising Jewish philosophers of Alexandria remained uninfluenced by the universal hope. Outside Palestine all eyes were directed towards Judaea, and each pilgrim band on its return, or wayfaring brother on his journey, might bring tidings of startling events. Within the

[11] We know that in the year 62 the contribution from these four extra-Palestinian communities: Apamea, Laodicea, Adramyttium, and Pergamos amounted to upwards of £8,000.

[12] For example, *Ant.* 10.276.

[13] Nothing can well be more interesting or important, but also more difficult, than the study of this literature, known as the pseudo-epigraphic writings. The present, however, is not the place for such inquiries, which must be reserved for much fuller discussion.

[14] Suet. *Vesp.* 4; Tac. *Hist.* v. 13.

land the feverish anxiety of those who watched the scene not unfrequently rose to delirium and frenzy. Only thus can we account for the appearance of so many false Messiahs and for the crowds which, despite repeated disappointments, were ready to cherish the most unlikely anticipations. It was thus that a *Theudas*[15] could persuade "a great part of the people" to follow him to the brink of Jordan, in the hope of seeing its waters once more miraculously divide, as before Moses, and an Egyptian impostor induce them to go out to the Mount of Olives in the expectation of seeing the walls of Jerusalem fall down at his command.[16] Nay, such was the infatuation of fanaticism, that while the Roman soldiers were actually preparing to set the Temple on fire, a false prophet could assemble 6,000 men, women, and children, in its courts and porches to await then and there a miraculous deliverance from heaven.[17] Nor did even the fall of Jerusalem quench these expectations, till a massacre, more terrible in some respects than that at the fall of Jerusalem, extinguished in blood the last public Messianic rising against Rome under *Bar Cochab*.[18]

For, however misdirected—so far as related to the person of the Christ and the nature of His kingdom—not to the fact or time of His coming, nor yet to the character of Rome—such thoughts could not be uprooted otherwise than with the history and religion of Israel. The New Testament proceeds upon them, as well as the Old; Christians and Jews alike cherished them. In the language of St. Paul, this was "the hope of the promise made of God unto our fathers: unto which our twelve tribes, instantly serving God day and night, hope to come" (Acts 26:6, 7). It was this which sent the thrill of expectancy through the whole nation, and drew crowds to Jordan, when

Now, a man that is in adversity does easily comply with such promises; for when a such a seducer makes him believe that he shall be delivered from those miseries which oppress him, then it is that the patient is full of hopes of such deliverance (Jos. Jewish War 6.287).

And so John came, baptizing in the desert region and preaching a baptism of repentance for the forgiveness of sins. The whole Judean countryside and all the people of Jerusalem went out to him. Confessing their sins, they were baptized by him in the Jordan River (Mark 1:4–5).

---

[15] Jos. *Ant.* 20.97–99. Of course this could not have been the Theudas of Acts 5:36, 37, but both the name and the movement were not solitary in Israel at the time.

[16] Jos. *Ant.* 20.167–172.

[17] Jos. *Jewish War,* 6.287.

[18] See my *History of the Jewish Nation,* pp. 215–227.

...and he sent them out to preach the kingdom of God and to heal the sick (Luke 9:2).

an obscure anchorite, who did not even pretend to attest his mission by any miracle, preached repentance in view of the near coming of the kingdom of God. It was this which turned all eyes to Jesus of Nazareth, humble and unpretending as were His origin, His circumstances, and His followers, and which diverted the attention of the people even from the Temple to the far-off lake of despised Galilee. And it was this which opened every home to the messengers whom Christ sent forth, by two and two, and even after the Crucifixion, every synagogue, to the apostles and preachers from Judaea. The title "Son of man" was familiar to those who had drawn their ideas of the Messiah from the well-known pages of Daniel. The popular apocalyptic literature of the period, especially the so-called "Book of Enoch," not only kept this designation in popular memory, but enlarged on the judgment which He was to execute on Gentile kings and nations.[19] "Wilt Thou at this time restore the kingdom to Israel?" was a question out of the very heart of Israel. Even John the Baptist, in the gloom of his lonely prison, staggered not at the person of the Messiah, but at the manner in which He seemed to found His kingdom.[20] He had expected to hear the blows of that axe which he had lifted fall upon the barren tree, and had to learn that the innermost secret of that kingdom—carried not in

---

[19] The following as a specimen must suffice for the present: "And this Son of man, whom thou hast seen, shall stir up the kings and the mighty from their layers, and the powerful from their thrones, and shall loose the bridles of the mighty and break in pieces the teeth of sinners. And He shall drive the kings from their thrones and from their empires, if they do not exalt nor praise Him, nor gratefully own from whence the kingdom has been entrusted to them. And He shall drive away the face of the mighty, and shame shall fill them: darkness shall be their dwelling and worms their bed, and they shall have no hope of rising from their beds, because they do not exalt the name of the Lord of spirits...And they shall be driven forth out of the homes of His congregation and of the faithful" (Book of Enoch, xlvi. 4, 5, 6, 8). A full discussion of this most important subject, and, indeed, of many kindred matters, must be reserved for a work on the Life and Times of our Lord.

[20] The passage above referred to has a most important apologetic interest. None but a truthful history would have recorded the doubts of John the Baptist; especially when they brought forward the real difficulties which the mission of Christ raised in the popular mind; least of all would it have followed up the statement of these difficulties by such an encomium as the Saviour passed upon John.

earthquake of wrath, nor in whirlwind of judgment, but breathed in the still small voice of love and pity— was comprehension, not exclusion; healing, not destruction.

As for the Rabbis, the leaders of public opinion, their position towards the kingdom was quite different. Although in the rising of Bar Cochab the great Rabbi Akiba acted as the religious standard-bearer, he may be looked upon as almost an exception. His character was that of an enthusiast, his history almost a romance. But, in general, the Rabbis did not identify themselves with the popular Messianic expectations. Alike the Gospel-history and their writings show not merely that anti-spiritual opposition to the Church which we might have expected, but coldness and distance in regard to all such movements. Legal rigorism and merciless bigotry are not fanaticism. The latter is chiefly the impulse of the ill-informed. Even their contemptuous turning away from "this people which knoweth not the law," as "accursed," proves them incapable of a fanaticism which recognises a brother in every one whose heart burns with the same fire, no matter what his condition otherwise. The great text-book of Rabbinism, the Mishnah, is almost entirely un-Messianic, one might say un-dogmatical. The method of the Rabbis was purely logical. Where not a record of facts or traditions, the Mishnah is purely a handbook of legal determinations in their utmost logical sequences, only enlivened by discussions or the tale of instances in point. The whole tendency of this system was anti-Messianic. Not but that in souls so devout and natures so ardent enthusiasm might be kindled, but that all their studies and pursuits went in the contrary direction. Besides, they knew full well how little of power was left them, and they dreaded losing even this. The fear of Rome constantly haunted them. Even at the destruction of Jerusalem the leading Rabbis aimed to secure their safety, and their after history shows, frequently recurring, curious instances of Rabbinical intimacy with their Roman oppressors. The Sanhedrim spoke their inmost apprehensions, when in that secret session they determined to kill Jesus from fear that, if He were allowed to go on, and all men were to believe on Him, the Romans would come and take away both their place and nation (John 11:48). Yet not one candid mind among them discussed the reality of His miracles; not one generous voice was raised to assert the principle of the Messiah's claims and kingdom, even though they had rejected those of Jesus of Nazareth! The question of the Messiah might come up as a speculative point; it might force itself upon the attention of the Sanhedrim; but it was not of personal, practical, life-interest to them. It may mark only one aspect of the question, and that an extreme one, yet even as such it is characteristic, when a Rabbi could assert that "between the present and the days of the Messiah there was only this difference, Israel's servitude."

If we let him go on like this, everyone will believe in him, and then the Romans will come and take away both our place and our nation (John 11:48).

Quite other matters engrossed the attention of the Rabbis. It was the present and the past, not the future, which occupied them—the *present* as fixing all legal determinations, and the *past* as giving sanction to this. Judaea proper was the only place where the *Shechinah* had dwelt, the land where Jehovah had caused His temple to be reared, the seat of the Sanhedrim, the place where alone learning and real piety were cultivated. From this point of view everything was judged. Judaea was "grain, Galilee straw, and beyond Jordan chaff." To be a Judaean was to be "an Hebrew of the Hebrews." It has already been stated what reproach the Rabbis attached to Galilee in regard to its language, manners, and neglect of regular study. In some respects the very legal observances, as certainly social customs, were different in Judaea from Galilee. Only in Judaea could Rabbis be ordained by the laying on of hands; only there could the Sanhedrim in solemn session declare and proclaim the commencement of each month, on which the arrangement of the festive calendar depended. Even after the stress of political necessity had driven the Rabbis to Galilee, they returned to Lydda for the purpose, and it needed a sharp struggle before they transferred the privilege of Judaea to

In Judea they used to do work until midday on the eves of Passover, but in Galilee they used to do nothing at all (Mishnah, Pesaḥim 4.5).

other regions in the third century of our era (*Jer. Sanh.* i. 1, 18). The wine for use in the Temple was brought exclusively from Judaea, not only because it was better, but because the transport through Samaria would have rendered it defiled. Indeed, the Mishnah mentions the names of the five towns whence it was obtained.[21] Similarly, the oil used was derived either from Judaea, or, if from Peraea, the olives only were brought, to be crushed in Jerusalem.[22]

The question what cities were really Jewish was of considerable importance, so far as concerned ritual questions, and it occupied the earnest attention of the Rabbis. It is not easy to fix the exact boundaries of Judaea proper towards the north-west. To include the sea-shore in the province of Samaria is a popular mistake. It certainly was never reckoned with it. According to Josephus (*Jewish War*, 3.35–58) Judaea proper extended along the sea-shore as far north as Ptolemais or Acco. The Talmud seems to exclude at least the northern cities. In the New Testament there is a distinction made between Caesarea and the province of Judaea (Acts 12:19; 21:10). This affords one of the indirect evidences not only of the intimate acquaintance of the writer with strictly Rabbinical views, but also of the early date of the composition of the Book of Acts. For, at a later period Caesarea was declared to belong to Judaea, although its harbour was excluded from such privileges, and all east and west of it pronounced "defiled." Possibly, it may have been added to the cities of Judaea, simply because afterwards so many celebrated Rabbis resided there. The importance attaching to Caesarea in connection with the preaching of the Gospel and the history of St. Paul, and the early and flourishing Christian churches there established give fresh interest to all notices of the place. Only those from Jewish sources can here engage our attention. It were out of place here to

Nor indeed is Judea destitute of such delights as come from the sea, since its maritime places extend as far as Ptolemais: it was parted into eleven portions, of which the royal city Jerusalem was the supreme, and presided over all the neighboring country, as the head does over the body. As to the other cities that were inferior to it, they presided over their several toparchies (Jos. Jewish War 3.53–54).

---

[21]Compare the discussion in M. Neubauer's *Géogr. du Talm.* p. 84, etc., and the Talmudical passages there quoted.

[22]*Ut supra.*

Philip, however, appeared at Azotus and traveled about, preaching the gospel in all the towns until he reached Caesarea (Acts 8:40).

describe the political importance of Caesarea, as the seat of the Roman power, or its magnificent harbour and buildings, or its wealth and influence. In Jewish writings it bears the same name by which we know it, though at times it is designated after its fortifications (Migdal Shur, M. Zor, M. Nassi), or after its harbour (Migdal Shina), once also by its ancient name, the tower of Straton. The population consisted of a mixture of Jews, Greeks, Syrians, and Samaritans, and tumults between them were the first signal of the great Jewish war. The Talmud calls it "the capital of the kings." As the seat of the Roman power it was specially hateful to the Jews. Accordingly it is designated as the "daughter of Edom—the city of abomination and blasphemy," although the district was, for its riches, called "the land of life." As might be expected, constant difficulties arose between the Jewish and Roman authorities in Caesarea, and bitter are the complaints against the unrighteousness of heathen judges. We can readily understand, that to a Jew Caesarea was the symbol of Rome, Rome of Edom—and Edom was to be destroyed! In fact, in their view Jerusalem and Caesarea could not really co-exist. It is in this sense that we account for the following curious passage: "If you are told that Jerusalem and Caesarea are both standing, or that they are both destroyed, believe it not; but if you are told that one of them is destroyed and the other standing, then believe it" (*Gitt.* 16 *a*; *Meg.* 6 *a*). It is interesting to know that on account of the foreign Jews resident in Caesarea, the Rabbis allowed the principal prayers to be said in Greek, as being the vernacular; and that, from the time of the evangelist Philip, good work was done for Christ among its resident Jews. Indeed, Jewish writings contain special notice of controversies there between Jews and Christians.

A brief summary of Jewish notices of certain other towns in Judaea, mentioned also in the New Testament, may throw some additional light on the sacred narratives. In general, the Mishnah divided Judaea proper into three parts—mountain, Shephelah, and valley (*Shev.* ix. 2), to which we must add the city of Jerusalem as a separate district.[23] And here we have another striking evidence of the authenticity of the New Testament, and especially of the writings of St. Luke. Only one intimately acquainted with the state of matters at the time would, with the Rabbis, have distinguished Jerusalem as a district separate from all the rest of Judaea, as St. Luke markedly does on several occasions (Luke 5:17; Acts 1:8; 10:39).[24] When the Rabbis speak of "the mountain," they refer to the district north-east and north of Jerusalem, also known as "the royal mount." The Shephelah, of course, is the country along the sea-shore. All the rest is included in the term "valley." It need scarcely be explained that, as the Jerusalem Talmud tells us, this is merely a general classification, which must not be too closely pressed. Of the eleven *toparchies* into which, according to Josephus,[25] Judaea proper was arranged, the Rabbis take no notice, although some of their names have been traced in Talmudical writings. These provinces were no doubt again subdivided into districts or hyparchies, just as the towns were into quarters or hegemonies, both terms occurring in the Talmud.[26] The Rabbis forbade the exportation of provisions from Palestine, even into Syria.

Travelling southward from Caesarea we are in the plain of Sharon, whose beauty and richness are so celebrated in Holy Scripture (Cant. 2:1; Isa. 35:2). This plain extends as far as Lydda, where it merges into that of *Darom*, which stretches farther southwards. In accordance with the statements of Holy Scripture (Isa. 65:10) the plain of Sharon was always celebrated for its pasturage. According to the Talmud most of the calves for sacrifices were brought from that district. The wine of Sharon was celebrated, and, for beverage, supposed to be mixed with one-third of

One day as he was teaching, Pharisees and teachers of the law, who had come from every village of Galilee and from Judea and Jerusalem, were sitting there. And the power of the LORD was present for him to heal the sick (Luke 5:17).

The desert and the parched land will be glad;
  the wilderness will rejoice and blossom.
Like the crocus, it will burst into bloom;
  it will rejoice greatly an shout for joy.
The glory of Lebanon will be given to it,
  the splendor of Carmel and Sharon;
they will see the glory of the LORD,
  the splendor of our God (Isa. 35:1–2).

---

[23] So in many passages. Compare, for example, *Cheth.* iv. 12.

[24] These, as the New Testament notices about Caesarea, have also been marked by M. Neubauer in his *Géogr. du Tal.* It is to be desired that the occasional inaccuracies, or rather, as we know, misprints in the Talmudic references should be corrected by the learned author.

[25] Pliny enumerates only ten. Compare *Relandus* (ed. Nuremb.) pp. 130, 131.

[26] See on this and generally Neubauer, p. 67, *et passim*.

water. The plain was also well known for the manufacture of pottery; but it must have been of an inferior
kind, since the Mishnah (*Baba K.* vi. 2) in enumerating for what proportion of damaged goods a
purchaser might not claim compensation, allows not
less than ten per cent for breakage in the pottery of
Sharon. In *Jer. Sotah* viii. 3, we read that the permission to return from war did not apply to those who
had built brick houses in Sharon, it being explained
that the clay was so bad, that the houses had to be
rebuilt within seven years. Hence also the annual
prayer of the high-priest on the Day of Atonement,
that the houses of the men of Sharon should not
become their graves.[27] *Antipatris,* the place where the
foot soldiers had left St. Paul in charge of the horsemen
(Acts 23:31), had once been the scene of a very different array. For it was here that, according to tradition
(*Yoma,* 69 *a*), the priesthood, under Simon the Just,
had met Alexander the Great in that solemn procession, which secured the safety of the Temple. In
Talmudical writings it bears the same name, which
was given it by Herod, in memory of his father
Antipater (*Ant.* 16.5.2). The name of Chephar Zaba,
however, also occurs, possibly that of an adjoining
locality. In *Sanh.* 94 *b*, we read that Hezekiah had
suspended a board at the entrance of the *Beth
Midrash* (or college), with the notification that
whoever studied not the Law was to be destroyed.
Accordingly they searched from Dan to Beersheba,
and found not a single unlettered person, nor yet
from Gebath to Antipatris, boy or girl, man or
woman, who was not fully versed in all the legal
ordinances concerning clean and unclean.

Another remarkable illustration of the New
Testament is afforded by *Lydda,* the Talmudical Lod
or Lud. We read that, in consequence of the labours
of St. Peter and the miracle wrought on Aeneas, "all
that dwelt at Lydda and Saron...turned to the Lord"
(Acts 9:35). The brief notice of Lydda given in this

*Sharon will become a
pasture for flocks,
and the Valley of Achor a
resting place for herds,
for my people who
seek me
(Isa. 65:10).*

[27]See my volume on *The Temple: Its Ministry and Services.* Compare also Neubauer's
Géogr. du Tal. in locum.

narrative of the apostle's labours, is abundantly confirmed by Talmudical notices, although, of course, we
must not expect them to describe the progress of
Christianity. We can readily believe that Lydda had its
congregation of "saints," almost from the first, since
it was (*Maas. Sh.* v. 2) within an easy day's journey
west of Jerusalem. Indeed, as the Talmud explains,
the second tithes (Deut. 14:22; 26:12) from Lydda
could not be converted into money, but had to be
brought to the city itself, so "that the streets of
Jerusalem might be garlanded with fruits." The same
passage illustrates the proximity of Lydda to the city,
and the frequent intercourse between the two,[28] by
saying that the women of Lydda mixed their dough,
went up to Jerusalem, prayed in the Temple, and
returned before it had fermented. Similarly, we infer
from Talmudical documents that Lydda had been the
residence of many Rabbis before the destruction of
Jerusalem. After that event, it became the seat of a
very celebrated school, presided over by some of the
leaders of Jewish thought. It was this school which
boldly laid it down, that, to avoid death, every ordinance of the Law might be broken, except those in
regard to idolatry, incest, and murder. It was in
Lydda, also, that two brothers voluntarily offered
themselves victims to save their co-religionists from
slaughter, threatened because a body had been found,
whose death was imputed to the Jews. It sounds like
a sad echo of the taunts addressed by "chief priests,"
"scribes and elders," to Jesus on the cross (Matt.
27:41–43) when, on the occasion just mentioned, the
Roman thus addressed the martyrs: "If you are of the
people of Ananias, Mishael, and Azarias, let your God
come, and save you from my hand!" (*Taan.* 18, 6.)

But a much more interesting chain of evidence
connects Lydda with the history of the founding of
the Church. It is in connection with Lydda and its
tribunal, which is declared to have been capable of

Be sure to set aside a tenth of all that your fields produce each year (Deut. 14:22).

In the same way the chief priests, the teachers of the law and the elders mocked him. "He saved others," they said, "but he can't save himself! He's the King of Israel! Let him come down now from the cross, and we will believe in him. He trusts in God. Let God rescue him now if he wants him, for he said, 'I am the Son of God' " (Matt. 27:41–43).

---

[28]The learned Lightfoot (*Cent. Chorogr. Matth. praemissa,* cxvi.) argues, that this was intended by the Rabbinists to show that no material damage was allowed to discourage the piety of the women of Lydda.

R. Tarfon taught at Lydda that [nothing less than an overcharge of] eight pieces of silver out of a sela, or one-third of the purchase-price, counts as defrauding, and the merchants of Lydda rejoiced (Mishnah, Baba Meṣiʿa iv. 3).

pronouncing sentence of death, that our blessed Lord and the Virgin Mother are introduced in certain Talmudical passages, though with studiously and blasphemously altered names.[29] The statements are, in their present form, whether from ignorance, design, or in consequence of successive alterations, confused, and they mix up different events and persons in Gospel history; among other things representing our Lord as condemned at Lydda.[30] But there can be no reasonable question that they refer to our blessed Lord and His condemnation for supposed blasphemy and seduction of the people, and that they at least indicate a close connection between Lydda and the founding of Christianity.[31] It is a curious confirmation of the gospel history, that the death of Christ is there described as having taken place "on the eve of the Passover," remarkably bearing out not only the date of that event as gathered from the synoptical gospels, but showing that the Rabbis at least knew nothing of those Jewish scruples and difficulties, by which modern Gentile writers have tried to prove the impossibility of Christ's condemnation on the Paschal night.[32] It has already been stated that, after the destruction of Jerusalem, many and most celebrated Rabbis chose Lydda for their residence. But the second century witnessed a great change. The inhabitants of Lydda are now charged with pride, ignorance, and neglect of their religion. The *Midrash* (Esther 1:3) has it, that there were "ten measures of

---

[29] A very ingenious attempt at explaining these names and designations has been made by Professor Cassel in his recent *brochure, Caricaturnamen Christi.*

[30] May there not perhaps be some historical foundation even for this statement? Could the secret gathering of "the chief priests and Pharisees," mentioned in John 11:47, have taken place in Lydda (compare vers. 54, 55)? Was it there, that Judas "communed with the chief priests and captains, how he might betray Him unto them?" There were at any rate obvious reasons for avoiding Jerusalem in all preliminary measures against Jesus; and we know that, while the Temple stood, Lydda was the only place out of Jerusalem which may be called a seat of the Rabbinical party.

[31] All the passages on the subject are collated and most ably argued upon in Buxtorf, *Lex. Talm.*

[32] See the discussion on the date of our Lord's crucifixion in the Appendix to my volume on *The Temple: Its Ministry and Services.*

wretchedness in the world. Nine of those belong to Lod, the tenth to all the rest of the world." Lydda was the last place in Judaea to which, after their migration into Galilee, the Rabbis resorted to fix the commencement of the month. Jewish legend has it, that they were met by the "evil eye," which caused their death. There may, perhaps, be an allegorical allusion in this. Certain it is, that, at the time, Lydda was the seat of a most flourishing Christian Church, and had its bishop. Indeed, a learned Jewish writer has connected the changed Jewish feeling towards Lod with the spread of Christianity.[33] Lydda must have been a very beautiful and a very busy place. The Talmud speaks in exaggerated terms of the honey of its dates,[34] and the Mishnah (*Baba M.* iv. 3) refers to its merchants as a numerous class, although their honesty is not extolled.[35]

Now that same day two of them were going to a village called Emmaus, about seven miles from Jerusalem (Luke 24:13).

Near Lydda, eastwards, was the village of *Chephar Tabi.* We might be tempted to derive from it the name of Tabitha (Acts 9:36), if it were not that the names Tabi and Tabitha had been so common at the time in Palestine. There can be no question of the situation of *Joppa,* the modern Jaffa, where Peter saw the vision which opened the door of the Church to the Gentiles. Many Rabbis are mentioned in connection with Joppa. The town was destroyed by Vespasian. There is a curious legend in the *Midrash* to the effect that Joppa was not overwhelmed by the deluge. Could this have been an attempt to insinuate the preservation and migration of men to distant parts of the earth? The exact location of *Emmaus,* for ever sacred to us by the manifestation of the Saviour to the two disciples (Luke 24:13), is matter of controversy. On the whole, the weight of evidence still inclines to the traditional site.[36] If so, it had a considerable Jewish population, although it was also

[33] Neubauer, p. 80.

[34] *Cheth.* iii. *a.*

[35] The Mishnah discusses how much profit a merchant is allowed to take on an article, and within what period a purchaser, who finds himself imposed upon, may return his purchase. The merchants of Lydda are certainly not placed in this discussion in the most advantageous light.

occupied by a Roman garrison. Its climate and waters were celebrated, as also its market-place. It is specially interesting to find that among the patrician Jewish families belonging to the laity, who took part in the instrumental music of the Temple, two—those of Pegarim and Zippariah—were from Emmaus, and also that the priesthood were wont to intermarry with the wealthy Hebrews of that place (*Er.* ii. 4). *Gaza,* on whose "desert" road[37] Philip preached to and baptized the Ethiopian eunuch, counted not fewer than eight heathen temples, besides an idol-shrine just outside the city. Still Jews were allowed to reside there, probably on account of its important market.

"In Bethlehem in Judea," they replied, "for this is what the prophet has written:
" 'But you, Bethlehem, in the land of Judah, are by no means least among the rulers of Judah;
for out of you will come a ruler
who will be the shepherd of my people Israel' "
(Matt. 2:5–6).

Only two names yet remain to be mentioned, but those of the deepest and most solemn interest. Bethlehem, the birthplace of our Lord, and Jerusalem, where He was crucified. It deserves notice, that the answer which the Sanhedrists of old gave to the inquiries of Herod (Matt. 2:5) is equally returned in many Talmudical passages,[38] and with the same reference to Micah 5:2. It may therefore be regarded as a settled point that, according to the Jewish fathers, Messiah, the Son of David, was to be born in Bethlehem of Judah. But there is one passage in the Mishnah which throws such peculiar light on the Gospel narrative, that it will be best to give it in its entirety. We know that, on the night in which our Saviour was born, the angels' message came to those who probably alone of all in or near Bethlehem were "keeping watch." For, close by Bethlehem, on the road to Jerusalem, was a tower, known as *Migdal Eder,* the "watch-tower of the flock." For here was the station where shepherds watched their flocks destined for sacrifices in the Temple. So well known was this, that if animals were found as far from Jerusalem as Migdal Eder, and within that circuit on

---

[36] Modern writers mostly identify it with the present *Kulonieh, colonia,* deriving the name from the circumstance that it was colonised by Roman soldiers. Lieut. Conder suggests the modern *Khamasa,* about eight miles from Jerusalem, as the site of Emmaus.

[37] Professor Robinson has given a most graphic description of that desert road.

[38] *Jer. Ber.* ii. 3 gives a most curious story connected with this.

every side, the males were offered as burnt-offerings, the females as peace-offerings.[39] R. Jehudah adds: "If suited for Paschal sacrifices, then they are Paschal sacrifices, provided it be not more than thirty days before the feast" (*Shekal.* vii. 4; compare also *Jer. Kid.* ii. 9). It seems of deepest significance, almost like the fulfilment of type, that those shepherds who first heard tidings of the Saviour's birth, who first listened to angels' praises, were watching flocks destined to be offered as sacrifices in the Temple. There was the type, and here the reality. At all times Bethlehem was among "the least" in Judah—so small that the Rabbis do not even refer to it in detail. The small village-inn was over-crowded, and the guests from Nazareth found shelter only in the stable,[40] whose manger became the cradle of the King of Israel. It was here that those who tended the sacrificial flocks, heaven-directed, found the Divine Babe—significantly the first to see Him, to believe, and to adore. But this is not all. It is when we remember, that presently these shepherds would be in the Temple, and meet those who came thither to worship and to sacrifice, that we perceive the full significance of what otherwise would have seemed scarcely worth while noticing in connection with humble shepherds: "And when they had seen it, they made known abroad the saying which was told them concerning this child. And all they that heard it wondered at those things which were told them by the shepherds" (Luke 2:17, 18). Moreover, we can understand the wonderful impression made on those in the courts of the Temple, as, while they selected their sacrifices, the shepherds told the devout of the speedy fulfilment of all these types in what they had themselves seen and heard in that night of

Broad-tailed sheep

[39] Formerly those who found such animals had out of their own means to supply the necessary drink-offerings. But as this induced some not to bring the animals to the Temple, it was afterwards decreed to supply the cost of the drink-offerings from the Temple treasury (*Shek.* vii. 5).

[40] In *Echa R.* 72 *a*, there is a tradition that the Messiah was to be born "in the Castle Arba of Bethlehem Judah." Caspari (*Chron. Geogr. Ant. ü. d. Leben Jesu,* p. 54) quotes this in confirmation that the present castellated monastery, in the cave of which is the traditional site of our Lord's birth, marks the real spot. In the East such caves were often used as stables.

Then Simeon blessed them and said to Mary, his mother: "This child is destined to cause the falling and rising of many in Israel, and to be a sign that will be spoken against, so that the thoughts of many hearts will be revealed. And a sword will pierce your own soul too" (Luke 2:34–35).

wonders; how eager, curious crowds might gather around to discuss, to wonder, perhaps to mock; how the heart of "just and devout" old Simeon would be gladdened within him, in expectation of the near realisation of a life's hopes and prayers; and how aged Anna, and they who like her "looked for redemption in Israel," would lift up their heads, since their salvation was drawing nigh. Thus the shepherds would be the most effectual heralds of the Messiah in the Temple, and both Simeon and Anna be prepared for the time when the infant Saviour would be presented in the sanctuary. But there is yet another verse which, as we may suggest, would find a fuller explanation in the fact that these shepherds tended the Temple flocks. When in Luke 2:20 we read that "the shepherds returned, glorifying and praising God," the meaning in that connection[41] seems somewhat difficult till we realise that, after bringing their flocks to the Temple, they would return to their own homes, and carry with them, joyfully and gratefully, tidings of the great salvation. Lastly, without entering into controversy, the passage from the Mishnah above quoted in great measure disposes of the objection against the traditional date of our Lord's birth, derived from the supposed fact, that the rains of December would prevent the flocks being kept all night "in the field." For, in the first place, these were flocks on their way to Jerusalem, and not regularly pasturing in the open at that season. And, secondly, the Mishnah evidently contemplates their being thus in the open thirty days before the Passover, or in the month of February, during which the average rainfall is quite the largest in the year.[42]

When they had seen him, they spread the word concerning what had been told them about this child, and all who heard it were amazed at what the shepherds said to them (Luke 2:17–18).

"Ten measures of beauty," say the Rabbis, "hath God bestowed upon the world, and nine of these fall

---

[41] Compare here verses 17, 18, which in point of time precede verse 20. The term *diagnōrizō*, rendered in the Authorised Version "make known abroad," and by Wahl "*ultro citroque narro*," does not seem exhausted by the idea of conversation with the party in the "stable," or with any whom they might meet in "the field."

[42] The average rainfall in Jerusalem for eight years amounts to fourteen inches in December, thirteen in January, and sixteen in February (Barclay, *City of the Great King*, p. 428). Compare Hamburger, *u.s. passim*.

Jerusalem, road to Bethlehem

to the lot of Jerusalem"—and again, "A city, the fame of which has gone out from one end of the world to the other."[43] "Thine, O Lord, is the greatness, the power, the glory, and eternity." This—explains the Talmud—"is Jerusalem." In opposition to her rival Alexandria, which was designated "the little," Jerusalem was called "the great." It almost reminds one of the title "eternal city," given to Rome, when we find the Rabbis speaking of Jerusalem as the "eternal house." Similarly, if a common proverb has it, that "all roads lead to Rome," it was a Jewish saying, "All coins come from Jerusalem." This is not the place to describe the city in its appearance and glory.[44] But one almost feels as if, on such a subject, one could understand, if not condone, the manifest exaggerations of the Rabbis. Indeed, there are indications that

[43] *Ber.* 38.
[44] For this compare the two first chapters of my volume on *The Temple: Its Ministry and Services.*

they scarcely expected their statements to be taken literally. Thus, when the number of its synagogues is mentioned as 460 or 480, it is explained that the latter number is the numerical equivalent of the word "full" in Isa. 1:21 ("it was full of judgment"). It is more interesting to know, that we find in the Talmud express mention of "the Synagogue of the Alexandrians," referred to in Acts 6:9—another important confirmation, if such were needed, of the accuracy of St. Luke's narratives. Of the hospitality of the inhabitants of Jerusalem accounts are given, which we can scarcely regard as much exaggerated; for the city was not reckoned to belong to any tribe in particular; it was to be considered as equally the home of all. Its houses were to be neither hired nor let, but freely thrown open to every brother. Nor did any one among the countless thousands who thronged it at feast-times ever lack room. A curtain hung before the entrance of a house intimated, that there was still room for guests; a table spread in front of it, that its board was still at their disposal. And, if it was impossible to accommodate within the walls of Jerusalem proper the vast crowds which resorted to the city, there can be no doubt that for sacred purposes *Bethany* and *Bethphage* were reckoned as within the circle of Jerusalem. It calls forth peculiar sensations, when we read in these Jewish records of Bethany and Bethphage as specially celebrated for their hospitality to pilgrim-guests, for it wakes the sacred memories of our Lord's sojourn with the holy family of Bethany, and especially of His last stay there and of His royal entrance into Jerusalem.

Opposition arose, however, from members of the Synagogue of the Freedmen (as it was called)—Jews of Cyrene and Alexandria as well as the provinces of Cilicia and Asia. These men began to argue with Stephen... (Acts 6:9).

In truth, every effort was used to make Jerusalem truly a city of delight. Its police and sanitary regulations were more perfect than in any modern city; the arrangements such as to keep the pilgrim free to give his heart and mind to sacred subjects. If, after all, "the townspeople," as they were called, were regarded as somewhat proud and supercilious, it was something to be a citizen of *Jerushalaimah,* as the Jerusalemites preferred to write its name. Their constant intercourse with strangers gave them a

Street scene in Jerusalem

knowledge of men and of the world. The smartness and cleverness of the young people formed a theme of admiration to their more shy and awkward country relatives. There was also a grandeur in their bearing— almost luxury; and an amount of delicacy, tact, and tenderness, which appeared in all their public dealings. Among a people whose wit and cleverness are proverbial, it was no mean praise to be renowned for these qualities. In short, Jerusalem was the ideal of the Jew, in whatever land of exile he might tarry. Her rich

Going to market

men would lavish fortunes on the support of Jewish learning, the promotion of piety, or the support of the national cause. Thus one of them would, when he found the price of sacrifices exceedingly high, introduce into the Temple-court the requisite animals at his own cost, to render the service possible for the poor. Or on another occasion he would offer to furnish the city for twenty-one months with certain provisions in her struggle against Rome. In the streets of Jerusalem men from the most distant countries met, speaking every variety of language and dialect. Jews and Greeks, Roman soldiers and Galilean peasants, Pharisees, Sadducees, and white-robed Essenes, busy merchants and students of abstruse theology, mingled, a motley crowd, in the narrow streets of the city of palaces. But over all the Temple, rising above the city, seemed to fling its shadow and its glory. Each morning the threefold blast of the priests' trumpets wakened the city with a call to prayer; each evening the same blasts closed the working day, as with sounds from heaven. Turn where you might, everywhere the holy buildings were in view, now with the smoke of sacrifices curling over the courts, or again with solemn stillness resting upon the sacred hills. It was the Temple which gave its character to Jerusalem, and which decided its fate. There is a remarkable passage in the Talmud, which, remembering that the time to which it refers was in all probability the very year in which our Lord died on the cross, reads like an unwilling confirmation of the Gospel narrative: "Forty years before the destruction of the Temple, its doors opened of their own accord. Jochanan,[45] the son of Saccai, rebuked them, saying: O Temple, why openest thou of thine own accord? Ah! I perceive that thine end is at hand; for it is written (Zech. 11:1): 'Open thy doors, O Lebanon, that the fire may devour thy cedars' " (*Yoma* 39 *b*). "And, behold, the veil of the Temple was rent in twain from the top to the bottom" (Matt. 27:51)—blessed be God, not merely in announcement of coming judgment, but henceforth to lay open unto all the way into the Holiest of All.

---

[45] Caspari suggests that this was the same as the high-priest Annas, the name having only the syllable indicating the name of Jehovah prefixed.

6
JEWISH HOMES

There is neither Jew nor Greek, slave nor free, male nor female, for you are all one in Christ Jesus. If you belong to Christ, then you are Abraham's seed, and heirs according to the promise (Gal. 3:28–29).

It may be safely asserted, that the grand distinction, which divided all mankind into Jews and Gentiles, was not only religious, but also social. However near the cities of the heathen to those of Israel, however frequent and close the intercourse between the two parties, no one could have entered a Jewish town or village without feeling, so to speak, in quite another world. The aspect of the streets, the building and arrangement of the houses, the municipal and religious rule, the manners and customs of the people, their habits and ways—above all, the family life, stood in marked contrast to what would be seen elsewhere. On every side there was evidence that religion here was not merely a creed, nor a set of observances, but that it pervaded every relationship, and dominated every phase of life.

Let us imagine a real Jewish town or village. There were many such, for Palestine had at all times a

External view of a city

far larger number of towns and villages than might have been expected from its size, or from the general agricultural pursuits of its inhabitants. Even at the time of its first occupation under Joshua we find somewhere about six hundred towns—if we may judge by the Levitical cities, of about an average circumference of two thousand cubits on each side, and with probably an average population of from two to three thousand.[1] But the number of towns and villages, as well as their populousness, greatly increased in later times. Thus Josephus (*Life*, 45) speaks of not fewer than two hundred and forty townships in Galilee alone in his days. This progress was, no doubt, due not only to the rapid development of society, but also to the love of building that characterised Herod and his family, and to which so many fortresses, palaces, temples, and towns owed their origin. Alike the New Testament, Josephus, and the Rabbis give us three names, which may be rendered by villages, townships, and towns—the latter being surrounded by walls, and again distinguished into those fortified already at the time of Joshua, and those of later date. A township might be either "great," if it had its synagogue, or small, if it wanted such; this being dependent on the residence of at least ten men, who could always be reckoned upon to form a quorum for the worship of the synagogue (the so-called Batlanin[2]); for service could not be celebrated with any less number of males. The villages had no synagogue; but their inhabitants were supposed to go to the nearest township for market on the Monday and Thursday of every week, when service was held for them, and the local Sanhedrim also sat (*Megill.* i. 1–3). A very curious law provided (*Cheth.* 110), that a man could not oblige his wife to follow him if he moved either from a township to a town, or the reverse. The reason of the former provision was, that

The Scroll [of Esther] is read on the 11th, 12th, 13th, 14th, or 15th [of Adar], never earlier and never later. Cities encompassed by a wall since the days of Joshua the son of Nun read it on the 15th. Villages and large towns read it on the 14th, save that villages [sometimes] read it earlier on a day of assembly (Mishnah, Megillah i. 1).

---

[1] Saalschütz, *Archaeol. d. Hebr.* ii. pp. 250, 251.

[2] From "betal," to cease—as the glossary to *Baba B.* 82 *a* explains: men without reproach, who gave up their work to give themselves wholly to the work of the synagogue. Such had a claim to support from the synagogue revenues.

in a town people lived together, and the houses were close to each other; hence there was a want of fresh, free air, and of gardens, which were enjoyed in townships. On the other hand, a woman might object to exchange residence in a town for one in a township, because in a town everything was to be got, and people met in the streets and market-place from all the neighbourhood.

Statements like these will give some idea of the difference between town and country life. Let us first think of the former. Approaching one of the ancient fortified towns, one would come to a low wall that protected a ditch. Crossing this moat, one would be at the city wall proper, and enter through a massive gate, often covered with iron, and secured by strong bars and bolts. Above the gate rose the watch-tower. "Within the gate" was the shady or sheltered retreat where "the elders" sat. Here grave citizens discussed public affairs or the news of the day, or transacted important business. The gates opened upon large squares, on which the various streets converged. Here was the busy scene of intercourse and trade. The country-people stood or moved about, hawking the produce of field, orchard, and dairy; the foreign

City gate

merchant or pedlar exposed his wares, recommend-ing the newest fashions from Rome or Alexandria, the latest luxuries from the far East, or the art produce of the goldsmith and the modeller at Jerusalem, while among them moved the crowd, idle or busy, chattering, chaffing, good-humoured, and bandying witticisms. Now they give way respectfully before a Pharisee; or their conversation is hushed by the weird appearance of an Essene or of some sectary—political or religious, —while low, muttered curses attend the stealthy steps of the publican, whose restless eyes wander around to watch that nothing escape the close meshes of the tax-gatherer's net. These streets are all named, mostly after the trades or guilds which have there their bazaars. For a guild always keeps together, whether in street or synagogue. In Alexandria the different trades sat in the synagogue arranged into guilds; and St. Paul could have no difficulty in meeting in the bazaar of his trade with the like-minded Aquila and Priscilla (Acts 18:2, 3), with whom to find a lodging. In these bazaars many of the workmen sat outside their shops, and, in the interval of labour, exchanged greetings or banter with the passers-by. For all Israel are brethren, and there is a sort of freemasonry even in the Jewish mode of salutation, which always embodied either an acknowledgment of the God of Israel, or a brotherly wish of peace. Excitable, impulsive, quick, sharp-witted, imaginative; fond of parable, pithy sayings, acute distinctions, or pungent wit; reverent towards God and man, respectful in the presence of age, enthusiastic of learning and of superior mental endowments, most delicately sensitive in regard to the feelings of others; zealous, with intensely warm Eastern natures, ready to have each prejudice aroused, hasty and violent in passion, but quickly assuaged—such is the motley throng around. And now, perhaps, the voice of a Rabbi, teaching in some shady retreat—although latterly Jewish pride of learning forbade the profanation of lore by popular-ising it for the "unlearned"—or, better far, at one time the presence of the Master, gathers and keeps them spell-bound, forgetful alike of the cravings of

There he met a Jew named Aquila, a native of Pontus, who had recently come from Italy with his wife Priscilla, because Claudius had ordered all the Jews to leave Rome. Paul went to see them, and because he was a tentmaker as they were, he stayed and worked with them (Acts 18:2–3).

The LORD *had said to Abram, "Leave your coun-try, your people and your father's household and go to the land I will show you.*
"I will make you into a
    great nation
    and I will bless you;
I will make your name
    great,
    and you will be a
    blessing.
I will bless those who
    bless you,
    and whoever curses you
    I will curse;
and all peoples on earth
    will be blessed through
    you"
(Gen. 12:1–3).

Well and bucket

You shall not make for yourself an idol in the form of anything in heaven above or on the earth beneath or in the waters below (Exod. 20:4).

But they threw themselves upon the ground, and laid their necks bare, and said they would take their death very willingly, rather than the wisdom of their laws should be transgressed; upon which Pilate was deeply affected with their firm resolution to keep their laws inviolable, and presently commanded the images to be carried back from Jerusalem to Cesarea (Jos. Antiquities 18.59).

hunger and of the lapse of time, till, the short Eastern day ended, the stars shining out on the deep blue sky must have reminded many among them of the promise to their father Abraham, now fulfilled in One greater than Abraham.

Back to the town in the cool of even to listen to the delicious murmur of well or fountain, as those crowd around it who have not cisterns in their own houses. The watchman is on the top of the tower above the gateway; presently, night-watchers will patrol the streets. Nor is there absolute darkness, for it is customary to keep a light burning all night in the house, and the windows (unlike those of modern Eastern dwellings) open chiefly on street and road. Those large windows are called Tyrian, the smaller ones Egyptian. They are not filled in with glass, but contain gratings or lattices. In the houses of the rich the window-frames are elaborately carved, and richly inlaid. Generally the woodwork is of the common sycamore, sometimes of olive or cedar, and in palaces even of Indian sandal-wood. The entablature is more or less curiously carved and ornamented. Only there must be no representation of anything in heaven or on earth. So deep was the feeling on this point, that even the attempt of Pilate to introduce by night into Jerusalem the effigies of Caesar on the top of the Roman standards led to scenes in which the Jews showed themselves willing to die for their convictions (Jos. *Ant.* 18.59); while the palace of Herod Antipas at Tiberias was burned by the mob because it was decorated with figures of animals (Jos. *Life,* 62–67). These extreme views, however, gave way, first, before the tolerant example of Gamaliel, the teacher of Paul, who made use of a public bath, although adorned by a statue of Venus, since, as he put it, the statue was intended for the embellishment of the bath, and not the bath for the sake of the statue. If this argument reminds us that Gamaliel was not a stranger to Christianity, the statement of his grandson, that an idol was nothing if its worship had been disclaimed by the heathen (*Ab. Sar.* 52), recalls still more strongly the teaching of St. Paul. And so we gradually come down to the modern orthodox doctrine, which allows the representation of plants, animals, etc., but prohibits that of sun, moon, and stars, except for purposes of study, while, though doubtfully, it admits those of men and even angels, provided they be in sunken, not in raised workmanship.

The rule of these towns and villages was exceedingly strict. The representatives of Rome were chiefly either military men, or else fiscal or political agents. We have, indeed, a notice that the Roman general Gabinius, about half a century before Christ, divided Palestine for juridical purposes into five districts, each presided over by a council (Jos. *Ant.* 14.91); but that arrangement was only of very short duration, and even while it lasted these councils seem to have been Jewish. Then every town had its Sanhedrim,[3] consisting of twenty-three members if the place numbered at least one hundred and twenty men, or of three members if the population were smaller.[4] These Sanhedrists were appointed directly by the supreme authority, or Great Sanhedrim, "the council," at Jerusalem, which consisted of seventy-one members. It is difficult to fix the limits of the actual power wielded by these Sanhedrims in criminal cases. But the smaller Sanhedrims are referred to in such passages as Matt. 5:22, 23; 10:17; Mark 13:9. Of course all ecclesiastical and, so to speak, strictly Jewish causes, and all religious questions were within their special cognisance. Lastly, there were also in every place what we may call municipal authorities, under the presidency of a mayor—the representatives of the "elders"—an institution so frequently mentioned in Scripture, and deeply rooted in Jewish society. Perhaps these may be referred to in Luke 7:3,

...and when he had ordained five councils, he distributed the nation into the same number of parts: so these councils governed the people; the first was at Jerusalem, the second at Gadara, the third at Amathus, the fourth at Jericho, and the fifth at Sepphoris, in Galilee. So the Jews were now freed from monarchic authority, and were governed by an aristocracy (Jos. Antiquities 14.91).

Be on your guard against men; they will hand you over to the local councils and flog you in their synagogues (Matt. 10:17).

---

[3] The name "Sanhedrin," or "Sunedrion," is undoubtedly of Greek derivation, although the Rabbis have tried to paraphrase it as "Sin" (=Sinai) "haderin," those who repeat or explain the law, or to trace its etymology, as being "those who *hate* to *accept* the persons of men in *judgment*" (the name being supposed to be composed of the Hebrew equivalents of the words italicised).

[4] An ingenious attempt has lately been made to show that the Sanhedrim of three members was not a regular court, but only arbitrators chosen by the parties themselves (see Schürer, *Neutest. Zeitgesch.* p. 403). But the argument, so far as it tries to prove that such was always the case, seems to me not to meet all the facts.

as sent by the centurion of Capernaum to intercede for him with the Lord.

What may be called the police and sanitary regulations were of the strictest character. Of Caesarea, for example, we know that there was a regular system of drainage into the sea, apparently similar to, but more perfect than that of any modern town (Jos. *Ant.* 15.340). The same holds true in regard to the Temple-buildings at Jerusalem. But in every town and village sanitary rules were strictly attended to. Cemeteries, tanneries, and whatever also might be prejudicial to health, had to be removed at least fifty cubits outside a town.[5] Bakers' and dyers' shops, or stables, were not allowed under the dwelling of another person. Again, the line of each street had to be strictly kept in building, nor was even a projection beyond it allowed. In general the streets were wider than those of modern Eastern cities. The nature of the soil, and the circumstance that so many towns were built on hills (at least in Judaea), would, of course, be advantageous in a sanitary point of view. It would also render the paving of the streets less requisite. But we know that certain towns *were* paved—Jerusalem with white stones (Jos. *Ant.* 20.219–223). To obviate

...nay, the very subterranean vaults and cellars had no less of architecture bestowed on them than had the buildings above ground. Some of these vaults carried things at even distances to the haven and to the sea; but one of them ran obliquely, and bound all the rest together, that both the rain and the filth of the citizens were together carried off with ease, and the sea itself, upon the flux of the tide from without, came into the city, and washed it all clean (Jos. Antiquities *15.340*).

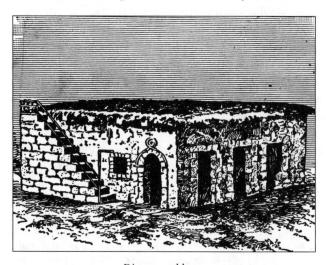

Dirt covered house

[5] See these and similar regulations chiefly in Mishnah (*Baba B.* i. and ii. *passim*).

occasions of dispute, neighbours were not allowed to have windows looking into the courts or rooms of others, nor might the principal entrance to a shop be through a court common to two or three dwellings.

These brief notices may help us better to realise the surroundings of Jewish town life. Looking up and down one of the streets of a town in Galilee or Judaea, the houses would be seen to differ in size and in elegance, from the small cottage, only eight or ten yards square, to the mansions of the rich, sometimes two or more stories high, and embellished by rows of pillars and architectural adornments. Suppose ourselves in front of a better-class dwelling, though not exactly that of a patrician, for it is built of brick, or perhaps of undressed, or even of dressed stone, but not of marble, nor yet of hewn stone; nor are its walls painted with such delicate colours as vermilion, but simply whitewashed, or, may be, covered with some neutral tint. A wide, sometimes costly, stair leads

Upper room

from the outside straight up to the flat roof, which is made to slope a little downwards, so as to allow the rainwater easily to flow through pipes into the cistern below. The roof is paved with brick, stone, or other hard substance, and surrounded by a balustrade, which, according to Jewish law, must be at least two cubits (three feet) high, and strong enough to bear the weight of a person. Police-regulations, conceived in the same spirit of carefulness, prohibited open wells and pits, insufficient ladders, rickety stairs, even dangerous dogs about a house. From roof to roof there might be a regular communication, called by the Rabbis "the road of the roofs" (*Baba Mez.* 88 *b*). Thus a person could make his escape, passing from roof to roof, till at the last house he would descend the stairs that led down its outside, without having entered any dwelling. To this "road of the roofs" our Lord no doubt referred in His warning to His followers (Matt. 24:17; Mark 13:15; Luke 17:31), intended to apply to the last siege of Jerusalem: "And let him that is on the housetop not go down into the house, neither enter therein." For ordinary intercourse the roof was the coolest, the airiest, the stillest place. Of

*House with platforms on
the roof for sleeping*

*What I tell you in the dark,
speak in the daylight; what
is whispered in your ear,
proclaim from the roofs
(Matt. 10:27).*

course, at times it would be used for purposes of domestic economy. But thither a man would retire in preference for prayer or quiet thinking; here he would watch, and wait, and observe whether friend or foe, the gathering of the storm, or—as the priest stationed on the pinnacle of the Temple before the morning sacrifice—how the red and golden light of dawn spread along the edge of the horizon. From the roof, also, it was easy to protect oneself against enemies, or to carry on dangerous fight with those beneath; and assuredly, if anywhere, it was "on the housetops" where secrets might be whispered, or, on the other hand, the most public "proclamation" of them be made (Matt. 10:27; Luke 12:3). The stranger's room was generally built on the roof, in order that, undisturbed by the household, the guest might go out and come in; and here, at the feast of Tabernacles, for coolness and convenience, the leafy "booths" were often reared, in which Israel dwelt in memory of their pilgrimage. Close by was "the upper chamber." On the roof the family would gather for converse, or else in the court beneath—with its trees spreading grateful shade, and the music of its plashing fountain falling soothingly on the ear, as you stood in the covered gallery that ran all around, and opened on the apartments of the household.

If the guest-chamber on the roof, which could be reached from the outside, without passing through the house, reminds us of Elisha and the Shunammite, and of the last Passover-supper, to which the Lord and His disciples could go, and which they could leave, without coming in contact with any in the house, the gallery that ran round the court under the roof recalls yet another most solemn scene. We remember how they who bore the man "sick of the palsy," when unable to "come nigh unto Jesus for the press," "uncovered the roof where He was," "and let him down through the tiling with his couch into the midst before Jesus" (Mark 2:4; Luke 5:19). We know, from many Talmudical passages, that the Rabbis resorted in preference to "the upper room" when discussing religious questions. It may have been so in this instance; and, unable to gain access through the door which led into the upper room, the bearers of the sick may have broken down the ceiling from the roof. Or, judging it more likely that the attendant multitude thronged the court beneath, while Jesus stood in the gallery that ran round the court and opened into the various apartments, they might have broken down the roof above Him, and so slowly let down their burden at His feet, and in sight of them all. There is a significant parallelism, or rather contrast, to this in a Rabbinical story (*Moed K.* 25 *a*), which relates how, when the bier on which a celebrated teacher was laid could not be passed out at the door, they carried up their burden and let it down from the roof—on its way, not to a new life, but to burial. Otherwise, there was also a stair which led from the roof into the court and house. Approaching a house, as visitors ordinarily would do, from the street, you would either pass through a large outer court, or else come straight to the vestibule or porch. Here the door opened into the inner court, which sometimes was shared by several families. A porter opened to callers on mentioning their names, as did Rhoda to Peter on the eventful night of his miraculous deliverance from prison (Acts 12:13, 14). Our Lord also applies this well-known fact of domestic life, when He says (Rev. 3:20), "Behold, I stand at the door, and knock: if any man hear My voice, and open the door, I will come into him, and will sup with him, and he with Me." Passing through this inner court, and through the gallery, you would reach the various rooms—the family room, the reception room, and the sleeping apartments—the most retired being occupied by the ladies, and the inner rooms used chiefly in winter. The furniture was much the same as that now in use, consisting of tables, couches, chairs, candlesticks, and lamps, varying in costliness according to the rank and wealth of the family. Among articles of luxury we mention rich cushions for the head and arms, ornaments, and sometimes even pictures. The doors, which moved on hinges fastened with wooden pins, were barred by wooden bolts,

Since they could not get him to Jesus because of the crowd, they made an opening in the roof above Jesus and, after digging through it, lowered the mat the paralyzed man was lying on. When Jesus saw their faith, he said to the paralytic, "Son, your sins are forgiven" (Mark 2:4–5).

Stone doorway

Remember the Sabbath day by keeping it holy (Exod. 20:8).

which could be withdrawn by check keys from the outside. The dining apartment was generally spacious, and sometimes employed for meetings.

We have been describing the arrangements and the appearance of towns and dwellings in Palestine. But it is not any of these outward things which gives a real picture of a Jewish home. Within, everything was quite peculiar. At the outset, the rite of circumcision separated the Jew from the nations around, and dedicated him to God. Private prayer, morning and evening, hallowed daily life, and family religion pervaded the home. Before every meal they washed and prayed; after it they "gave thanks." Besides, there were what may be designated as specially family feasts. The return of the Sabbath sanctified the week of labour. It was to be welcomed as a king, or with songs as a bridegroom; and each household observed it as a season of sacred rest and of joy. True, Rabbinism made all this a matter of mere externalism, converting it into an unbearable burden, by endless injunctions of what constituted work and of that which was supposed to produce joy, thereby utterly changing its sacred character. Still, the fundamental idea remained, like a broken pillar that shows where the palace had stood, and what had been its noble proportions. As the head of the house returned on the Sabbath-eve from the synagogue to his home, he found it festively adorned, the Sabbath lamp brightly burning, and the table spread with the richest each household could afford. But first he blessed each child with the blessing of Israel. And next evening, when the Sabbath light faded out, he made solemn "separation" between the hallowed day and the working week, and so commenced his labour once more in the name of the Lord. Nor were the stranger, the poor, the widow, or the fatherless forgotten. How fully they were provided for, how each shared in what was to be considered not a burden but a privilege, and with what delicacy relief was administered—for all Israel were brethren, and fellow-citizens of their

Jerusalem—those know best who have closely studied Jewish life, its ordinances and practices.[6]

But this also is rather a sketch of religious than of family life. At the outset, we should here say, that even the Hebrew name for "woman," given her at her creation (Gen. 2:23), marked a wife as the companion of her husband, and his equal ("Ishah," a woman, from "Ish," a man). But it is when we consider the relations between man and wife, children and parents, the young and the aged, that the vast difference between Judaism and heathenism so strikingly appears. Even the relationship in which God presented Himself to His people, as their Father, would give peculiar strength and sacredness to the bond which connected earthly parents with their offspring. Here it should be borne in mind that, so to speak, the whole purpose of Israel as a nation, with a view to the appearance of the Messiah from among them, made it to each household a matter of deepest interest that no light in Israel should be extinguished through want of succession. Hence, such an expression as (Jer. 22:10), "Weep sore for him that goeth away: for he shall return no more," was applied to those who died childless (*Moed K.* 27). Similarly, it was said that he who had no child was like one dead. Proverbial expressions in regard to the "parental relation" occur in Rabbinical writings, which in their higher application remind us that the New Testament writers were Jews. If, in the impassioned strain of happy assurance concerning our Christian safety, we are told (Rom. 8:33), "Who shall lay anything to the charge of God's elect? It is God that justifieth," we may believe that St. Paul was familiar with a saying like this: "Shall a father bear witness against his son?" (*Abod S.* 3). The somewhat similar question, "Is there a father who hateth his own son?" may recall to our minds the comfort which the Epistle to the Hebrews ministers to those who are in suffering (Heb. 12:7), "If ye endure chastening, God dealeth with you as

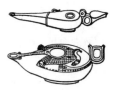

Lamps

*The man said,
"This is now bone of my bones
and flesh of my flesh;
she shall be called
'woman,'
for she was taken out
of man"
(Gen. 2:23).*

*Sons are a heritage from
the LORD,
children a reward
from him
(Ps. 127:3).*

---

[6]The reader must remember that these are but "sketches." A full elaboration of all these subjects, in their various bearings, must be reserved for a larger work.

with sons; for what son is he whom the father chasteneth not?"

Speaking of the relation between parents and children, it may be safely asserted, that no crime was more severely reprobated than any breach of the fifth commandment. The Talmud, with its usual punctiliousness, enters into details, when it lays down as a rule that "a son is bound to feed his father, to give him drink, to clothe him, to protect him, to lead him in, and to conduct him out, and to wash his face, his hands, and his feet;" to which the Jerusalem Gemara adds, that a son is even bound to beg for his father—although here also Rabbinism would give preference to a spiritual before a natural parent, or rather to one who teaches the law before a father! The general state of Jewish society shows us parents as fondly watching over their children, and children as requiting their care by bearing with the foibles, and even the trials, arising from the caprices of old age and infirmity. Such things as undutifulness, or want of loving consideration for parents, would have wakened a thrill of horror in Jewish society. As for crimes against parents, which the law of God visited with the utmost penalty, they seem happily to have been almost unknown. The Rabbinical ordinances, however, also specified the obligation of parents, and limited their power. Thus a son was considered independent whenever he could gain his own living; and, although a daughter remained in the power of her father till marriage, she could not, after she was of age, be given away without her own express and free consent. A father might chastise his child, but only while young, and even then not to such extent as to destroy self-respect. But to beat a grown-up son was forbidden on pain of excommunication; and the apostolic injunction (Eph. 6:4), "Fathers, provoke not your children to wrath," finds almost its literal counterpart in the Talmud (*Moed K.* 17 *a*). Properly speaking, indeed, the Jewish law limited the absolute obligation of a father[7] to feed, clothe, and house his child to his sixth

Honor your father and your mother, so that you may live long in the land the LORD *your God is giving you (Exod. 20:12).*

---

[7]A mother was free from such legal obligation.

year, after which he could only be admonished to it as one of the duties of love, but not legally constrained (*Chethub.* 49 *b*; 65 *b*). In case of separation of the parents, the mother had charge of the daughters, and the father of the sons; but the latter also might be intrusted to the mother, if the judges considered it for the advantage of the children.

A few notices as to the reverence due to age will appropriately close this brief sketch of Jewish home life. It was a beautiful thought—however some may doubt its exegetical correctness—that just as the pieces of the broken tables of the law were kept in the ark, so old age should be venerated and cherished, even though it should be broken in mind or memory (*Ber.* 8 *b*). Assuredly, Rabbinism went to the utmost verge in this matter when it recommended reverence for age, even though it were in the case of one ignorant of the law, or of a Gentile. There were, however, diverging opinions on this point. The passage, Lev. 19:32, "Thou shalt rise up before the hoary head, and honour the face of the old man," was explained to refer only to sages, who alone were to be regarded as old. If R. Jose compared such as learned of young men to those who ate unripe grapes and drank of new wine, R. Jehudah taught, "Look not at the bottles, but at what they contain. There are new bottles full of old wine, and old bottles which contain not even new wine" (*Ab.* iv. 20). Again, if in Deut. 13:1, 2, and also, 18:21, 22, the people were directed to test a prophet by the signs which he showed—a misapplication of which was made by the Jews, when they asked Christ what sign He showed unto them (John 2:18; 6:30)—while in Deut. 17:10 they were told simply "to do according to all that they of that place inform thee," it was asked, What, then, is the difference between an old man and a prophet? To this the reply was: A prophet is like an ambassador, whom you believe in consequence of his royal credentials; but an ancient is one whose word you receive without requiring such evidence. And it was strictly enjoined that proper outward marks of respect should be shown to old age, such as to rise in the presence of older men, not to

You may say to yourselves, "How can we know when a message has not been spoken by the LORD?" If what a prophet proclaims in the name of the LORD does not take place or come true, that is a message the LORD has not spoken. That prophet has spoken presumptuously. Do not be afraid of him (Deut. 18:21–22).

So they asked him, "What miraculous sign then will you give that we may see it and believe you? What will you do?" (John 6:30).

For God said, "Honor your father and mother" and "Anyone who curses his father or mother must be put to death." But you say that if a man says to his father or mother, "Whatever help you might otherwise have received from me is a gift devoted to God," he is not to "honor his father" with it. Thus you nullify the word of God for the sake of your tradition (Matt. 15:4–6).

occupy their seats, to answer them modestly, and to assign to them the uppermost places at feasts.

After having thus marked how strictly Rabbinism watched over the mutual duties of parents and children, it will be instructive to note how at the same time traditionalism, in its worship of the letter, really destroyed the spirit of the Divine law. An instance will here suffice; and that which we select has the double advantage of illustrating an otherwise difficult allusion in the New Testament, and of exhibiting the real characteristics of traditionalism. No commandment could be more plainly in accordance, alike with the spirit and the letter of the law, than this: "He that curseth father or mother, let him die the death." Yet our Lord distinctly charges traditionalism with "transgressing" it (Matt. 15:4–6). The following quotation from the Mishnah (*Sanh.* vii. 8) curiously illustrates the justice of His accusation: "He that curseth his father or his mother is not guilty, unless he curses them with express mention of the name of Jehovah." In any other case the sages declare him absolved! And this is by no means a solitary instance of Rabbinical perversion. Indeed, the moral systems of the synagogue leave the same sad impression on the mind as its doctrinal teaching. They are all elaborate chains of casuistry, of which no truer description could be given than in the words of the Saviour (Matt. 15:6): "Ye have made the commandment of God of none effect by your tradition."

7

THE UPBRINGING OF JEWISH CHILDREN

The tenderness of the bond which united Jewish parents to their children appears even in the multiplicity and pictorialness of the expressions by which the various stages of child-life are designated in the Hebrew. Besides such general words as "ben" and "bath"—"son" and "daughter"—we find no fewer than nine different terms, each depicting a fresh stage of life.[1] The first of these simply designates the babe as the newly-"born"—the "jeled," or, in the feminine, "jaldah"—as in Exod. 2:3, 6, 8. But the use of this term throws a fresh light on the meaning of some passages of Scripture. Thus we remember that it is applied to our Lord in the prophecy of His birth (Isa. 9:6): "For a babe ('jeled') is born unto us, a son ('ben') is given to us;" while in Isa. 2:6 its employment adds a new meaning to the charge: "They please themselves (or strike hands) with the 'jalde'—the 'babes'—of strangers"—marking them, so to speak, as not only the children of strangers, but as unholy from their very birth. Compare also the pictorial, or else the poetical, use of the word "jeled" in such passages as Isa. 29:23; 57:4; Jer. 31:20; Eccl. 4:13; 1 Kings 12:8; 2 Kings 2:24; Gen. 42:22; and others. The next child-name, in point of time, is "jonek," which means, literally, "a suckling," being also sometimes used figuratively of plants, like our English "sucker," as in Isa. 53:2: "He shall grow up before Him as a sucker"—"jonek." The word "jonek"

But when she could hide him no longer, she got a papyrus basket for him and coated it with tar and pitch. Then she placed the child in it and put it among the reeds along the bank of the Nile (Exod. 2:3).

When they see among them their children,
the work of my hands,
they will keep my name holy;
they will acknowledge the holiness of the Holy One of Jacob,
and will stand in awe of the God of Israel (Isa. 29:23).

---

[1]Compare Hamburger, *Real-Encycl.* vol. i. p. 642.

*O LORD, our LORD,
how majestic is your
name in all the earth!
You have set your glory
above the heavens.
From the lips of children
and infants
you have ordained praise
because of your enemies,
to silence the foe and
the avenger
(Ps. 8:1–2).*

*But I have stilled and
quieted my soul;
like a weaned child with
its mother,
like a weaned child is my
soul within me
(Ps. 131:2).*

*Therefore the LORD himself
will give you a sign: The
virgin will be with child
and will give birth to a
son, and will call him
Immanuel (Isa. 7:14).*

occurs, for example, in Isa. 11:8, and in Ps. 8:2. On the other hand, the expression in the latter passage, rendered "babes" in our Authorised Version, marks a yet third stage in the child's existence, and a farther advancement in the babe-life. This appears from many passages. As the word implies, the "olel" is still "sucking;" but it is no longer satisfied with only this nourishment, and is "asking bread," as in Lam. 4:4: "The tongue of the 'jonek' cleaves to the roof of his mouth for thirst: the 'olalim' ask bread." A fourth designation represents the child as the "gamul," or "weaned one" (Ps. 131:2; Isa. 11:8; 28:9), from a verb which primarily means to complete, and secondarily to wean. As we know, the period of weaning among the Hebrews was generally at the end of two years (*Chethub.* 60), and was celebrated by a feast. After that the fond eye of the Hebrew parent seems to watch the child as it is clinging to its mother—as it were, ranging itself by her—whence the fifth designation, "taph" (Esther 3:13, "The 'taph' and the women in one day;" Jer. 40:7; Ezek. 9:6). The sixth period is marked by the word "elem" (in the feminine, "almah," as in Isa. 7:14, of the virgin-mother), which denotes becoming firm and strong. As one might expect, we have next the "naar," or youth— literally, he who shakes off, or shakes himself free. Lastly, we find the child designated as "bachur," or the "ripened one;" a young warrior, as in Isa. 31:8; Jer. 18:21; 15:8, etc. Assuredly, those who so keenly watched child-life as to give a pictorial designation to each advancing stage of its existence, must have been fondly attached to their children.

There is a passage in the Mishnah (*Aboth.* v. 21), which quaintly maps out and, as it were, labels the different periods of life according to their characteristics. It is worth reproducing, if only to serve as introduction to what we shall have to say on the upbringing of children. Rabbi Jehudah, the son of Tema, says: "At five years of age, reading of the Bible; at ten years, learning the Mishnah; at thirteen years, bound to the commandments; at fifteen years, the study of the Talmud; at eighteen years, marriage; at twenty, the pursuit of trade or business (active life); at thirty years, full vigour; at forty, maturity of reason; at fifty, for counsel; at sixty, commencement of agedness; at seventy, grey age; at eighty, advanced old age; at ninety, bowed down; at a hundred, as if he were dead and gone, and taken from the world." In the passage just quoted the age of five is mentioned as that when a child is expected to commence reading the Bible—of course, in the original Hebrew. But different opinions also prevailed. Generally speaking, such early instruction was regarded as only safe in the case of very healthy and strong children; while those of average constitution were not to be set to regular work till six years old. There is both common sense and sound experience in this Talmudical saying (*Cheth.* 50), "If you set your child to regular study before it is six years old, you shall always have to run after, and yet never get hold of it." This chiefly has reference to the irreparable injury to health caused by such early strain upon the mind. If, on the other hand, we come upon an admonition to begin teaching a child when it is three years old, this must refer to such early instruction as that of certain passages of Scripture, or of small isolated portions and prayers, which a parent would make his child repeat from tenderest years. As we shall show in the sequel, six or seven was the age at which a parent in Palestine was legally bound to attend to the schooling of his son.

But, indeed, it would have been difficult to say when the instruction of the Hebrew child really commenced. Looking back, a man must have felt that the teaching which he most—indeed, one might almost say, which he exclusively—valued had mingled with the first waking thoughts of his consciousness. Before the child could speak—before it could almost understand what was taught, in however elementary language—before it would even take in the domestic rites of the recurring weekly festival, or those of the annual feasts—it must have been attracted by the so-called "Mesusah," which was fastened at the

Figure of mother and child

These commandments that I give you today are to be upon your hearts...Write them on the doorframes of your houses and on your gates (Deut. 6:6, 9).

Phylacteries

They are also to inscribe the principal blessings they have received from God upon their doors,...that God's readiness to bless them may appear everywhere conspicuous about them (Jos. Antiquities 4.213).

Hear, O Israel: The LORD our God, the LORD is one. Love the LORD your God with all your heart and with all your soul and with all your strength (Deut. 6:4–5).

door-post of every "clean" apartment,[2] and at the entrance of such houses as were inhabited by Jews exclusively. The "Mesusah" was a kind of phylactery for the house, serving a purpose kindred to that of the phylactery for the person, both being derived from a misunderstanding and misapplication of the Divine direction (Deut. 6:9; 11:20), taking in the letter what was meant for the spirit. But while we gladly concede that the earlier Jewish practice was free from some of the present almost semi-heathenish customs,[3] and further, that many houses in Palestine were without it, there can be little doubt that, even at the time of Christ, this "Mesusah" would be found wherever a family was at all Pharisaically inclined. For, not to speak of what seems an allusion to it, so early as in Isa. 57:8, we have the distinct testimony of Josephus (*Ant.* 4.213) and of the Mishnah to their use (*Ber.* iii. 3; *Megill.* i. 8; *Moed K.* iii. 4; *Men.* iii. 7—in the last-mentioned place, even with superstitious additions). Supposing the "Mesusah" to have been somewhat as at present, it would have consisted of a small, longitudinally-folded parchment square, on which, on twenty-two lines, these two passages were written: Deut. 6:4–9, and 11:13–21. Inclosed in a shining metal case, and affixed to the door-post, the child, when carried in arms, would naturally put out its hand to it; the more so, that it would see the father and all others, on going out or in, reverently touch the case, and afterwards kiss the finger, speaking at the same time a benediction. For, from early times, the presence of the "Mesusah" was connected with the Divine protection, this verse being specially applied to it: "The Lord shall preserve thy going out and thy coming in from this time forth, and even for

---

[2] The "Mesusah" was not affixed to any that were not "diroth cavod"— dwellings of honour. Thus not to bath rooms, wash-houses, tanneries, dyeworks, etc. The "Mesusah" was only attached to dwelling-places, not to synagogues.

[3] The tractate *Massecheth Mesusah* (Kirchheim, *Septem libri Talm. parvi Hieros.* pp. 12–16) cannot be regarded as an authority for early times. But even the "Sohar" contains much that is little better than heathen superstition on the supposed efficacy of the "Mesusah." Among later superstitions connected with it, are the writing of the name "Cuso bemuchsas cuso" (supposed to be that of Israel's watching angel), the etymology of that name, etc.

evermore" (Ps. 121:8). Indeed, one of the most interesting ancient literary monuments in existence—
"Mechilta," a Jewish commentary on the book of
Exodus, the substance of which is older than the
Mishnah itself, dating from the beginning of the
second century of our era, if not earlier—argues the
efficacy of the "Mesusah" from the fact that, since the
destroying angel passed over the doors of Israel which
bore the covenant-mark, a much higher value must
attach to the "Mesusah," which embodied the name
of the Lord no less than ten times, and was to be
found in the dwellings of Israel day and night through
all their generations. From this to the magical mysticism of the "Kabbalah," and even to such modern
superstitions as that, if dust or dirt were kept within
a cubit of the "Mesusah," no less a host than three
hundred and sixty-five demons would come, there is
a difference of degree rather than of kind.

The blood will be a sign for you on the houses where you are; and when I see the blood, I will pass over you. No destructive plague will touch you when I strike Egypt (Exod. 12:13).

But to return. As soon as the child had any
knowledge, the private and the united prayers of the
family, and the domestic rites, whether of the weekly
Sabbath or of festive seasons, would indelibly impress
themselves upon his mind. It would be difficult to say
which of those feasts would have the most vivid effect
upon a child's imagination. There was "Chanukah,"
the feast of the Dedication, with its illumination of
each house, when (in most cases) the first evening
one candle would be lit for each member of the
household, the number increasing each night, till, on
the eighth, it was eight times that of the first. Then
there was "Purim," the feast of Esther, with the good
cheer and boisterous merriment which it brought;
the feast of Tabernacles, when the very youngest of
the house had to live out in the booth; and, chiefest of
feasts, the week of the Passover, when, all leaven
being carefully purged out, every morsel of food, by
its difference from that ordinarily used, would show
the child that the season was a special one. From the
moment a child was at all capable of being instructed
—still more, of his taking any part in the services—
the impression would deepen day by day. Surely no
one who had ever worshipped within the courts of

Jehovah's house at Jerusalem could ever have forgotten the scenes he had witnessed, or the words he had heard. Standing in that gorgeous, glorious building, and looking up its terraced vista, the child would watch with solemn awe, not unmingled with wonderment, as the great throng of white-robed priests busily moved about, while the smoke of the sacrifice rose from the altar of burnt-offering. Then, amid the hushed silence of that vast multitude, they had all fallen down to worship at the time of incense. Again, on those steps that led up to the innermost sanctuary the priests had lifted their hands and spoken over the people the words of blessing; and then, while the drink-offering was poured out, the Levites' chant of Psalms had risen and swelled into a mighty volume; the exquisite treble of the Levite children's voices being sustained by the rich round notes of the men, and accompanied by instrumental music. The Jewish child knew many of these words. They had been the earliest songs he had heard— almost his first lesson when clinging as a "taph" to his mother. But now, in those white-marbled, gold-adorned halls, under heaven's blue canopy, and with such surroundings, they would fall upon his ear like sounds from another world, to which the prolonged threefold blasts from the silver trumpets of the priests would seem to waken him. And *they were* sounds from another world; for, as his father would tell him, all that he saw was after the exact pattern of heavenly things which God had shown to Moses on Mount Sinai; all that he heard was God-uttered, spoken by Jehovah Himself through the mouth of His servant David, and of the other sweet singers of Israel. Nay, that place and that house were God-chosen; and in the thick darkness of the Most Holy Place—there afar off, where the high-priest himself entered on one day of the year only, and in simple pure white vesture, not in those splendid golden garments in which he was ordinarily arrayed—had once stood the ark, with the veritable tables of the law, hewn and graven by the very hand of God; and between the cherubim had then throned in the cloud the visible presence of

Candlestick

Jehovah. Verily this Temple with its services was heaven upon earth!

Nor would it have been easy to lose the impression of the first Paschal Supper which a child had attended. There was that about its symbols and services which appealed to every feeling, even had it not been that the law expressly enjoined full instruction to be given as to every part and rite of the service, as well as to the great event recorded in that supper. For in that night had Israel been born as a nation, and redeemed as the "congregation" of the Lord. Then also, as in a mould, had their future history been cast to all time; and there, as in type, had its eternal meaning and import for all men been outlined, and with it God's purpose of love and work of grace foreshadowed. Indeed, at a certain part of the service it was expressly ordained, that the youngest at the Paschal table should rise and formally ask what was the meaning of all this service, and how that night was distinguished from others; to which the father was to reply, by relating, in language suited to the child's capacity, the whole national history of Israel, from the calling of Abraham down to the deliverance from Egypt and the giving of the law; "and the more fully," it is added, "he explains it all, the better." In view of all this, Philo might indeed, without exaggeration, say that the Jews "were from their swaddling clothes, even before being taught either the sacred laws or the unwritten customs, trained by their parents, teachers, and instructors to recognise God as Father and as the Maker of the world" (*Legat. ad Cajum*, sec. 16); and that, "having been taught the knowledge (of the laws) from earliest youth, they bore in their souls the image of the commandments" (*ibid*. sec. 31). To the same effect is the testimony of Josephus, that "from their earliest consciousness" they had "learned the laws, so as to have them, as it were, engraven upon the soul" (*Ag. Apion*, 2.18); although, of course, we do not believe it, when, with his usual boastful magniloquence, he declares that at the age of fourteen he had been "frequently" consulted by "the high priests and principal men of the city...about the accurate under-

And when your children ask you, "What does this ceremony mean to you?" then tell them, "It is the Passover sacrifice to the LORD, *who passed over the houses of the Israelites in Egypt and spared our homes when he struck down the Egyptians"* (Exod. 12:26–27a).

standing of points of the law" (*Life*, 7–12; compare also *Ant.* 4.31; *Ag. Apion*, 1.60–68; 2.199–203).

But there is no need of such testimony. The Old Testament, the Apocrypha, and the New Testament, leading us progressively from century to century, indicate the same carefulness in the upbringing of children. One of the earliest narratives of Scripture records how God said to Abraham, "I know him, that he will command his children, and his household after him, and they shall keep the way of Jehovah, to do justice and judgment" (Gen. 18:19)—a statement which, we may note by the way, implies the distinction between the seed of Abraham after the flesh and after the spirit.[4] How thoroughly the spirit of this Divine utterance was carried out under the law, appears from a comparison of such passages as Exod. 12:26; 13:8, 14; Deut. 4:9, 10; 6:7, 20; 11:19; 31:13; Ps. 78:5, 6. It is needless to pursue the subject farther, or to show how even God's dealings with His people were regarded as the basis and model of the parental relationship. But the book in the Old Testament which, if properly studied, would give us the deepest insight into social and family life under the old dispensation—we mean the book of Proverbs—is so full of admonitions about the upbringing of children, that it is sufficient to refer the reader generally to it. He will find there the value of such training, its object, in the acquisition of true wisdom in the fear and service of Jehovah, and the opposite dangers most vividly portrayed—the practical bearing of all being summed up in this aphorism, true to all times: "Train up a child in the way he should go, and when he is old he will not depart from it" (Prov. 22:6); of which we have this New Testament application: "Bring up (your children) in the nurture and admonition of the Lord" (Eph. 6:4).

The book of Proverbs brings before us yet another phase of deepest interest. It contains the fullest appreciation of woman in her true dignity, and of her position and influence in the family-life. It is

Only be careful, and watch yourselves closely so that you do not forget the things your eyes have seen or let them slip from your heart as long as you live. Teach them to your children and to their children after them (Deut. 4:9).

The father of a righteous man has great joy; he who has a wise son delights in him (Prov. 23:24).

---

[4] See Oehler, *Theol. d. A. Test.* vol. i. p. 91.

quite true, as we shall presently show, that the obligation to train the child rested primarily upon the
father, and that both by the law of God and by the
ordinances of the Rabbis. But even the patriarchal
story will prepare an attentive reader to find, especially in the early upbringing of children, that
constant influence of woman, which, indeed, the
nature of the maternal relationship implies, provided
the family-life be framed on the model of the Word of
God. Lovelier pictures of this than the mother of
Samuel and the pious Shunammite hostess of Elisha
can scarcely be conceived. But the book of Proverbs
shows us, that even in the early times of the Jewish
monarchy this characteristic of Old Testament life
also appeared outside the bounds of the Holy Land,
wherever pious Israelites had their settlements. The
subject is so deeply interesting, historically and
religiously, and perhaps so new to some readers, that
a slight digression may be allowed us.

> *She said to her husband,*
> *"I know that this man who*
> *often comes our way is a*
> *holy man of God. Let's*
> *make a small room on the*
> *roof and put in it a bed*
> *and a table, a chair and a*
> *lamp for him. Then he can*
> *stay there whenever he*
> *comes to us" (2 Kgs. 4:9–10).*

Beyond the limits of the Holy Land, close by
Dumah, lay the land or district of Massa (Gen. 25:14),
one of the original seats of the Ishmaelites (1 Chron.
1:30). From Isa. 21:11 we gather that it must have
been situate beyond Seir—that is, to the south-east of
Palestine, in Northern Arabia. Whether the
Ishmaelites of Massa had come to the knowledge of
Jehovah, the true God; whether Massa was occupied
by a Jewish colony, which there established the
service of the Lord;[5] or whether, through the influence of Hebrew immigrants, such a religious change
had been brought about, certain it is, that the two last
chapters of the book of Proverbs introduce the royal
family of Massa as deeply imbued with the spiritual
religion of the Old Testament, and the queen- mother
as training the heir to the throne in the knowledge
and fear of the Lord.[6] Indeed, so much is this the case,

> *These are the names of*
> *the sons of Ishmael, listed*
> *in the order of their birth:*
> *Nebaioth the firstborn*
> *of Ishmael, Kedar, Adbeel,*
> *Mibsam, Mishma, Dumah,*
> *Massa, Hadad, Tema,*
> *Jetur, Naphish and*
> *Kedemah (Gen. 25:13–15).*

---

[5] From 1 Chron. 4:38–43 we infer colonisation in that direction, especially on the part of
the tribe of Simeon. Utterances in the prophets (such as in Isa. 21 and Micah 1) seem also to
indicate a very wide spread of Jewish settlers. It is a remarkable fact that, according to mediaeval
Jewish and Arab writers, the districts of Massa and Dumah were largely inhabited by Jews (see
Ritter, *Arabien*, p. 406.

[6] There can be no question that the word rendered in the Authorised Version (Prov. 30:1
and 31:1) by "prophecy" is simply the name of a district, "Massa."

A wife of noble character who can find? She is worth far more than rubies (Prov. 31:10).

that the instruction of the queen of Massa, and the words of her two royal sons, are inserted in the book of Proverbs as part of the inspired records of the Old Testament. According to the best criticism, Prov. 30:1 should be thus rendered: "The words of Agur, the son of her whom Massa obeys. Spake the man to God-with-me—God with me, and I was strong."[7] Then Prov. 31 embodies the words of Agur's royal brother, even "the words of Lemuel, king of Massa, with which his mother taught him." If the very names of these two princes—Agur, "exile," and Lemuel, "for God," or "dedicated to God"—are significant of her convictions, the teaching of that royal mother, as recorded in Prov. 31:2–9, is worthy of a "mother in Israel." No wonder that the record of her teaching is followed by an enthusiastic description of a godly woman's worth and work (Prov. 31:10–31), each verse beginning with a successive letter of the Hebrew alphabet,[8] like the various sections of Ps. 119—as it were, to let her praises ring through every letter of speech.

As might have been expected, the spirit of the Apocryphal books is far different from that which breathes in the Old Testament. Still, such a composition as Ecclesiasticus shows that even in comparatively late and degenerate times the godly upbringing of children occupied a most prominent place in religious thinking. But it is when we approach the New Testament, that a fresh halo of glory seems to surround woman. And here our attention is directed to the spiritual influence of mothers rather than of fathers. Not to mention "the mother of Zebedee's children," nor the mother of John Mark, whose home at Jerusalem seems to have been the meeting-place and the shelter of the early disciples, and that in times of the most grievous persecution; nor yet "the elect lady and her children," whom not only St. John, "but

---

[7] Or, according to another rendering, "Spake the man: I diligently searched after God, and I am become weary." This, of course, is not the place for critical discussion; but we may say that we have followed the general conclusions adopted alike by Delitzsch and Zöckler, and by Ewald, Hitzig, and Bertheau.

[8] The Hebrew alphabet has twenty-two letters.

also all they that know the truth," loved in truth (2 John 1), and her similarly elect sister with her children (ver. 13), two notable instances will occur to the reader. The first of these presents a most touching instance of a mother's faith, and prayers, and labour of love, to which the only parallel in later history is that of Monica, the mother of St. Augustine. How Eunice, the daughter of the pious Lois, had come to marry a heathen,[9] we know as little as the circumstances which may have originally led the family to settle at Lystra (Acts 16:1; compare 14:6, etc.), a place where there was not even a synagogue. At most then two or three Jewish families lived in that heathen city. Perhaps Lois and Eunice were the only worshippers of Jehovah there; for we do not even read of a meeting-place for prayer, such as that by the river-side where Paul first met Lydia. Yet in such adverse circumstances, and as the wife of a Greek, Eunice proved one to whom royal Lemuel's praise applied in the fullest sense: "Her children arise up and call her blessed," and "Her works praise her in the gates"—of the new Jerusalem. Not a truer nor more touching portraiture of a pious Jewish home could have been drawn than in these words of St. Paul: "I call to remembrance the unfeigned faith that is in thee, which dwelt first in thy grandmother Lois, and thy mother Eunice;" and again, "From a child thou hast known the Holy Scriptures" (2 Tim. 1:5; 3:15). There was, we repeat, no synagogue in Lystra where Timothy might have heard every Sabbath, and twice in the week, Moses and the Prophets read, and derived other religious knowledge; there was, so far as we can see, neither religious companionship nor means of instruction of any kind, nor religious example, not even from his father; but all around quite the contrary. But there was one influence for highest good—constant, unvarying, and most powerful. It was that of a "mother of Israel." From the time that as a "taph" he

...and how from infancy you have known the holy Scriptures, which are able to make you wise for salvation through faith in Christ Jesus (2 Tim. 3:15).

---

[9] The language of the New Testament leads to the inference that Timothy's father was not only by birth, but continued a Greek—being not merely a heathen, but not even a Jewish proselyte.

clung to her—even before that, when a "gamul," an "olel," and a "jonek"—had Eunice trained Timothy in the nurture and admonition of the Lord. To quote again the forcible language of St. Paul, "From an infant"[10] (or baby) "thou hast known the Holy Scriptures, which are able to make thee wise unto salvation, through faith which is in Christ Jesus."

From the Apocrypha, from Josephus, and from the Talmud we know what means of instruction in the Scriptures were within reach of a pious mother at that time. In a house like that of Timothy's father there would, of course, be no phylacteries, with the portions of Scripture which they contained, and probably no "Mesusah," although, according to the Mishnah (*Ber.* iii. 3), the latter duty was incumbent, not only upon men but upon women. The Babylon Talmud (*Ber.* 20 *b*) indeed gives a very unsatisfactory reason for the latter provision. But may it not be that the Jewish law had such cases in view as that of Eunice and her son, without expressly saying so, from fear of lending a sanction to mixed marriages? Be this as it may, we know that at the time of the Syrian persecutions, just before the rising of the Maccabees, the possession of portions or of the whole of the Old Testament by private families was common in Israel. For, part of those persecutions consisted in making search for these Scriptures and destroying them (1 Macc. i. 57), as well as punishing their possessors (Jos. *Ant.* 12.256). Of course, during the period of religious revival which followed the triumph of the Maccabees, such copies of the Bible would have greatly multiplied. It is by no means an exaggeration to say that, if perhaps only the wealthy possessed a complete copy of the Old Testament, written out on parchment or on Egyptian paper, there would scarcely be a pious home, however humble, which did not cherish as its richest treasure some portion of the Word of God—whether the five books of the Law, or

Women and slaves and minors are exempt from reciting the Shema, and from wearing phylacteries, but they are not exempt from saying the Tefillah, from the law of the Mezuzah or from saying the Benediction after meals (Mishnah, Berakot iii. 3).

And if there were any sacred book of the law found, it was destroyed; and those with whom they were found miserably perished also (Jos. Antiquities 12.256).

---

[10]The Greek term means literally "a baby," and is so used, not only by classical writers, but in all the passages in which it occurs in the New Testament, which are as follows: Luke 1:41, 44; 2:12, 16; 18:15; Acts 7:19; 2 Tim. 3:15; and 1 Pet. 2:2.

the Psalter, or a roll of one or more of the Prophets. Besides, we know from the Talmud[11] that at a later period, and probably at the time of Christ also, there were little parchment rolls specially for the use of children, containing such portions of Scripture as the "Shema"[12] (Deut. 6:4–9; 11:13–21; Num. 15:37–41), the "Hallel"(Ps. 113–118), the history of the Creation to that of the Flood, and the first eight chapters of the book of Leviticus. Such means of instruction there would be at the disposal of Eunice in teaching her son.

Praise the LORD. Praise, O servants of the LORD, praise the name of the LORD (Ps. 113:1).

And this leads us to mention, with due reverence, the other and far greater New Testament instance of maternal influence in Israel. It is none less than that of the mother of our blessed Lord Himself. While the fact that Jesus became subject to His parents, and grew in wisdom and in favour both with God and man, forms part of the unfathomable mystery of His self-humiliation, the influence exerted upon His early education, especially by His mother, seems implied throughout the gospel history. Of course, His was a pious Jewish home; and at Nazareth there was a synagogue, to which, as we shall by-and-by explain, a school was probably attached. In that synagogue Moses and the Prophets would be read, and, as afterwards by Himself (Luke 4:16), discourses or addresses be delivered from time to time. What was taught in these synagogue-schools, and how, will be shown in another chapter. But, whether or not Jesus had attended such a school, His mind was so thoroughly imbued with the Sacred Scriptures—He was so familiar with them in their every detail—that we cannot fail to infer that the home of Nazareth possessed a precious copy of its own of the entire Sacred Volume, which from earliest childhood formed, so to speak, the meat and drink of the God-Man. More than that, there is clear evidence that He was familiar with the art of

He went to Nazareth, where he had been brought up, and on the Sabbath day he went into the synagogue, as was his custom. And he stood up to read (Luke 4:16).

---

[11]Compare Herzfeld, *Gesch. d. Volk. Jes.* vol. iii. p. 267, note.

[12]The "Shema"—so called from the first word, "Shema" ("Hear, O Israel")—forms part of the regular prayers; as the section called "Hallel" ("praise") was appointed to be sung at certain seasons.

I tell you the truth, until heaven and earth disappear, not the smallest letter, not the least stroke of a pen, will by any means disappear from the Law until everything is accomplished (Matt. 5:18).

The Books [of Scripture] differ from phylacteries and Mezuzahs only in that the Books may be written in any language, while phylacteries and Mezuzahs may be written in the Assyrian writing only (Mishnah, Megillah i. 8).

writing, which was by no means so common in those days as reading. The words of our Lord, as reported both by St. Matthew (Matt. 5:18) and by St. Luke (Luke 16:17), also prove that the copy of the Old Testament from which He had drawn was not only in the original Hebrew, but written, like our modern copies, in the so-called Assyrian, and not in the ancient Hebrew-Phoenician characters. This appears from the expression "one iota or one little hook"—erroneously rendered "tittle" in our Authorised Version—which can only apply to the modern Hebrew characters. That our Lord taught in Aramaean, and that He used and quoted the Holy Scriptures in the Hebrew, perhaps sometimes rendering them for popular use into Aramaean,[13] there can be little doubt on the part of careful and unprejudiced students, though some learned men have held the opposite. It is quite true that the Mishnah (*Megill.* i. 8) seems to allow the writing of Holy Scripture in any language; but even Simeon, the son of Gamaliel (the teacher of St. Paul), confined this concession to the Greek—no doubt with a view to the LXX., which was so widely spread in his time. But we also know from the Talmud, how difficult it was for a Rabbi to defend the study or use of Greek, and how readily popular prejudice burst into a universal and sweeping condemnation of it.[14] The same impression is conveyed not only from the immediate favourable change which the use of the Aramaean by St. Paul produced upon the infuriated people (Acts 21:40), but also from the fact that only an appeal to the Hebrew Scriptures could have been of authority in discussion with the Pharisees and Scribes, and that it alone gave point to the frequent expostulations of Christ: "Have ye not read?" (Matt. 12:3; 19:4; 21:13, 16, 42; 22:31).

[13]Keim (*u.s.*), p. 430, rightly instances Matt. 27:46 as an instance of "the Aramaean colouring" of the Hebrew text. We quote Keim the more readily, as being a strong opponent of the orthodox view; although his work is far more careful and reverent than others that have of late issued, especially from the French press, which it is scarcely possible to read without astonishment at the power of assertion, and moral indignation at what is asserted.

[14]The fact that the Evangelists so frequently quote from the LXX. does not in the least affect the argument that our LORD used the Hebrew text.

This familiarity from earliest childhood with the Scriptures in the Hebrew original also explains how at the age of twelve Jesus could be found "in the Temple; sitting in the midst of the doctors, both hearing them and asking them questions" (Luke 2:46). In explaining this seemingly strange circumstance, we may take the opportunity of correcting an almost universal mistake. It is generally thought that, on the occasion referred to, the Saviour had gone up, as being "of age," in the Jewish sense of the expression, or, to use their own terms, as a "Bar Mizvah," or "son of the commandment," by which the period was marked when religious obligations and privileges devolved upon a youth, and he became a member of the congregation. But the legal age for this was not twelve, but thirteen (*Ab.* v. 21). On the other hand, the Rabbinical law enjoined (*Yoma*, 82 *a*) that even before that—two years, or at least one year—lads should be brought up to the Temple, and made to observe the festive rites.[15] Unquestionably, it was in conformity with this universal custom that Jesus went on the occasion named to the Temple. Again, we know that it was the practice of the members of the various Sanhedrims—who on ordinary days sat as judicatories, from the close of the morning to the time of the evening sacrifice (*Sanh.* 88 *b*)—to come out upon the Sabbaths and feast-days on "the terrace of the Temple," and there publicly to teach and expound, the utmost liberty being given of asking questions, discussing, objecting, and otherwise taking intelligent part in these lectures. On the occasion of Christ's presence, these discussions would, as usual, be carried on during the "Moed Katon," or minor festive days, intervening between the second and the last day of the Paschal week. Joseph and Mary, on the other hand, had, as allowed by the law, returned towards Nazareth on the third day of the Paschal week, while Jesus remained behind. These circumstances also explain why His appearance in the midst

At five years old [one is fit] for the Scripture, at ten years for the Mishnah, at thirteen for [the fulfilling of] the commandments, at fifteen for the Talmud, at eighteen for the bride-chamber, at twenty for pursuing [a calling], at thirty for authority, at forty for discernment, at fifty for counsel, at sixty for to be an elder, at seventy for grey hairs, at eighty for special strength, at ninety for bowed back, and at a hundred a man is as one that has [already] died and passed away and ceased from the world (Mishnah, 'Abot v. 21).

---

[15]Compare Altingius, *Academ. Dissert.* p. 336, who is almost the only one correct on this point.

of the doctors, although very remarkable considering His age, did not at once command universal attention. In point of fact, the only qualification requisite, so far as learning was concerned, would be a thorough knowledge of the Scriptures in the Hebrew, and a proper understanding of them.[16]

What we have hitherto described will have conveyed to the reader that the one branch of instruction aimed after or desired by the Jews at the time of Christ was religious knowledge. What was understood by this, and how it was imparted—whether in the family or in the public schools—must form the subject of special investigation.

---

[16]Lightfoot (*Hora Hebr. in Luc.* ii. 46) gives an entirely fanciful and erroneous view of the matter, representing the Saviour as either actually teaching or at least qualified to take part in the regular discussions and instructions of the Rabbis. The note of Wetstein (*Nov. Test.* i. p. 668) approximates more nearly the correct view.

8

SUBJECTS OF STUDY. HOME EDUCATION IN ISRAEL; FEMALE EDUCATION. ELEMENTARY SCHOOLS, SCHOOLMASTERS, AND SCHOOL ARRANGEMENTS.

If a faithful picture of society in ancient Greece or Rome were to be presented to view, it is not easy to believe that even they who now most oppose the Bible could wish their aims success. For this, at any rate, may be asserted, without fear of gainsaying, that no other religion than that of the Bible has proved competent to control an advanced, or even an advancing, state of civilisation. Every other bound has been successively passed and submerged by the rising tide; how deep only the student of history knows. Two things are here undeniable. In the case of heathenism every advance in civilisation has marked a progressive lowering of public morality, the earlier stages of national life always showing a far higher tone than the later. On the contrary, the religion of the Bible (under the old as under the new dispensation) has increasingly raised, if not uniformly the public morals, yet always the tone and standard of public morality; it has continued to exhibit a standard never yet attained, and it has proved its power to control public and social life, to influence and to mould it.

Scroll

Strange as it may sound, it is strictly true that, beyond the boundaries of Israel, it would be scarcely possible to speak with any propriety of family life, or even of the family, as we understand these terms. It is significant, that the Roman historian Tacitus should mark it as something special among the Jews[1]—

---

[1] Tacitus, *Hist.* v. 5. In general this fifth book is most interesting, as showing the strange mixture of truth and error, and the intense hatred of the Jewish race even on the part of such men as Tacitus.

They exchanged the truth of God for a lie, and worshiped and served created things rather than the Creator—who is forever praised. Amen (Rom. 1:25).

which they only shared with the ancient barbarian Germans[2]—that they regarded it as a crime to kill their offspring! This is not the place to describe the exposure of children, or the various crimes by which ancient Greece and Rome, in the days of their highest culture, sought to rid themselves of what was regarded as superfluous population. Few of those who have learned to admire classical antiquity have a full conception of any one phase in its social life—whether of the position of woman, the relation of the sexes, slavery, the education of children, their relation to their parents, or the state of public morality. Fewer still have combined all these features into one picture, and that not merely as exhibited by the lower orders, or even among the higher classes, but as fully owned and approved by those whose names have descended in the admiration of ages as the thinkers, the sages, the poets, the historians, and the statesmen of antiquity. Assuredly, St. Paul's description of the ancient world in the first and second chapters of his Epistle to the Romans must have appeared to those who lived in the midst of it as Divine even in its tenderness, delicacy, and charity; the full picture under bright sunlight would have been scarcely susceptible of exhibition. For such a world there was only one alternative—either the judgment of Sodom, or the mercy of the Gospel and the healing of the Cross.[3]

When we pass from the heathen world into the homes of Israel, even the excess of their exclusiveness seems for the moment a relief. It is as if we turned from enervating, withering, tropical heat into a darkened room, whose grateful coolness makes us for the

---

[2] *De Germania,* xix.

[3] Let it not be thought that we have been guilty of the slightest exaggeration. The difficulty here is to tell the truth and yet find moderate terms in which to express it. That Christianity should have laid its hold on such a society, found there its brightest martyrs and truest followers, and finally subdued and transformed it, is quite as great a miracle as that of the breaking down of the middle wall of partition among the Jews, or their spiritual transformation of mind and heart from self-righteousness and externalism. In either case, to the student of history the miracle will seem greater than if "one rose from the dead." The general reader who wishes more details about the state of heathenism is referred to the admirable work of Döllinger, *Heidenthum u. Judenth.* pp. 679–728.

moment forget that its gloom is excessive, and cannot continue as the day declines. And this shutting out of all from without, this exclusiveness, applied not only to what concerned their religion, their social and family life, but also to their knowledge. In the days of Christ the pious Jew had no other knowledge, neither sought nor cared for any other—in fact, denounced it—than that of the law of God. At the outset, let it be remembered that, in heathenism, theology, or rather mythology, had no influence whatever on thinking or life—was literally submerged under their waves. To the pious Jew, on the contrary, the knowledge of God was everything; and to prepare for or impart that knowledge was the sum total, the sole object of his education. This was the life of his soul—the better, and only true life, to which all else as well as the life of the body were merely subservient, as means towards an end. His religion consisted of two things: knowledge of God, which by a series of inferences, one from the other, ultimately resolved itself into theology, as they understood it; and service, which again consisted of the proper observance of all that was prescribed by God, and of works of charity towards men—the latter, indeed, going beyond the bound of what was strictly due (the Chovoth) into special merit or "righteousness" (Zedakah). But as service presupposed knowledge, theology was again at the foundation of all, and also the crown of all, which conferred the greatest merit. This is expressed or implied in almost innumerable passages of Jewish writings. Let one suffice, not only because it sounds more rationalistic, but because it is to this day repeated each morning in his prayers by every Jew: "These are the things of which a man eats the fruit in this world, but their possession[4] continueth for the next world: to honour father and mother, pious works, peacemaking between man and man, and the study of the law, which is equivalent to them all" (*Peah.* i. 1).

And literally "equivalent to them all" was such study to the Jew. The circumstances of the times

God said to Solomon, "Since this is your heart's desire and you have not asked for wealth, riches or honor, nor for the death of your enemies, and since you have not asked for a long life but for wisdom and knowledge to govern my people over whom I have made you king, therefore wisdom and knowledge will be given you" (2 Chron. 1:11–12a).

Worship the LORD *with gladness; come before him with joyful songs (Ps. 100:2).*

---

[4]The capital sum, as it were.

And thus used Hillel to say: He that makes wordly [sic] use of the crown shall perish. Thus thou mayest learn that he that makes profit out of the words of the Law removes his life from the world (Mishnah, 'Abot iv. 5).

forced him to learn Greek, perhaps also Latin, so much as was necessary for intercourse; and to tolerate at least the Greek translation of the Scriptures, and the use of any language in the daily prayers of the Shema, of the eighteen benedictions, and of the grace after meat.[5] But the blessing of the priests might not be spoken, nor the phylacteries nor the Mesusah written, in other than the Hebrew language (*Megil.* i. 8; *Sotah*, vii. 1, 2); while heathen science and literature were absolutely prohibited. To this, and not to the mere learning of Greek, which must have been almost necessary for daily life, refer such prohibitions as that traced to the time of Titus (*Sotah*, ix. 14), forbidding a man to teach his son Greek. The Talmud itself (*Men.* 99 *b*) furnishes a clever illustration of this, when, in reply to the question of a younger Rabbi, whether, since he knew the whole "Thorah" (the law), he might be allowed to study "Greek wisdom," his uncle reminded him of the words (Josh. 1:8), "Thou shalt meditate therein day and night." "Go, then, and consider," said the older Rabbi, "which is the hour that is neither of the day nor of the night, and in it thou mayest study Grecian wisdom." This, then, was one source of danger averted. Then, as for the occupations of ordinary life, it was indeed quite true that every Jew was bound to learn some trade or business. But this was not to divert him from study; quite the contrary. It was regarded as a profanation— or at least declared such[6]—to make use of one's learning for secular purposes, whether of gain or of honour. The great Hillel had it (*Ab.* i. 13): "He who serves himself by the crown (the 'Thorah') shall fade away." To this Rabbi Zadok added the warning, "Make study neither a crown by which to shine, nor yet a spade with which to dig"—the Mishnah inferring that such attempts would only lead to the shortening of life (*Ab.* iv. 5). All was to be merely subsidiary to the one grand object; the one was of

---

[5] These are the oldest elements of the Jewish liturgy.

[6] Such, at any rate, was the profession; the practice, it is to be feared, was often far different, as the reader of the New Testament will infer from Mark 12:40; Luke 16:14; 20:47.

time, the other of eternity; the one of the body, the other of the soul;[7] and its use was only to sustain the body, so as to give free scope to the soul on its upward path. Every science also merged in theology. Some were not so much sciences as means of livelihood, such as medicine and surgery; others were merely handmaidens to theology. Jurisprudence was in reality a kind of canon law; mathematics and astronomy were subservient to the computations of the Jewish calendar; literature existed not outside theological pursuits; and as for history, geography, or natural studies, although we mark, in reference to the latter, a keenness of observation which often led instinctively to truth, we meet with so much ignorance, and with so many gross mistakes and fables, as almost to shake the belief of the student in the trustworthiness of any Rabbinical testimony.

Beware of the teachers of the law. They like to walk around in flowing robes and love to be greeted in the marketplaces and have the most important seats in the synagogues and the places of honor at banquets (Luke 20:46).

From what has been stated, three inferences will be gathered, all of most material bearing on the study of the New Testament. It will be seen how a mere knowledge of the law came to hold such place of almost exclusive importance that its successful prosecution seemed to be well-nigh all in all. Again, it is easy now to understand why students and teachers of theology enjoyed such exceptional honour (Matt. 23:6, 7; Mark 12:38, 39; Luke 11:43; 20:46). In this respect the testimonies of Onkelos, in his paraphrastic rendering of the Scriptures, of the oldest "Targumim," or paraphrastic commentaries, of the Mishnah, and of the two Talmuds, are not only unanimous, but most extravagant. Not only are miracles supposed to be performed in attestation of certain Rabbis, but such a story is actually ventured upon (*Bab. Mes.* 86 *a*), as that on the occasion of a discussion in the academy of heaven, when the Almighty and His angels were of different opinions in regard to a special point of law, a Rabbi famed for his knowledge of that subject was summoned up by the angel of death to decide the matter between them! The story is altogether too

---

[7] There is here a most instructive passage in *Kidd.* iv. 14.

Act according to the law they teach you and the decisions they give you. Do not turn aside from what they tell you, to the right or to the left (Deut. 17:11).

Nay, indeed, the law does not permit us to make festivals at the births of our children, and thereby afford occasion of drinking to excess; but it ordains that the very beginning of our education should be immediately directed to sobriety. It also commands us to bring those children up in learning and to exercise them in the laws, and make them acquainted with the acts of their predecessors, in order to their imitation of them, and that they may be nourished up in the laws from their infancy, and might neither transgress them, nor yet have any pretense for their ignorance of them (Jos. Against Apion 2.204).

blasphemous for details, and indeed the whole subject is too wide for treatment in this connection. If such was the exalted position of a Rabbi, this direction of the Mishnah seems quite natural, that in case of loss, of difficulties, or of captivity, a teacher was to be cared for before a father, since to the latter we owed only our existence in this world, but to the former the life of the world to come (*Bab. Mez.* ii. 11). It is curious how in this respect also Roman Catholicism and Pharisaism arrive at the same ultimate results. Witness this saying of the celebrated Rabbi, who flourished in the thirteenth century, and whose authority is almost absolute among the Jews. The following is his glossary on Deut. 17:11: "Even if a Rabbi were to teach that your left hand was the right, and your right hand the left, you are bound to obey."

The third inference which the reader will draw is as to the influence which such views must have exercised upon education, alike at home and in schools. It is no doubt only the echo of the most ancient mode of congratulating a parent when to this day those who are present at a circumcision, and also the priest when the first-born is redeemed from him, utter this: "As this child has been joined to the covenant" (or, as the case may be, "attained this redemption"), "so may it also be to him in reference to the 'thorah,' the 'chuppah,'[8] and to good works." The wish marks with twofold emphasis the life that is to come, as compared with the life that now is. This quite agrees with the account of Josephus, who contrasts the heathen festivals at the birth of children with the Jewish enactments by which children were from their very infancy nourished up in the laws of God (*Ag. Apion,* 1.38–68; 2.173–205).

There can be no question that, according to the law of Moses, the early education of a child devolved upon the father; of course, always bearing in mind that his first training would be the mother's (Deut. 11:19, and many other passages). If the father were

---

[8] The marriage-baldacchino, under which the regular marriage ceremony is performed.

not capable of elementary teaching, a stranger would be employed. Passing over the Old Testament period, we may take it that, in the days of Christ, home-teaching ordinarily began when the child was about three years old. There is reason for believing that, even before this, that careful training of the memory commenced, which has ever since been one of the mental characteristics of the Jewish nation.[9] Verses of Scripture, benedictions, wise sayings, etc., were impressed on the child, and mnemonic rules devised to facilitate the retention of what was so acquired. We can understand the reason of this from the religious importance attaching to the exact preservation of the very words of tradition. The Talmud describes the *beau ideal* of a student when it compares him to a well-plastered cistern, which would not let even a single drop escape. Indeed, according to the Mishnah, he who from negligence "forgets any one thing in his study of the Mishnah, Scripture imputes it to him as if he had forfeited his life;" the reference here being to Deut. 4:9 (*Ab.* iii. 10). And so we may attach some credit even to Josephus' boast about his "wonderful memory" (*Life*, 2.8).

Only be careful, and watch yourselves closely so that you do not forget the things your eyes have seen or let them slip from your heart as long as you live. Teach them to your children and to their children after them (Deut. 4:9).

In teaching to read, the alphabet was to be imparted by drawing the letters on a board, till the child became familiar with them. Next, the teacher would point in the copy read with his finger, or, still better, with a style, to keep up the attention of the pupil. None but well-corrected manuscripts were to be used, since, as was rightly said, mistakes impressed upon the young mind were afterwards not easily corrected. To acquire fluency, the child should be made to read aloud. Special care was to be bestowed on the choice of good language, in which respect, as we know, the inhabitants of Judaea far excelled those of Galilee, who failed not only in elegance of diction, but even in their pronunciation. At five years of age the Hebrew Bible was to be begun; commencing,

...I made mighty proficiency in the improvements of my learning, and appeared to have both a great memory and understanding (Jos. Life 2.8).

---

[9] Gfrörer, *Jahrh. d. Heils*, vol. i. p. 170, proposes as a curious test that all copies of the Talmud should be destroyed, feeling sure that any twelve learned Rabbis would be able to restore it verbatim from memory!

however, not with the book of Genesis, but with that of Leviticus. This not (as Altingius suggests in his *Academ. Dissert.* p. 335) to teach the child his guilt, and the need of justification, but rather because Leviticus contained those ordinances which it behoved a Jew to know as early as possible. The history of Israel would probably have been long before imparted orally, as it was continually repeated on all festive occasions, as well as in the synagogue.

When he takes the throne of his kingdom, he is to write for himself on a scroll a copy of this law, taken from that of the priests, who are Levites (Deut. 17:18).

It has been stated in a former chapter that writing was not so common an accomplishment as reading. Undoubtedly, the Israelites were familiar with it from the very earliest period of their history, whether or not they had generally acquired the art in Egypt. We read of the graving of words on the gems of the high-priest's breastplate, of the record of the various genealogies of the tribes, etc.; while such passages as Deut. 6:9; 11:20; 24:1, 3, imply that the art was not confined to the priesthood (Num. 5:23), but was known to the people generally. Then we are told of copies of the law (Deut. 17:18; 28:58, etc.), while in Josh. 10:13 we have a reference to a work called "the book of Jasher." In Josh. 18:9 we find mention of a description of Palestine "in a book," and in 24:26 of what Joshua "wrote in the book of the law of God." From Judges 8:14 (margin) it would appear that in the time of Gideon the art of writing was very generally known. After that, instances occur so frequently and applied to so many relationships, that the reader of the Old Testament can have no difficulty in tracing the progress of the art. This is not the place to follow the subject farther, nor to describe the various materials employed at that time, nor the mode of lettering. At a much later period the common mention of "scribes" indicates the popular need of such a class. We can readily understand that the Oriental mind would delight in writing enigmatically, that is, conveying by certain expressions a meaning to the initiated which the ordinary reader would miss, or which, at any rate, would leave the explanation to the exercise of ingenuity. Partially in the same class we might reckon the custom of designating a word by its initial letter.

All these were very early in practice, and the subject has points of considerable interest. Another matter deserves more serious attention. It will scarcely be credited how general the falsification of signatures and documents had become. Josephus mentions it (*Ant.* 16.317–319); and we know that St. Paul was obliged to warn the Thessalonians against it (2 Thess. 2:2), and at last to adopt the device of signing every letter which came from himself. There are scarcely any ancient Rabbinical documents which have not been interpolated by later writers, or, as we might euphemistically call it, been recast and re-edited. In general, it is not difficult to discover such additions; although the vigilance and acuteness of the critical scholar are specially required in this direction to guard against rash and unwarrantable inferences. But without entering on such points, it may interest the reader to know what writing materials were employed in New Testament times. In Egypt red ink seems to have been used; but assuredly the ink mentioned in the New Testament was black, as even the term indicates ("melan," 2 Cor. 3:3; 2 John 12; 3 John 13). Josephus speaks of writing in gold letters (*Ant.* 12.324–329); and in the Mishnah (*Meg.* ii. 2) we read of mixed colours, of red, of sympathetic ink, and of certain chemical compositions. Reed quills are mentioned in 3 John 13. The best of these came from Egypt; and the use of a penknife would of course be indispensable. Paper (from the Egyptian "papyrus") is mentioned in 2 John 12; parchment in 2 Tim. 4:13. Of this there were three kinds, according as the skin was used either whole, or else split up into an outer and an inner skin. The latter was used for the Mesusah. Shorter memoranda were made on tablets, which in the Mishnah (*Shab.* xii. 4) bear the same name as in Luke 1:63.

Before passing to an account of elementary schools, it may be well, once and for all, to say that the Rabbis did not approve of the same amount of instruction being given to girls as to boys. More particularly they disapproved of their engaging in legal studies—partly because they considered woman's

After this writing was produced, Herod had no doubt about the treacherous designs of his sons against him; but Alexander said that Diophantus, the scribe, had imitated his hand, and that the paper was maliciously drawn up by Antipater; for Diophantus appeared to be very cunning in such practices; and as he was afterward convicted of forging other papers, he was put to death for it (Jos. Antiquities *16.319).*

I have much to write you, but I do not want to do so with pen and ink (3 John 13).

Parchment, case, and rolls

He had been instructed in the way of the LORD, and he spoke with great fervor and taught about Jesus accurately, though he knew only the baptism of John. He began to speak boldly in the synagogue. When Priscilla and Aquila heard him, they invited him to their home and explained to him the way of God more adequately (Acts 18:25–26).

mission and duties as lying in other directions, partly because the subjects were necessarily not always suitable for the other sex, partly because of the familiar intercourse between the sexes to which such occupations would have necessarily led, and finally—shall we say it?—because the Rabbis regarded woman's mind as not adapted for such investigations. The unkindest thing, perhaps, which they said on this score was, "Women are of a light mind;" though in its oft repetition the saying almost reads like a semi-jocular way of cutting short a subject on which discussion is disagreeable. However, instances of Rabbinically learned women do occur. What their Biblical knowledge and what their religious influence was, we learn not only from the Rabbis, but from the New Testament. Their attendance at all public and domestic festivals, and in the synagogues, and the circumstance that certain injunctions and observances of Rabbinic origin devolved upon them also, prove that, though not learned in the law, there must have been among them not a few who, like Lois and Eunice, could train a child in the knowledge of the Scripture, or, like Priscilla, be qualified to explain even to an Apollos the way of God more perfectly.

Supposing, then, a child to be so far educated at home; suppose him, also, to be there continually taught the commandments and observances, and, as the Talmud expressly states, to be encouraged to repeat the prayers aloud, so as to accustom him to it. At six years of age he would be sent to school; not to an academy, or "beth hammedrash," which he would only attend if he proved apt and promising; far less to the class-room of a great Rabbi, or the discussions of the Sanhedrim, which marked a very advanced stage of study. We are here speaking only of primary or elementary schools, such as even in the time of our Lord were attached to every synagogue in the land. Passing over the supposed or real Biblical notices of schools, and confining our attention strictly to the period ending with the destruction of the Temple, we have first a notice in the Talmud (*Bab. B.* 21 *b*), ascribing to Ezra an ordinance, that as many school-

masters as chose should be allowed to establish themselves in any place, and that those who had formerly
been settled there might not interfere with them.
In all likelihood this notice should not be taken in its
literal sense, but as an indication that the encouragement of schools and of education engaged the attention
of Ezra and of his successors. Of the Grecianised
academies which the wicked high-priest Jason tried to
introduce in Jerusalem (2 Macc. iv. 12, 13) we do not
speak, because they were anti-Jewish in their spirit,
and that to such extent, that the Rabbis, in order to
"make a hedge," forbade all gymnastic exercises. The
farther history and progress of Jewish schools are
traced in the following passage of the Talmud
(*Bab. B.* 21, *a*): "If any one has merit, and deserves
that his name should be kept in remembrance, it is
Joshua, the son of Gamaliel. Without him the law
would have fallen into oblivion in Israel. For they
used to rest on this saying of the law (Deut. 11:19),
'Ye shall teach them.' Afterwards it was ordained that
masters be appointed at Jerusalem for the instruction
of youth, as it is written (Isa. 2:3), 'Out of Zion shall
go forth the law.' But even so the remedy was not
effectual, only those who had fathers being sent to
school, and the rest being neglected. Hence it was
arranged that Rabbis should be appointed in every
district, and that lads of sixteen or seventeen years
should be sent to their academies. But this institution
failed, since every lad ran away if he was chastised by
his master. At last Joshua the son of Gamaliel
arranged, that in every province and in every town
schoolmasters be appointed, who should take charge
of all boys from six or seven years of age." We may
add at once, that the Joshua here spoken of was
probably the high-priest of that name who flourished before the destruction of the Temple, and that
unquestionably this farther organisation implied
at least the existence of elementary schools at an
earlier period.

Every place, then, which numbered twenty-five
boys of a suitable age, or, according to Maimonides,
one hundred and twenty families, was bound to

See that you do not look down on one of these little ones. For I tell you that their angels in heaven always see the face of my Father in heaven (Matt. 18:10).

appoint a schoolmaster. More than twenty-five pupils or thereabouts he was not allowed to teach in a class. If there were forty, he had to employ an assistant; if fifty, the synagogue authorities appointed two teachers. This will enable us to understand the statement, no doubt greatly exaggerated, that at the destruction of Jerusalem there were no fewer than four hundred and eighty schools in the metropolis. From another passage, which ascribes the fall of the Jewish state to the neglect of the education of children, we may infer what importance popular opinion attached to it. But indeed, to the Jew, child-life was something peculiarly holy, and the duty of filling it with thoughts of God specially sacred. It almost seems as if the people generally had retained among them the echo of our Lord's saying, that their angels continually behold the face of our Father which is in heaven. Hence the religious care connected with education. The grand object of the teacher was moral as well as intellectual training. To keep children from all intercourse with the vicious; to suppress all feelings of bitterness, even though wrong had been done to one's parents;[10] to punish all real wrong-doing; not to prefer one child to another; rather to show sin in its repulsiveness than to predict what punishment would follow, either in this or the next world, so as not to "discourage" the child—such are some of the rules laid down.[11] A teacher was not even to promise a child anything which he did not mean to perform, lest its mind be familiarised with falsehood. Everything that might call up disagreeable or indelicate thoughts was to be carefully avoided. The teacher must not lose patience if his pupil understood not readily, but rather make the lesson more plain. He might, indeed, and he should, punish when necessary, and, as one of the Rabbis put it, treat the child

---

[10]To this day there is this beautiful prayer in the Jewish liturgy: "In regard to those who curse, let my soul be silent; yea, let my soul be like the dust towards all."

[11]The references here are too numerous to be given. In general, compare Hamburger, *Real. Enc.* vol. i. p. 340; my *History of the Jewish Nation*, p. 298; and the pamphlet by Ehrmann, *Beitr. zur Gesch. d. Schulen.*

HEBREW		GREEK		
Nîsān	נִיסָן	*Xanthikos*	Ξανθικός	March–April
'iyyār	אִיָּר	*Artemisios*	'Αρτεμίσιος	April–May
Sîwān	סִיוָן	*Daisios*	Δαίσιος	May–June
Tammûz	תַּמּוּז	*Panemos*	Πάνεμος	June–July
'āb	אָב	*Lōos*	Λῷος	July–August
'elûl	אֱלוּל	*Gorpiaios*	Γορπιαῖος	August–September
Tišrî	תִּשְׁרִי	*Hyperberetaios*	'Υπερβερεταῖος	September–October
Marḥešwān	מַרְחֶשְׁוָן	*Dios*	Δῖος	October–November
Kislēv	כִּסְלֵו	*Apellaios*	'Απελλαῖος	November–December
Ṭēbēt	טֵבֵת	*Audynaios*	Αὐδυναῖος	December–January
Šebāṭ	שְׁבָט	*Peritios*	Περίτιος	January–February
'adār	אֲדָר	*Dystros*	Δύστρος	February–March

Calendar of Months Used in the Postexilic Period

like a young heifer whose burden was daily increased. But excessive severity was to be avoided; and we are told of one teacher who was actually dismissed from office for this reason. Where possible, try kindness; and if punishment was to be administered, let the child be beaten with a strap, but never with a rod. At ten the child began to study the Mishnah; at fifteen he must be ready for the Talmud, which would be explained to him in a more advanced academy. If after three, or at most five, years of tuition the child had not made decided progress, there was little hope of his attaining to eminence. In the study of the Bible the pupil was to proceed from the book of Leviticus to the rest of the Pentateuch, thence to the Prophets, and lastly to the Hagiographa. This regulation was in accordance with the degree of value which the Rabbis attached to these divisions of the Bible.[12] In the case of advanced pupils the day was portioned out—one part being devoted to the Bible, the other two to the Mishnah and the Talmud. Every parent was also advised to have his child taught swimming.

It has already been stated that in general the school was held in the synagogue. Commonly its teacher was the "chazan," or "minister" (Luke 4:20); by which expression we are to understand not a spiritual office, but something like that of a beadle. This officer was salaried by the congregation; nor was

---

[12]The full explanation of this must be reserved to a larger work.

he allowed to receive fees from his pupils, lest he should show favour to the rich. The expenses were met by voluntary and charitable contributions; and in case of deficiency the most distinguished Rabbis did not hesitate to go about and collect aid from the wealthy. The number of hours during which the junior classes were kept in school was limited. As the close air of the school-room might prove injurious during the heat of the day, lessons were intermitted between ten A.M. and three P.M. For similar reasons, only four hours were allowed for instruction between the seventeenth of Thamuz and the ninth of Ab (about July and August), and teachers were forbidden to chastise their pupils during these months. The highest honour and distinction attached to the office of a teacher, if worthily discharged. Want of knowledge or of method was regarded as sufficient cause for removing a teacher; but experience was always deemed a better qualification than mere acquirements. No teacher was employed who was not a married man. To discourage unwholesome rivalry, and to raise the general educational standard, parents were prohibited from sending their children to other than the schools of their own towns.

A very beautiful trait was the care bestowed on the children of the poor and on orphans. In the Temple there was a special receptacle—that "of the secret"—for contributions, which were privately applied for the education of the children of the pious poor. To adopt and bring up an orphan was regarded as specially a "good work." This reminds us of the apostolic description of a "widow indeed," as one "well reported for good works;" who "had brought up children, lodged strangers, washed the saints' feet, relieved the afflicted, diligently followed every good work" (1 Tim. 5:10). Indeed, orphans were the special charge of the whole congregation—not thrust into poor-houses,—and the parochial authorities were even bound to provide a fixed dowry for female orphans.

Such were the surroundings, and such the atmosphere, in which Jesus of Nazareth moved while tabernacling among men.

9

MOTHERS, DAUGHTERS, AND WIVES IN ISRAEL

Israelite woman in full dress

In order accurately to understand the position of woman in Israel, it is only necessary carefully to peruse the New Testament. The picture of social life there presented gives a full view of the place which she held in private and in public life. Here we do not find that separation, so common among Orientals at all times, but a woman mingles freely with others both at home and abroad. So far from suffering under social inferiority, she takes influential and often leading part in all movements, specially those of a religious character. Above all, we are wholly spared those sickening details of private and public immorality with which contemporary classical literature abounds. Among Israel woman was pure, the home happy, and the family hallowed by a religion which consisted not only in public services, but entered into daily life, and embraced in its observances every member of the household. It was so not only in

New Testament times but always in Israel. St. Peter's reference to "the holy women" "in the old time" (1 Pet. 3:5) is thoroughly in accordance with Talmudical views. Indeed, his quotation of Gen. 18:12, and its application: "Even as Sara obeyed Abraham, calling him lord," occur in precisely the same manner in Rabbinical writings (*Tanch.* 28, 6), where her respect and obedience are likewise set forth as a pattern to her daughters.[1]

So Sarah laughed to herself as she thought, "After I am worn out and my master is old, will I now have this pleasure?" (Gen. 18:12).

Some further details may illustrate the matter better than arguments. The creation of woman from the rib of Adam is thus commented on:[2] "It is as if Adam had exchanged a pot of earth for a precious jewel." This, although Jewish wit caustically had it: "God has cursed woman, yet all the world runs after her; He has cursed the ground, yet all the world lives of it." In what reverence "the four mothers," as the Rabbis designate Sarah, Rebekah, Leah, and Rachel, were held, and what influence they exercised in patriarchal history, no attentive reader of Scripture can fail to notice. And as we follow on the sacred story, Miriam, who had originally saved Moses, leads the song of deliverance on the other side of the flood, and her influence, though not always for good, continued till her death (compare Micah 6:4). Then "the women whose heart stirred them up in wisdom" contribute to the rearing of the Tabernacle;[3] Deborah works deliverance, and judgeth in Israel; and the piety of Manoah's wife is at least as conspicuous, and more intelligent, than her husband's (Judg. 13:23). So also is that of the mother of Samuel. In the times of the kings the praises of Israel's maidens stir the jealousy of Saul; Abigail knows how to avert the danger of her husband's folly; the wise woman of Tekoah is sent for

I brought you up out of Egypt and redeemed you from the land of slavery. I sent Moses to lead you, also Aaron and Miriam (Mic. 6:4).

Deborah, a prophetess, the wife of Lappidoth, was leading Israel at that time. She held court under the Palm of Deborah between Ramah and Bethel in the hill country of Ephraim, and the Israelites came to her to have their disputes decided (Judg. 4:4–5).

---

[1] The following illustration also occurs: A certain wise woman said to her daughter before her marriage: "My child, stand before thy husband and minister to him. If thou wilt act as his maiden he will be thy slave, and honour thee as his mistress; but if thou exalt thyself against him, he will be thy master, and thou shalt become vile in his eyes, like one of the maidservants."

[2] *Shab.* 23.

[3] There is a Jewish tradition that the women had contributed of their substance to the Tabernacle, but refused to do so for making the golden calf, which is deduced from the account in Exod. 32:2 compared with verse 3.

to induce the king to fetch his banished home; and the conduct of a woman "in her wisdom" puts an end to the rebellion of Sheba. Later on, the constant mention of queen mothers, and their frequent interference in the government, shows their position. Such names as that of Huldah the prophetess, and the idyllic narrative of the Shunammite, will readily occur to the memory. The story of a woman's devotion forms the subject of the Book of Ruth; that of her pure and faithful love, the theme or the imagery of the Song of Songs; that of her courage and devotion the groundwork of the Book of Esther: while her worth and virtues are enumerated in the closing chapter of the Book of Proverbs. Again, in the language of the prophets the people of God are called "the daughter," "the virgin daughter of Zion," "the daughter of Jerusalem," "the daughter of Judah," etc.; and their relationship to God is constantly compared to that of the married state. The very terms by which woman is named in the Old Testament are significant. If the man is *Ish*, his wife is *Ishah*, simply his equal; if the husband is *Gever*, the ruler, the woman is, in her own domain, *Gevirah* and *Gevereth*, the mistress (as frequently in the history of Sarah and in other passages), or else *the dweller at home* (*Nevath bayith*, Ps. 68:12).[4] Nor is it otherwise in New Testament times. The ministry of woman to our blessed Lord, and in the Church, has almost become proverbial. Her position there marks really not a progress upon, but the full carrying out of, the Old Testament idea; or, to put the matter in another light, we ask no better than that any one who is acquainted with classical antiquity should compare what he reads of a Dorcas, of the mother of Mark, of Lydia, Priscilla, Phoebe, Lois, or Eunice, with what he knows of the noble women of Greece and Rome at that period.

David said to Abigail, "Praise be to the LORD, the God of Israel, who has sent you today to meet me" (1 Sam. 25:32).

The LORD announced the word, and great was the company of those who proclaimed it: "Kings and armies flee in haste; in the camps men divide the plunder" (Ps. 68:11–12).

---

[4] Similar expressions are *Sarah* and *Shiddah*, both from roots meaning *to rule*. Nor is this inconsistent with the use of the word *Baal*, to marry, and *Beulah*, the married one, from *Baal*, a lord—even as Sarah "called Abraham lord" (1 Pet. 3:6, the expression used of her to Abimelech, Gen. 20:3, being *Beulah*). Of course it is not meant that these are the only words for females. But the others, such as *Bath* and *Naarah*, are either simply feminine terminations, or else, as *Bethulah, Levush, Nekevah, Almah, Rachem*, descriptive of their physical state.

In Joppa there was a disciple named Tabitha (which, when translated, is Dorcas), who was always doing good and helping the poor (Acts 9:36).

I have been reminded of your sincere faith, which first lived in your grandmother Lois and in your mother Eunice and, I am persuaded, now lives in you also (2 Tim. 1:5).

You ask, "Why?" It is because the LORD is acting as the witness between you and the wife of your youth, because you have broken faith with her, though she is your partner, the wife of your marriage covenant (Mal. 2:14).

Of course, against all this may be set the permission of *polygamy*, which undoubtedly was in force at the time of our Lord, and the ease with which *divorce* might be obtained. In reference to both these, however, it must be remembered that they were temporary concessions to "the hardness" of the people's heart. For, not only must the circumstances of the times and the moral state of the Jewish and of neighbouring nations be taken into account, but there were progressive stages of spiritual development. If these had not been taken into account, the religion of the Old Testament would have been unnatural and an impossibility. Suffice it, that "from the beginning it was not so," nor yet intended to be so in the end—the intermediate period thus marking the gradual progress from the perfectness of the idea to the perfectness of its realisation. Moreover, it is impossible to read the Old, and still more the New Testament without gathering from it the conviction, that polygamy was not the rule but the rare exception, so far as the people generally were concerned. Although the practice in reference to divorce was certainly more lax, even the Rabbis surrounded it with so many safeguards that, in point of fact, it must in many cases have been difficult of accomplishment. In general, the whole tendency of the Mosaic legislation, and even more explicitly that of later Rabbinical ordinances, was in the direction of recognising the rights of woman, with a scrupulousness which reached down even to the Jewish slave, and a delicacy that guarded her most sensitive feelings. Indeed, we feel warranted in saying, that in cases of dispute the law generally leant to her side. Of *divorce* we shall have to speak in the sequel. But what the religious views and feelings both about it and monogamy were at the time of Malachi, appears from the pathetic description of the altar of God as covered with the tears of "the wife of youth," "the wife of thy covenant," "thy companion," who had been "put away" or "treacherously dealt" with (Mal. 2:13 to

end). The whole is so beautifully paraphrased by the
Rabbis that we subjoin it:[5]

"If death hath snatched from thee the wife of youth,
It is as if the sacred city were,
And e'en the Temple, in thy pilgrim days,
Defiled, laid low, and levelled with the dust.
The man who harshly sends from him
His first-woo'd wife, the loving wife of youth,
For him the very altar of the Lord
Sheds forth its tears of bitter agony."

When he [Samson] returned, he said to his father and mother, "I have seen a Philistine woman in Timnah; now get her for me as my wife" (Judg. 14:2).

Where the social intercourse between the sexes
was nearly as unrestricted as among ourselves, so far
as consistent with Eastern manners, it would, of
course, be natural for a young man to make personal
choice of his bride. Of this Scripture affords abundant
evidence. But, at any rate, the woman had, in case of
betrothal or marriage, to give her own free and
expressed consent, without which a union was
invalid. *Minors*—in the case of girls up to twelve years
and one day—might be betrothed or given away by
their father. In that case, however, they had afterwards the right of insisting upon divorce. Of course,
it is not intended to convey that woman attained her
full position till under the New Testament. But this is
only to repeat what may be said of almost every social
state and relationship. Yet it is most marked how
deeply the spirit of the Old Testament, which is
essentially that of the New also, had in this respect
also penetrated the life of Israel. St. Paul's warning
(2 Cor. 6:14) against being "unequally yoked together,"
which is an allegorical application of Lev. 19:19; Deut.
22:10, finds to some extent a counterpart in mystical
Rabbinical writings,[6] where the last-mentioned
passage is expressly applied to spiritually unequal
marriages. The admonition of 1 Cor. 7:39 to marry
"only in the Lord," recalls many similar Rabbinical

Keep my decrees. Do not mate different kinds of animals. Do not plant your field with two kinds of seed. Do not wear clothing woven of two kinds of material (Lev. 19:19).

---

[5] After the elegant poetical version of Dr. Sachs (*Stimmen vom Jordan u. Euphrat.* p. 347). We select this one poetic description of Jewish wedded love and respect for woman from among many that might be given.

[6] The somewhat similar reference to Lev. 19:19 in *Philo. de Creat. Princ.* (ed Francof.) pp. 730, 731, mentioned in Wetstein, *Nov. Test.* ii. p. 193, does not seem sufficiently parallel for quotation.

For the unbelieving husband has been sanctified through his wife, and the unbelieving wife has been sanctified through her believing husband. Otherwise your children would be unclean, but as it is, they are holy (1 Cor. 7:14).

warnings, from which we select the most striking. Men, we are told,[7] are wont to marry for one of four reasons—for passion, wealth, honour, or the glory of God. As for the first-named class of marriages, their issue must be expected to be "stubborn and rebellious" sons, as we may gather from the section referring to such following upon that in Deut. 21:11. In regard to marriages for wealth, we are to learn a lesson from the sons of Eli, who sought to enrich themselves in such manner, but of whose posterity it was said (1 Sam. 2:36) that they should "crouch for a piece of silver and a morsel of bread." Of marriages for the sake of connection, honour, and influence, King Jehoram offered a warning, who became King Ahab's son-in-law, because that monarch had seventy sons, whereas upon his death his widow Athaliah "arose and destroyed all the seed royal" (2 Kings 11:1). But far otherwise is it in case of marriage "in the name of heaven." The issue of such will be children who "preserve Israel." In fact, the Rabbinical references to marrying "in the name of heaven," or "for the name of God,"—in God and for God—are so frequent and so emphatic, that the expressions used by St. Paul must have come familiarly to him. Again, much that is said in 1 Cor. 7 about the married estate, finds striking parallels in Talmudical writings. One may here be mentioned, as explaining the expression (ver. 14): "Else were your children unclean; but now are they holy." Precisely the same distinction was made by the Rabbis in regard to proselytes, whose children, if begotten before their conversion to Judaism, were said to be "unclean;" if after that event to have been born "in holiness," only that, among the Jews, *both* parents required to profess Judaism, while St. Paul argues in the contrary direction, and concerning a far different holiness than that which could be obtained through any mere outward ceremony.

Some further details, gathered almost at random, will give glimpses of Jewish home life and of current views. It was by a not uncommon, though irreverent,

---

[7]Yalkut on Deut. 21:15.

mode of witticism, that two forms of the same verb, sounding almost alike, were made to express opposite experiences of marriage. It was common to ask a newly-married husband: "*Maza* or *Moze?*"—"findeth" or "found;" the first expression occurring in Prov. 18:22, the second in Eccles. 7:26. A different sentiment is the following from the Talmud (*Yeb.* 62 *b*; *Sanh.* 76 *b*), the similarity of which to Eph. 5:28 will be immediately recognised: "He that loveth his wife as his own body, honoureth her more than his own body, brings up his children in the right way, and leads them in it to full age—of him the Scripture saith: 'Thou shalt know that thy tabernacle shall be in peace' (Job 5:24)." Of all qualities those most desired in woman were meekness, modesty, and shamefacedness. Indeed, brawling, gossip in the streets, and immodest behaviour in public were sufficient grounds for divorce. Of course, Jewish women would never have attempted "teaching" in the synagogue, where they occupied a place separate from the men—for Rabbinical study, however valued for the male sex, was disapproved of in the case of women. Yet this direction of St. Paul (1 Tim. 2:12): "I suffer not a woman to usurp authority over the man" findeth some kind of parallel in the Rabbinical saying: "Whoever allows himself to be ruled by his wife, shall call out, and no one will make answer to him."

It is on similar grounds that the Rabbis argue, that man must seek after woman, and not a woman after a man; only the reason which they assign for it sounds strange. Man, they say, was formed from the ground—woman from man's rib; hence, in trying to find a wife man only looks after what he had lost! This formation of man from soft clay, and of woman from a hard bone, also illustrated why man was so much more easily reconcilable than woman. Similarly, it was observed, that God had not formed woman out of the head, lest she should become proud; nor out of the eye, lest she should lust; nor out of the ear, lest she should be curious; nor out of the mouth, lest she should be talkative; nor out of the heart, lest she should be jealous; nor out of the hand, lest she should

He who finds a wife finds what is good and receives favor fro the LORD (Prov. 18:22).

In this same way, husbands ought to love their wives as their own bodies. He who loves his wife loves himself (Eph. 5:28).

be covetous; nor out of the foot, lest she be a busy-body; but out of the rib, which was always covered. Modesty was, therefore, a prime quality. It was no doubt chiefly in jealous regard for this, that women were interdicted engaging in Rabbinical studies; and a story is related to show how even the wisest of women, Beruria, was thereby brought to the brink of extreme danger. It is not so easy to explain why women were dispensed from all positive obligations (commands, but not prohibitions) that were not general in their bearing (*Kidd.* i. 7, 8), but fixed to certain periods of time (such as wearing the phylacteries, etc.), and from that of certain prayers, unless it be that woman was considered not her own mistress but subject to others, or else that husband and wife were regarded as one, so that his merits and prayers applied to her as well. Indeed, this view, at least so far as the meritorious nature of a man's engagement with the law is concerned, is expressly brought forward, and women are accordingly admonished to encourage their husbands in all such studies.

We can understand how, before the coming of the Messiah, marriage should have been looked upon as of religious obligation. Many passages of Scripture were at least *quoted* in support of this idea. Ordinarily, a young man was expected to enter the wedded state (according to Maimonides) at the age of sixteen or seventeen, while the age of twenty may be regarded as the utmost limit conceded, unless study so absorbed time and attention as to leave no leisure for the duties of married life. Still it was thought better even to neglect study than to remain single. Yet money cares on account of wife and children were dreaded. The same comparison is used in reference to them, which our Lord applies to quite a different "offence," that against the "little ones" (Luke 17:2). Such cares are called by the Rabbis, "a millstone round the neck" (*Kidd.* 29 *b*). In fact, the expression seems to have become proverbial, like so many others which are employed in the New Testament.

We read in the Gospel that, when the Virgin-mother "was espoused to Joseph, before they came

The rites of the laying on of hands, waving, bringing-near [the Meal-offering], taking the Handful and burning it, and wringing the necks of the Bird-offerings, sprinkling the blood and receiving the blood are performed by men but not by women, excepting in the Meal-offerings of the Suspected Adulteress and of the female Nazirite, for which they themselves perform the act of waving (Mishnah, Qiddusin i. 8).

It would be better for him to be thrown into the sea with a millstone tied around his neck than for him to cause one of these little ones to sin (Luke 17:2).

together, she was found with child of the Holy Ghost. Then Joseph her husband, being a just man, and not willing to make her a public example, was minded to put her away privily" (Matt. 1:18, 19). The narrative implies a distinction between *betrothal* and *marriage*—Joseph being at the time betrothed, but not actually married to the Virgin-mother. Even in the Old Testament a distinction is made between *betrothal* and *marriage*. The former was marked by a bridal present (or *Mohar*, Gen. 34:12; Exod. 22:17; 1 Sam. 18:25), with which the father, however, would in certain circumstances dispense. From the moment of her betrothal a woman was treated as if she were actually married. The union could not be dissolved, except by regular divorce; breach of faithfulness was regarded as adultery; and the property of the woman became virtually that of her betrothed, unless he had expressly renounced it (*Kidd.* ix. 1). But even in that case he was her natural heir. It is impossible here to enter into the various legal details, as, for example, about property or money which might come to a woman after betrothal or marriage. The law adjudicated this to the husband, yet with many restrictions, and with infinite delicacy towards the woman, as if reluctant to put in force the rights of the stronger (*Kidd.* viii. 1, etc.). From the Mishnah (*Bab. B.* x. 4) we also learn that there were regular *Shitre Erusin*, or writings of betrothal, drawn up by the authorities (the costs being paid by the bridegroom). These stipulated the mutual obligations, the dowry, and all other points on which the parties had agreed. The *Shitre Erusin* were different from the regular *Chethubah* (literally, *writing*), or marriage contract, without which the Rabbis regarded a marriage as merely legalised concubinage (*Cheth.* v. 1). The *Chethubah* provided a settlement of at least two hundred denars for a maiden, and one hundred denars for a widow, while the priestly council at Jerusalem fixed four hundred denars for a priest's daughter. Of course these sums indicate only the legal *minimum*, and might be increased indefinitely at pleasure, though opinions differ whether any larger

Make the price for the bride and the gift I am to bring as great as you like, and I'll pay whatever you ask me. Only give me the girl as my wife (Gen. 34:12).

They may not write deeds of betrothal or marriage save with the consent of both the parties; and the bridegroom must pay the fee (Mishnah, Baba Bathra x. 4).

Denarius of Tiberius

sums might be legally exacted, if matters did not go beyond betrothal. The form at present in use among the Jews sets forth, that the bridegroom weds his bride "according to the law of Moses and of Israel;" that he promises "to please, to honour, to nourish, and to care for her, as is the manner of the men of Israel," adding thereto the woman's consent, the document being signed by two witnesses. In all probability this was substantially the form in olden times. In Jerusalem and in Galilee—where it was said that men in their choice had regard to "a fair degree," while in the rest of Judaea they looked a good deal after money—widows had the right of residence in their husband's house secured to them.

On the other hand, a father was bound to provide a dowry (*nedan, nedanjah*) for his daughter conformable to her station in life; and a second daughter could claim a portion equal to that of her elder sister, or else one-tenth of all immovable property. In case of the father's death, the sons, who, according to Jewish law, were his sole heirs, were bound to maintain their sisters, even though this would have thrown them upon public charity, and to endow each with a tenth part of what had been left. The dowry, whether in money, property, or jewellery, was entered into the marriage contract, and really belonged to the wife, the husband being obliged to add to it one-half more, if it consisted of money or money's value; and if of jewellery, etc., to assign to her four-fifths of its value. In case of separation (not divorce) he was bound to allow her a proper aliment, and to re-admit her to his table and house on the Sabbath-eve. A wife was entitled to one-tenth of her dowry for pin-money. If a father gave away his daughter without any distinct statement about her dowry, he was bound to allow her at least fifty *sus*; and if it had been expressly stipulated that she was to have no dowry at all, it was delicately enjoined that the bridegroom should, *before marriage*, give her sufficient for the necessary outfit. An orphan was to receive a dowry of at least fifty *sus* from the parochial authorities. A husband could not oblige his wife to leave the Holy Land nor the city of Jerusalem, nor yet to change a town for a country residence, or *vice versâ,* nor a good for a bad house. These are only a few of the provisions which show how carefully the law protected the interests of women. To enter into farther details would lead beyond our present object. All this was substantially settled at the betrothal, which, in Judaea at least, seems to have been celebrated by a feast. Only a *bonâ fide* breach of these arrangements, or wilful fraud, was deemed valid ground for dissolving the bond once formed. Otherwise, as already noted, a regular divorce was necessary.

According to Rabbinical law certain formalities were requisite to make a betrothal legally valid. These consisted either in handing to a woman, directly or through messengers, a piece of money, however small, or else a letter,[8] provided it were in each case expressly stated before witnesses, that the man thereby intended to espouse the woman as his wife. The marriage followed after a longer or shorter interval, the limits of which, however, were fixed by law. The ceremony itself consisted in leading the bride into the house of the bridegroom, with certain formalities, mostly dating from very ancient times. Marriage with a maiden was commonly celebrated on a Wednesday afternoon, which allowed the first days of the week for preparation, and enabled the husband, if he had a charge to prefer against the previous chastity of his bride, to make immediate complaint before the local Sanhedrim, which sat every Thursday. On the other hand, the marriage of a widow was celebrated on Thursday afternoon, which left three days of the week for "rejoicing with her." This circumstance enables us, with some certainty, to arrange the date of the events which preceded the marriage in Cana. Inferring from the accompanying festivities that it was the marriage of a maiden, and therefore took place on a Wednesday, we have the following succession of events:—On *Thursday* (beginning as every

Bride

---

[8]There was also a third mode of espousal—simply by cohabitation, but this was very strongly disapproved by the Rabbis.

Jewish day with the previous evening), testimony of the Baptist to the Sanhedrim-deputation from Jerusalem. On *Friday* (John 1:29), "John seeth Jesus coming unto him," and significantly preacheth the first sermon about "the Lamb of God which taketh away the sin of the world." On *Saturday* (ver. 35), John's second sermon on the same text; the consequent conversion of St. John and St. Andrew, and the calling of St. Peter. On *Sunday* (ver. 43), our Lord Himself preacheth His first Messianic sermon, and calls Philip and Nathanael. On "the third day" after it, that is, on *Wednesday,* was the marriage in Cana of Galilee. The significance of these dates, when compared with those in the week of our Lord's Passion, will be sufficiently evident.

On the third day a wedding took place at Cana in Galilee (John 2:1a).

But this is not all that may be learned from the account of the marriage in Cana. Of course, there was a "marriage-feast," as on all these occasions. For this reason, marriages were not celebrated either on the Sabbath, or on the day before or after it, lest the Sabbath-rest should be endangered. Nor was it lawful to wed on any of the three annual festivals, in order, as the Rabbis put it, "not to mingle one joy (that of the marriage) with another (that of the festival)." As it was deemed a religious duty to give pleasure to the newly-married couple, the merriment at times became greater than the more strict Rabbis approved. Accordingly, it is said of one, that to produce gravity he broke a vase worth about £25; of another, that at his son's wedding he broke a costly glass; and of a third, that being asked to sing, he exclaimed, Woe to us, for we must all die! For, as it is added (*Ber.* 31 *a*): "It is forbidden to man, that his mouth be filled with laughter in this world (dispensation), as it is written, 'Then our mouth was filled with laughter, and our tongue with singing.' When is that to be? At the time when 'they shall sing among the heathen, The Lord hath done great things for them.' "

It deserves notice, that at the marriage in Cana there is no mention of "the friends of the bridegroom," or, as we would call them, the groomsmen. This was in strict accordance with Jewish custom, for groomsmen were customary in *Judaea,* but not in Galilee (*Cheth.* 25 *a*). This also casts light upon the locality where John 3:29 was spoken, in which "the friend of the bridegroom" is mentioned. But this expression is quite different from that of "children of the bridechamber," which occurs in Matt. 9:15, where the scene is once more laid in Galilee. The term "children of the bridechamber" is simply a translation of the Rabbinical "*bene Chuppah,*" and means the guests invited to the bridal. In Judaea there were at every marriage *two* groomsmen or "friends of the bridegroom"—one for the bridegroom, the other for his bride. Before marriage, they acted as a kind of intermediaries between the couple; at the wedding they offered gifts, waited upon the bride and bridegroom, and attended them to the bridal chamber, being also, as it were, the guarantors of the bride's virgin chastity. Hence, when St. Paul tells the Corinthians (2 Cor. 11:2): "I am jealous over you with godly jealousy; for I have espoused you to one husband, that I may present you as a chaste virgin to Christ," he speaks, as it were, in the character of groomsman or "bridegroom's friend," who had acted as such at the spiritual union of Christ with the Corinthian Church. And we know that it was specially the duty of the "friend of the bridegroom" so to present to him his bride. Similarly it was his also, after marriage, to maintain proper terms between the couple, and more particularly to defend the good fame of the bride against all imputations. It may interest some to know that this custom also was traced up to highest authority. Thus, in the spiritual union of Israel with their God, Moses is spoken of as "the friend of the bridegroom" who leads out the bride (Exod. 19:17); while Jehovah, as the bridegroom, meets His Church at Sinai (Ps. 68:7; *Pirke di R. El.* 41). Nay, in some mystic writings God is described as acting "the friend of the bridegroom," when our first parents met in Eden. There is a touch of poetry in the application of Ezek. 28:13 to that scene, when angels led the choir, and decked and watched the bridal-bed (*Ab. de R. Nathan* iv. and xii.). According to another

The bride belongs to the bridegroom. The friend who attends the bridegroom waits and listens for him, and is full of joy when he hears the bridegroom's voice. That joy is mine, and it is now complete (John 3:29).

Jesus answered, "How can the guests of the bridegroom mourn while he is with them? The time will come when the bridegroom will be taken from them; then they will fast" (Matt. 9:15).

Then Moses led the people out of the camp to meet with God, and they stood at the foot of the mountain (Exod. 19:17).

You were in Eden,
    the garden of God;
every precious stone
    adorned you:
ruby, topaz and emerald,
    chrysolite, onyx and
    jasper, sapphire,
    turquoise and beryl.
Your settings and mount-
    ings were made of gold;
on the day you were
    created they were
    prepared
(Ezek. 28:13).

Gather the people,
consecrate the assembly;
bring together the elders,
gather the children,
those nursing at the
breast.
Let the bridegroom leave
his room
and the bride her chamber
(Joel 2:16).

And every woman who
prays or prophesies with
her head uncovered dis-
honors her head—it is just
as though her head were
shaved. If a woman does
not cover her head, she
should have her hair cut
off; and if it is a disgrace
for a woman to have her
hair cut or shaved off, she
should cover her head
(1 Cor. 11:5–6).

For this reason, and
because of the angels, the
woman ought to have a
sign of authority on her
head (1 Cor. 11:10).

ancient Rabbinical commentary (*Ber. R.* viii.), God Almighty Himself took the cup of blessing and spoke the benediction, while Michael and Gabriel acted the "bridegroom's friends" to our first parents when they wedded in Paradise.

With such a "benediction," preceded by a brief formula, with which the bride was handed over to her husband (Tobit vii. 13), the wedding festivities commenced.[9] And so the pair were led towards the bridal chamber (*Cheder*) and the bridal bed (*Chuppah*).[10] The bride went with her hair unloosed. Ordinarily, it was most strictly enjoined upon women to have their head and hair carefully covered. This may throw some light upon the difficult passage, 1 Cor. 11:1–10. We must bear in mind that the apostle there argues with Jews, and that *on their own ground,* convincing them by a reference to their own views, customs, and legends of the propriety of the practice which he enjoins. From that point of view the propriety of a woman having her head "covered" could not be called in question. The opposite would, to a Jew, have indicated immodesty. Indeed, it was the custom in the case of a woman accused of adultery to have her hair "shorn or shaven," at the same time using this formula: "Because thou hast departed from the manner of the daughters of Israel, who go with their head covered;…therefore that has befallen thee which thou hast chosen." This so far explains verses 5 and 6. The expression "power," as applied in verse 10 to the head of woman, seems to refer to this covering, indicating, as it did, that she was under the power of her husband, while the very difficult addition, "because of the angels," may either allude to the presence of the angels and to the well-known Jewish view (based, no doubt, on truth) that those angels may be grieved or offended by our conduct, and bear the sad tidings before the throne of God, or it may possibly refer to the very ancient Jewish belief, that the evil spirits

---

[9] It is, to say the least, doubtful whether the Rabbinical form of this benediction and of that at betrothal dates from earliest times. However beautiful, seems far too elaborate for that.

[10] The distinction is marked in Joel 2:16; the *Chuppah* is also mentioned in Ps. 19:5.

gained power over a woman who went with her head bare.

The custom of a bridal veil—either for the bride alone, or spread over the couple—was of ancient date. It was interdicted for a time by the Rabbis after the destruction of Jerusalem. Still more ancient was the wearing of crowns (Cant. 3:11; Isa. 61:10; Ezek. 16:12), which was also prohibited after the last Jewish war. Palm and myrtle branches were borne before the couple, grain or money was thrown about, and music preceded the procession, in which all who met it were, as a religious duty, expected to join.[11] The Parable of the Ten Virgins, who, with their lamps, were in expectancy of the bridegroom (Matt. 25:1), is founded on Jewish custom. For, according to Rabbinical authority, such lamps carried on the top of staves were frequently used, while *ten* is the number always mentioned in connection with public solemnities.[12] The marriage festivities generally lasted a week, but the bridal days extended over a full month.[13]

Having entered thus fully on the subject of marriage, a few further particulars may be of interest. The bars to marriage mentioned in the Bible are sufficiently known. To these the Rabbis added others, which have been arranged under two heads—as farther extending the laws of kindred (to their *secondary* degrees), and as intended to guard morality. The former were extended over the whole line of forbidden kindred, where that line was direct, and to one link farther where the line became indirect—as, for example, to the wife of a maternal uncle, or to the step- mother of a wife. In the category of guards to morality we include such prohibitions as that a divorced woman might not marry her seducer, nor a man the woman to whom he had brought her letter

I delight greatly in the
LORD;
my soul rejoices in my
God.
For he has clothed me with
garments of salvation
and arrayed me in a robe
of righteousness,
as a bridegroom adorns his
head like a priest,
and as a bride adorns
herself with her jewels
(Isa. 61:10).

---

[11] See my article on "Marriage" in Cassell's *Bible Educator,* vol. iv. pp. 267–270.

[12] According to R. Simon (on *Chel.* ii. 8) it was an Eastern custom that, when the bride was led to her future home, "they carried before the party about ten" such lamps.

[13] The practice of calling a wife a bride during the first year of her marriage is probably based on Deut. 24:5.

"Teacher," they said, "Moses wrote for us that if a man's brother dies and leaves a wife but no children, the man must marry the widow and have children for his brother" (Mark 12:19).

But I tell you that anyone who divorces his wife, except for marital unfaithfulness, causes her to become an adulteress, and anyone who marries the divorced woman commits adultery (Matt. 5:32).

of divorce, or in whose case he had borne testimony; or of marriage with those not in their right senses, or in a state of drunkenness; or of the marriage of minors, or under fraud, etc. A widower had to wait over three festivals, a widow three months, before re-marrying, or if she was with child or gave suck, for two years. A woman might not be married a third time; no marriage could take place within thirty days of the death of a near relative, nor yet on the Sabbath, nor on a feast-day, etc. Of the marriage to a deceased husband's brother (or the next of kin), in case of childlessness, it is unnecessary here to speak, since although the Mishnah devotes a whole tractate to it (*Yebamoth*), and it was evidently customary at the time of Christ (Mark 12:19, etc.), the practice was considered as connected with the territorial possession of Palestine, and ceased with the destruction of the Jewish commonwealth (*Bechar.* i. 7). A priest was to inquire into the legal descent of his wife (up to four degrees if the daughter of a priest, otherwise up to five degrees), except where the bride's father was a priest in actual service, or a member of the Sanhedrim. The high-priest's bride was to be a maid not older than six months beyond her puberty.

The fatal ease with which divorce could be obtained, and its frequency, appear from the question addressed to Christ by the Pharisees: "Is it lawful for a man to put away his wife for every cause?"[14] (Matt. 19:3), and still more from the astonishment with which the disciples had listened to the reply of the Saviour (ver. 10). That answer was much wider in its range than our Lord's initial teaching in the Sermon on the Mount (Matt. 5:32).[15] To the latter no Jew could have had any objection, even though its morality would have seemed elevated beyond their highest standard, represented in this case by the school of

---

[14]This other reading has been proposed: "for every offence." This would certainly tally better with the spirit of the Pharisees than the reading in our *textus receptus*.

[15]Rabbinical ordinances so limited the Mosaic law in regard to an adulteress, that the trial and punishment could only have been of the very rarest occurrence. Into these laws and distinctions we cannot, however, at present enter.

Shammai, while that of Hillel, and still more Rabbi
Akiba, presented the lowest opposite extreme. But in
reply to the Pharisees, our Lord placed the whole
question on grounds which even the strictest
Shammaite would have refused to adopt. For the
farthest limit to which he would have gone would
have been to restrict the cause of divorce to "a matter
of uncleanness" (Deut. 24:1), by which he would
probably have understood not only a breach of the
marriage vow, but of the laws and customs of the
land. In fact, we know that it included every kind of
impropriety, such as going about with loose hair,
spinning in the street, familiarly talking with men,
ill-treating her husband's parents in his presence,
brawling, that is, "speaking to her husband so loudly
that the neighbours could hear her in the adjoining
house" (*Chethub.* vii. 6), a general bad reputation, or
the discovery of fraud before marriage. On the other
hand, the wife could insist on being divorced if her
husband were a leper, or affected with polypus, or
engaged in a disagreeable or dirty trade, such as that
of a tanner or coppersmith. One of the cases in which
divorce was obligatory was, if either party had
become heretical, or ceased to profess Judaism. But
even so, there were at least checks to the danger of
general lawlessness, such as the obligation of paying
to a wife her portion, and a number of minute ordinances about formal *letters of divorce,* without which
no divorce was legal,[16] and which had to be couched
in explicit terms, handed to the woman herself, and
that in presence of two witnesses, etc.

If he selects her for his son, he must grant her the rights of a daughter. If he marries another woman, he must not deprive the first one of her food, clothing and marital rights (Exod. 21:9–10).

According to Jewish law there were four obligations incumbent on a wife towards her husband, and
ten by which he was bound. Of the latter, three are
referred to in Exod. 21:9, 10; the other seven include
her settlement, medical treatment in case of sickness,
redemption from captivity, a respectable funeral,
provision in his house so long as she remained a
widow and had not been paid her dowry, the support

---

[16]The Jews have it that a woman "is loosed from the law of her husband" by only one of
two things: death or a letter of divorce; hence Rom. 7:2, 3.

of her daughters till they were married, and a provision that her sons should, besides receiving their portion of the father's inheritance, also share in what had been settled upon her. The obligations upon the wife were, that all her gains should belong to her husband, as also what came to her after marriage by inheritance; that the husband should have the usufruct of her dowry, and of any gains by it, provided he had the administration of it, in which case, however, he was also responsible for any loss; and that he should be considered her heir-at-law.[17]

What the family life among the godly in Israel must have been, how elevated its tone, how loving its converse, or how earnestly devoted its mothers and daughters, appears sufficiently from the gospel story, from that in the book of Acts, and from notices in the apostolic letters. Women, such as the Virgin-mother, or Elisabeth, or Anna, or those who enjoyed the privilege of ministering to the Lord, or who, after His death, tended and watched for His sacred body, could not have been quite solitary in Palestine; we find their sisters in a Dorcas, a Lydia, a Phoebe, and those women of whom St. Paul speaks in Phil. 4:3, and whose lives he sketches in his Epistles to Timothy and Titus. Wives such as Priscilla, mothers such as that of Zebedee's children, or of Mark, or like St. John's "elect lady," or as Lois and Eunice, must have kept the moral atmosphere pure and sweet, and shed precious light on their homes and on society, corrupt to the core as it was under the sway of heathenism. What and how they taught their households, and that even under the most disadvantageous outward circumstances, we learn from the history of Timothy. And although they were undoubtedly in that respect without many of the opportunities which we enjoy, there was one sweet practice of family religion, going beyond the prescribed prayers, which enabled them to teach their children from tenderest years to intertwine the Word of God with their daily devotion and daily life. For it was the custom to teach a child some

Yes, and I ask you, loyal yokefellow, help these women who have contended at my side in the cause of the gospel, along with Clement and the rest of my fellow workers, whose names are in the book of life (Phil. 4:3).

---

[17] This is not the place to enter into the legal details, fully discussed by the Rabbis.

verse of Holy Scripture beginning or ending with precisely the same letters as its Hebrew name, and this birthday text or guardian-promise the child was day by day to insert in its prayers.[18] Such guardian words, familiar to the mind from earliest years, endeared to the heart by tenderest recollections, would remain with the youth in life's temptations, and come back amid the din of manhood's battle. Assuredly, of Jewish children so reared, so trained, so taught, it might be rightly said: "Take heed that ye despise not one of these little ones; for I say unto you, That in heaven their angels do always behold the face of My Father which is in heaven."

He called a little child and had him stand among them. And he said: "I tell you the truth, unless you change and become like little children, you will never enter the kingdom of heaven. Therefore, whoever humbles himself like this child is the greatest in the kingdom of heaven. (Matt. 18:2–4)

---

[18] *Kol Kore*, by R. El. Soloweycyk, p. 184. Compare *Taan.* 9 a.

10
IN DEATH AND AFTER DEATH

Jesus said to her, "I am the resurrection and the life. He who believes in me will live, even though he dies; and whoever lives and believes in me will never die. Do you believe this?" (John 11:25–26).

Interior of tombs of the kings

A sadder picture could scarcely be drawn than that of the dying Rabbi Jochanan ben Saccai, that "light of Israel" immediately before and after the destruction of the Temple, and for two years the president of the Sanhedrim. We read in the Talmud (*Ber.* 28 *b*) that, when his disciples came to see him on his death-bed, he burst into tears. To their astonished inquiry why he, "the light of Israel, the right pillar of the Temple, and its mighty hammer," betrayed such signs of fear, he replied: "If I were now to be brought before an earthly king, who lives to-day and dies to-morrow, whose wrath and whose bonds are not everlasting, and whose sentence of death, even, is not that to everlasting death, who can be assuaged by arguments, or perhaps bought off by money—I should tremble and weep; how much more reason have I for it, when about to be led before the King of kings, the Holy One, blessed be He, Who liveth and abideth for ever, Whose chains are chains for evermore, and Whose sentence of death killeth for ever, Whom I cannot assuage with words, nor bribe by money! And not only so, but there are before me two ways, one to paradise and the other to hell, and I know not which of the two ways I shall have to go—whether to paradise or to hell: how, then, shall I not shed tears?" Side by side with this we may place the opposite saying of R. Jehudah, called the Holy, who, when he died, lifted up both his hands to heaven, protesting that none of those ten fingers had broken the law of God! It were difficult to say which of these two is more contrary to the light and liberty of the Gospel— the utter hopelessness of the one, or the apparent presumption of the other.

Enter through the narrow gate. For wide is the gate and broad is the road that leads to destruction, and many enter through it. But small is the gate and narrow the road that leads to life, and only a few find it (Matt. 7:13–14).

And yet these sayings also recall to us something in the Gospel. For there also we read of two ways— the one to paradise, the other to destruction, and of fearing not those who can kill the body, but rather Him who, after He hath killed the body, hath power to cast into hell. Nor, on the other hand, was the assurance of St. Stephen, of St. James, or of St. Paul, less confident than that of Jehudah, called the Holy, though it expressed itself in a far different manner and rested on quite other grounds. Never are the voices of the Rabbis more discordant, and their utterances more contradictory or unsatisfying than in view of the great problems of humanity: sin, sickness, death, and the hereafter. Most truly did St. Paul, taught at the feet of Gamaliel in all the traditions and wisdom of the fathers, speak the inmost conviction of every Christian Rabbinist, that it is only our Saviour Jesus Christ Who "hath brought life and immortality to light through the Gospel" (2 Tim. 1:10).

When the disciples asked our Lord, in regard to the "man which was blind from his birth:" "Master, who did sin, this man, or his parents, that he was born blind?" (John 9:1, 2) we vividly realise that we

And you have forgotten that word of encouragement that addresses you as sons:
"My son, do not make light of the LORD's discipline,
and do not lose heart when he rebukes you,...
Moreover, we have all had human fathers who disciplined us and we respected them for it. How much more should we submit to the Father of our spirits and live!" (Heb. 12:5, 9).

Blessed is the man you discipline, O LORD, the man you teach from your law (Ps. 94:12).

Praise be to God, who has not rejected my prayer or withheld his love from me (Ps. 66:20)!

hear a strictly Jewish question. It was just such as was likely to be raised, and it exactly expressed Jewish belief. That children benefited or suffered according to the spiritual state of their parents was a doctrine current among the Jews. But they also held that an unborn child might contract guilt, since the *Yezer ha-ra,* or evil disposition which was present from its earliest formation, might even then be called into activity by outward circumstances. And sickness was regarded as alike the punishment for sin and its atonement. But we also meet with statements which remind us of the teaching of Heb. 12:5, 9. In fact, the apostolic quotation from Prov. 3 is made for exactly the same purpose in the Talmud (*Ber.* 5 *a*), in how different a spirit will appear from the following summary. It appears that two of the Rabbis had disagreed as to what were "the chastisements of love," the one maintaining, on the ground of Ps. 94:12, that they were such as did not prevent a man from study, the other inferring from Ps. 66:20 that they were such as did not hinder prayer. Superior authority decided that both kinds were "chastisements of love," at the same time answering the quotation from Ps. 94 by proposing to read, not "teachest *him,*" but "teachest *us* out of Thy law." But that the law teaches us that chastisements are of great advantage might be inferred as follows: If, according to Ex. 21:26, 27, a slave obtained freedom through the chastisement of his master—a chastisement which affected only one of his members—how much more must those chastisements effect which purified the whole body of man? Moreover, as another Rabbi reminds us, the "covenant" is mentioned in connection with salt (Lev. 2:13), and also in connection with chastisements (Deut. 28:58). "As is the covenant," spoken of in connection with salt, which gives taste to the meat, so also is "the covenant" spoken of in connection with chastisements, which purge away all the sins of a man. Indeed, as a third Rabbi says: "Three good gifts hath the Holy One—blessed be He!—given to Israel, and each of them only through sufferings—the law, the land of Israel, and the world to come." The law, according to Ps. 94:12; the land, according to Deut. 8:5, which is immediately followed by ver. 7; and the world to come, according to Prov. 6:23.

As on most other subjects, the Rabbis were accurate and keen observers of the laws of health, and their regulations are often far in advance of modern practice. From many allusions in the Old Testament we infer that the science of medicine, which was carried to comparatively great perfection in Egypt, where every disease had its own physician, was also cultivated in Israel. Thus the sin of Asa, in trusting too much to earthly physicians, is specially reproved (2 Chron. 16:12). In New Testament times we read of the woman who had spent all her substance, and suffered so much at the hands of physicians (Mark 5:26); while the use of certain remedies, such as oil and wine, in the treatment of wounds (Luke 10:34), seems to have been popularly known. St. Luke was a "physician" (Col. 4:14); and among the regular Temple officials there was a medical man, whose duty it was to attend to the priesthood who, from ministering barefoot, must have been specially liable to certain diseases. The Rabbis ordained that every town must have at least one physician, who was also to be qualified to practise surgery, or else a physician and a surgeon. Some of the Rabbis themselves engaged in medical pursuits: and, in theory at least, every practitioner ought to have had their licence. To employ a heretic or a Hebrew Christian was specially prohibited, though a heathen might, if needful, be called in. But, despite their patronage of the science, caustic sayings also occur. "Physician, heal thyself," is really a Jewish proverb; "Live not in a city whose chief is a medical man"—he will attend to public business and neglect his patients; "The best among doctors deserves Gehenna"—for his bad treatment of some, and for his neglect of others. It were invidious to enter into a discussion of the remedies prescribed in those times, although, to judge from what is advised in such cases, we can scarcely wonder that the poor woman in the gospel was nowise benefited, but rather the worse of them (Mark 5:26). The means recommended were

Know then in your heart that as a man disciplines his son, so the LORD your God disciplines you... For the LORD your God is bringing you into a good land—a land with streams and pools of water, with springs flowing in the valleys and hills (Deut. 8:5, 7).

For these commands are a lamp, this teaching is a light, and the corrections of discipline are the way to life (Prov. 6:23).

In the thirty-ninth year of his reign Asa was afflicted with a disease in his feet. Though his disease was severe, even in his illness he did not seek help from the LORD, but only from the physicians (2 Chron. 16:12).

And a woman was there who had been subject to bleeding for twelve years. She had suffered a great deal under the care of many doctors and had spent all she had, yet instead of getting better she grew worse (Mark 5:25–26).

And Moses the servant of the LORD died there in Moab, as the LORD had said (Deut. 34:5).

either generally hygienic—and in this respect the Hebrews contrast favourably even with ourselves—or purely medicinal, or else sympathetic, or even magical. The prescriptions consisted of *simples* or of *compounds*, vegetables being far more used than minerals. Cold-water compresses, the external and internal use of oil and of wine, baths (medicated and other), and a certain diet, were carefully indicated in special diseases. Goats'-milk and barley-porridge were recommended in all diseases attended by wasting. Jewish surgeons seem even to have known how to operate for cataract.

Ordinarily, life was expected to be protracted, and death regarded as alike the punishment and the expiation of sin. To die within fifty years of age was to be cut off; within fifty-two, to die the death of Samuel the prophet; at sixty years of age, it was regarded as death at the hands of Heaven; at seventy, as that of an old man; and at eighty, as that of strength. Premature death was likened to the falling off of unripe fruit, or the extinction of a candle. To depart without having a son was to *die*, otherwise it was to *fall asleep*. The latter was stated to have been the case with David; the former with Joab. If a person had finished his work, his was regarded as the death of the righteous, who is gathered to his fathers. Tradition (*Ber.* 8 *a*) inferred, by a peculiar Rabbinical mode of exegesis, from a word in Ps. 62:12, that there were 903 different kinds of dying. The worst of these was *angina*, which was compared to tearing out a thread from a piece of wool; while the sweetest and gentlest, which was compared to drawing a hair out of milk, was called "death by a kiss." The latter designation originated from Num. 33:38 and Deut. 34:5, in which Aaron and Moses are respectively said to have died "according to the word"—literally, "by the mouth of Jehovah." Over six persons, it was said, the angel of death[1] had had no power—viz., Abraham, Isaac, and Jacob, because they had seen their work quite completed; and over Miriam, Aaron, and Moses, who had died

---

[1]We purposely do not enter on the Rabbinical views about the "angel of death." The Babylon Talmud, however, has a curious passage about anointing the eyes of the dying with oil.

by "the kiss of God." If premature death was the pun-ishment of sin, the righteous died because others were to enter on their work—Joshua on that of Moses, Solomon on that of David, etc. But, when the time for death came, anything might serve for its infliction, or, to put it in Rabbinical language, "O Lord, all these are Thy servants;" for "whither a man was to go, thither his feet would carry him."

Certain signs were also noted as to the time and manner of dying. Sudden death was called "being swallowed up," death after one day's illness, that of rejection; after two days', that of despair; after four days', that of reproof; after five days', a natural death. Similarly, the posture of the dying was carefully marked. To die with a happy smile, or at least with a bright countenance, or looking upward, was a good omen; to look downward, to seem disturbed, to weep, or even to turn to the wall, were evil signs.[2] On recov-ering from illness, it was enjoined to return special thanks. It was a curious superstition (*Ber.* 55 *b*), that, if any one announced his illness on the first day of its occurrence, it might tend to make him worse, and that only on the second day should prayers be offered for him. Lastly, we may mention in this connection, as possibly throwing light on the practice referred to by St. James (Jas. 5:14), that it was the custom to anoint the sick with a mixture of oil, wine, and water, the preparation of which was even allowed on the Sabbath (*Jer. Ber.* ii. 2).

When our Lord mentioned visitation of the sick among the evidences of that religion which would stand the test of the judgment day (Matt. 25:36), He appealed to a principle universally acknowledged among the Jews. The great Jewish doctor Maimonides holds that this duty takes precedence of all other good works, and the Talmud goes even so far as to assert, that whoever visits the sick shall deliver his soul from Gehenna (*Ned.* 40 *a*). Accordingly, a Rabbi, dis-cussing the meaning of the expression, "Ye shall walk

Is any one of you sick? He should call the elders of the church to pray over him and anoint him with oil in the name of the Lord (Jas. 5:14).

I was sick and you looked after me, I was in prison and you came to visit me (Matt. 25:36b).

---

[2]An account of the manner of "setting one's house in order" (2 Sam. 17:23; 2 Kings 20:1), would lead beyond our present purpose.

He who is kind to the poor lends to the LORD, and he will reward him for what he has done (Prov. 19:17).

He who mocks the poor shows contempt for their Maker; whoever gloats over disaster will not go unpunished (Prov. 17:5).

At that moment she fell down at his feet and died. Then the young men came in and, finding her dead, carried her out and buried her beside her husband (Acts 5:10).

Myrrh

after the Lord your God" (Deut. 13:4), arrives at the conclusion, that it refers to the imitation of what we read in Scripture of His doings. Thus God clothed the naked (Gen. 3:21), and so should we; He visited the sick (Gen. 18:1); He comforted the mourners, (Gen. 25:11); and He buried the dead (Deut. 35:6); leaving us in all this an ensample that we should follow in His footsteps (*Sota* 14 *a*). It was possibly to encourage to this duty, or else in reference to the good effects of sympathy upon the sick, that we are told, that whoever visits the sick takes away a sixtieth part of his sufferings (*Ned.* 39 *b*). Nor was the service of love to stop here; for, as we have seen, the burial of the dead was quite as urgent a duty as the visitation of the sick. As the funeral procession passed, every one was expected, if possible, to join the convoy. The Rabbis applied to the observance of this direction Prov. 14:32, and 19:17; and to its neglect Prov. 17:5 (*Ber.* 18 *a*). Similarly, all reverence was shown towards the remains of the dead, and burying-places were kept free from every kind of profanation, and even from light conversation.

Burial followed generally as soon as possible after death (Matt. 9:23; Acts 5:6, 10; 8:2), no doubt partly on sanitary grounds. For special reasons, however (Acts 9:37, 39), or in the case of parents, there might be a delay even of days. The preparations for the burial of our Lord, mentioned in the gospels—the ointment against His burial (Matt. 26:12), the spices and ointments (Luke 23:56), the mixture of myrrh and aloes—find their literal confirmation in what the Rabbis tell us of the customs of the period (*Ber.* 53 *a*). At one time the wasteful expenditure connected with funerals was so great as to involve in serious difficulties the poor, who would not be outdone by their neighbours. The folly extended not only to the funeral rites, the burning of spices at the grave, and the depositing of money and valuables in the tomb, but even to luxury in the wrappings of the dead body. At last a much-needed reform was introduced by Rabbi Gamaliel, who left directions that he was to be buried in simple linen garments. In recognition of this a cup is to this day emptied to his memory at funeral meals. His grandson limited even the number of grave-clothes to *one* dress. The burial-dress is made of the most inexpensive linen, and bears the name of (*Tachrichin*) "wrappings," or else the "travelling-dress." At present it is always white, but formerly any other colour might be chosen, of which we have some curious instances. Thus one Rabbi would not be buried in white, lest he might seem like one glad, nor yet in black, so as not to appear to sorrow, but in red; while another ordered a white dress, to show that he was not ashamed of his works; and yet a third directed that he should have his shoes and stockings, and a stick, to be ready for the resurrection! As we know from the gospel, the body was wrapped in "linen clothes," and the face bound about with a napkin (John 11:44; 20:5, 7).

The body having been properly prepared, the funeral rites proceeded, as described in the gospels. From the account of the funeral procession at Nain, which the Lord of life arrested (Luke 7:11–15), many interesting details may be learned. *First,* burying-places were always *outside* cities (Matt. 8:28; 27:7, 52, 53; John 11:30, 31). Neither watercourses nor public roads were allowed to pass through them, nor sheep to graze there. We read of *public* and *private* burying-places—the latter chiefly in gardens and caves. It was the practice to visit the graves (John 11:31) partly to mourn and partly to pray. It was unlawful to eat or drink, to read, or even to walk irreverently among them. *Cremation* was denounced as a purely heathen practice, contrary to the whole spirit of Old Testament teaching. *Secondly,* we know that, as at Nain, the body was generally carried open on a bier, or else in an open coffin, the bearers frequently changing to give an opportunity to many to take part in a work deemed so meritorious. Graves in fields or in the open were often marked by memorial columns. Children less than a month old were carried to the burying by their mothers; those under twelve months were borne on a bed or stretcher. *Lastly,* the order in which the procession seems to have wound out of

Soon afterward, Jesus went to a town called Nain, and his disciples and a large crowd went along with him. As he approached the town gate, a dead person was being carried out—the only son of his mother, and she was a widow. And a large crowd from the town was with her. When the Lord saw her, his heart went out to her and he said, "Don't cry."

Then he went up and touched the coffin, and those carrying it stood still. He said, "Young man, I say to you, get up!" The dead man sat up and began to talk, and Jesus gave him back to his mother (Luke 7:11–15).

Funeral procession

Nain exactly accords with what we know of the customs of the time and place. It was outside the city gate that the Lord with His disciples met the sad array. Had it been in Judaea the hired mourners and musicians would have preceded the bier; in Galilee they followed. First came the women, for, as an ancient Jewish commentary explains—woman, who brought death into our world, ought to lead the way in the funeral procession. Among them our Lord readily recognised the widowed mother, whose only treasure was to be hidden from her for ever. Behind the bier followed, obedient to Jewish law and custom, "much people of the city." The sight of her sorrow touched the compassion of the Son of Man; the presence of death called forth the power of the Son of God. To her only He spoke, what in the form of a question He said to the woman who mourned at His own grave, ignorant that death had been swallowed up in victory, and what He still speaks to us from heaven, "Weep not!" He bade not the procession halt, but, as He touched the bier, they that bore on it the dead body stood still. It was a marvellous sight outside the gate of Nain. The Rabbi and His disciples should reverently have joined the procession; they arrested it. One word of power burst inwards the sluices of Hades, and out flowed once again the tide of life. "He that was dead sat up on his bier, and began to speak"—what words of wonderment we are not told. It must have been like the sudden wakening, which leaves not on the consciousness the faintest trace of the dream. Not of that world but of this would his speech be, though he knew he had been over there, and its dazzling light made earth's sunshine so dim, that ever afterwards life must have seemed to him like the sitting up on his bier, and its faces and voices like those of the crowd which followed him to his burying.

At the grave, on the road to which the procession repeatedly halted, when short addresses were occasionally delivered, there was a funeral oration. If the grave were in a public cemetery, at least a foot and a half must intervene between each sleeper. The caves, or rock-hewn sepulchres, consisted of an antechamber in which the bier was deposited, and an inner or rather lower cave in which the bodies were deposited, in a recumbent position, in niches. According to the Talmud these abodes of the dead were usually six feet long, nine feet wide, and ten feet high. Here there were niches for eight bodies: three on each side of the entrance, and two opposite. Larger sepulchres held thirteen bodies. The entrance to the sepulchres was guarded by a large stone or by a door (Matt. 27:66; Mark 15:46; John 11:38, 39). This structure of the tombs will explain some of the particulars connected with the burial of our Lord, how the women coming early to the grave had been astonished in finding the "very great stone" "rolled away from the door of the sepulchre," and then, when they entered the outer cave, were affrighted to see what seemed "a young man sitting on the right side, clothed in a long white garment" (Mark 16:4, 5). Similarly, it explains the events as they are successively recorded in John 20:1–12, how Mary Magdalene, "when it was yet dark," had come to the sepulchre, in every sense waiting for the light, but even groping had felt that the stone was rolled away, and fled to tell the disciples they had, as she thought, taken away the Lord out of the sepulchre. If she knew of the sealing of that stone and of the Roman guard, she must have felt as if the hatred of man would now deprive their

Sealed stone at entrance to a tomb

So Joseph bought some linen cloth, took down the body, wrapped it in the linen, and placed it in a tomb cut out of rock. Then he rolled a stone against the entrance of the tomb (Mark 15:46).

Early on the first day of the week, while it was still dark, Mary Magdalene went to the tomb and saw that the stone had been removed from the entrance. So she came running to Simon Peter and the other disciple, the one Jesus loved, and said, "They have taken the LORD out of the tomb, and we don't know where they have put him!" (John 20:1–2).

A pair of tomb entrances

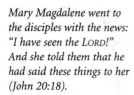

Mary Magdalene went to the disciples with the news: "I have seen the LORD!" And she told them that he had said these things to her (John 20:18).

love even of the sacred body of their Lord. And yet, through it all, the hearts of the disciples must have treasured hopes, which they scarce dared confess to themselves. For those other two disciples, witnesses of all His deeds on earth, companions of His shame in Caiaphas' palace, were also waiting for the daybreak —only at home, not like her at the grave. And now "they both ran together." But on that morning, so near the night of betrayal, "the other disciple did out-run Peter." Grey light of early spring had broken the heavy curtain of cloud and mist, and red and golden sunlight lay on the edge of the horizon. The garden was still, and the morning air stirred the trees which in the dark night had seemed to keep watch over the dead, as through the unguarded entrance, by which lay "the very great stone" rolled away, John passed, and "stooping down" into the inner cave "saw the linen clothes lying." "Then cometh Simon Peter," not to wait in the outer cave, but to go into the sepulchre, presently to be followed thither by John. For that empty sepulchre was not a place to look into, but to go into and believe. That morn had witnessed many wonders—wonders which made the Magdalene long for yet greater—for the wonder of wonders, the Lord Himself. Nor was she disappointed. He Who alone could answer her questions fully, and dry her tears, spake first to her who loved so much.

Thus also did our blessed Lord Himself fulfil most truly that on which the law and Jewish tradition laid so great stress: to comfort the mourners in their affliction (comp. James 1:27). Indeed, tradition has it, that there was in the Temple a special gate by which mourners entered, that all who met them might discharge this duty of love. There was a custom, which deserves general imitation, that mourners were not to be tormented by talk, but that all should observe silence till addressed by them. Afterwards, to obviate foolish remarks, a formula was fixed, according to which, in the synagogue the leader of the devotions, and in the house some one, began by asking, "Inquire for the ground of mourning;" upon which one of those present—if possible, a Rabbi—answered, "God is a just Judge," which meant, that He had removed a near relative. Then, in the synagogue, a regular fixed formula of comfort was spoken, while in the house kind expressions of consolation followed.

Religion that God our Father accepts as pure and faultless is this: to look after orphans and widows in their distress and to keep oneself from being polluted by the world (Jas. 1:27).

The Rabbis distinguish between the *Onen* and the *Avel*—the sorrowing or suffering one, and the bowed down, fading one, or mourner; the former expression applying only to the day of the funeral, the latter to the period which followed. It was held, that the law of God only prescribed mourning for the first day, which was that of death and burial (Lev. 22:4, 6), while the other and longer period of mourning that followed was enjoined by the elders. So long as the dead body was actually in the house, it was forbidden to eat meat or drink wine, to put on the phylacteries, or to engage in study. All necessary food had to be prepared outside the house, and was, if possible, not to be eaten in presence of the dead. The first duty was to rend the clothes, which might be done in one or more of the inner garments, but not in the outer dress. The rent is made standing, and in front; it is generally about a hand-breadth in length. In the case

The high priest, the one among his brothers who has had the anointing oil poured on his head and who has been ordained to wear the priestly garments, must not let his hair become unkempt or tear his clothes. He must not enter a place where there is a dead body. He must not make himself unclean, even for his father or mother (Lev. 21:10–11).

For I could wish that I myself were cursed and cut off from Christ for the sake of my brothers, those of my own race (Rom. 9:3).

of parents it is never closed up again; but in that of others it is mended after the thirtieth day. Immediately after the body is carried out of the house all chairs and couches are reversed, and the mourners sit (except on the Sabbath, and on the Friday only for one hour) on the ground or on a low stool. A threefold distinction was here made. Deep mourning was to last for seven days, of which the first three were those of "weeping." During these seven days it was, among other things, forbidden to wash, to anoint oneself, to put on shoes, to study, or to engage in any business. After that followed a lighter mourning of thirty days. Children were to mourn for their parents a whole year; and during eleven months (so as not to imply that they required to remain a full year in purgatory) to say the "prayer for the dead." The latter, however, does *not* contain any intercession for the departed. The anniversary of the day of death was also to be observed. An apostate from the Jewish faith was not to be mourned; on the contrary, white dress was to be worn on the occasion of his decease, and other demonstrations of joy to be made. It is well known under what exceptional circumstances priests and the high-priest were allowed to mourn for the dead (Lev. 21:10, 11; 1–4). In the case of the highpriest it was customary to say to him, "May we be thy expiation!" ("Let us suffer what ought to have befallen thee;") to which he replied, "Be ye blessed of Heaven" (*Sanh.* ii. 1). It is noted that this mode of address to the high-priest was intended to indicate the greatness of their affection; and the learned *Otho* suggests (*Lexic. Rabb.*, p. 343), that this may have been in the mind of the apostle when he would have wished himself *Anathema* for the sake of his brethren (Rom. 9:3). On the return from the burial, friends or neighbours prepared a meal for the mourners, consisting of bread, hard-boiled eggs, and lentils—round and coarse fare; round like life, which is rolling on unto death. This was brought in and served up in earthenware. On the other hand, the mourners' friends partook of a funeral meal, at which no more than ten cups were to be emptied—two before the meal, five at it, and three afterwards (*Jer. Ber.* iii. 1). In modern times the religious duty of attending to the dying, the dead, and mourners, is performed by a special "holy brotherhood," as it is called, which many of the most religious Jews join for the sake of the pious work in which it engages them.

We add the following, which may be of interest. It is expressly allowed (*Jer. Ber.* iii. 1), on Sabbaths and feast-days to walk beyond the Sabbath limits, and to do all needful offices for the dead. This throws considerable light on the evangelical account of the offices rendered to the body of Jesus on the eve of the Passover. The chief mourning rites, indeed, were intermitted on Sabbaths and feast-days; and one of the most interesting, and perhaps the earliest Hebrew non-Biblical record—the *Megillath Taanith,* or roll of fasts—mentions a number of other days on which mourning was prohibited, being the anniversaries of joyous occasions. The Mishnah (*Moed K.* iii. 5–9) contains a number of regulations and limitations of mourning observances on greater and lesser feasts, which we do not quote, as possessing little interest save in Rabbinical casuistry. The loss of slaves was not to be mourned.

But what after death and in the judgment? And what of that which brought in, and which gives such terrible meaning to death and the judgment—*sin?* It were idle, and could only be painful here to detail the various and discordant sayings of the Rabbis, some of which, at least, may admit of an allegorical interpretation. Only that which may be of use to the New Testament student shall be briefly summarised. Both the Talmud (*Pes.* 54 *a*; *Ned.* 39 *b*), and the Targum teach that paradise and hell were created before this world. One quotation from the Jerusalem Targum (on Gen. 3:24) will not only sufficiently prove this, but show the general current of Jewish teaching. "Two thousand years," we read, "before the world was made, God created the Law and Gehenna, and the Garden of Eden. He made the Garden of Eden for the righteous, that they might eat of the fruits thereof, and delight themselves in them, because in this world

…he will swallow up death forever. The Sovereign LORD will wipe away the tears from all faces; he will remove the disgrace of his people from all the earth. The LORD has spoken (Isa 25:8).

After he drove the man out, he placed on the east side of the Garden of Eden cherubim and a flaming sword flashing back and forth to guard the way to the tree of life (Gen. 3:24).

they had kept the commandments of the law. But for the wicked He prepared Gehenna, which is like a sharp two-edged destroying sword. He put within it sparks of fire and burning coals, to punish the wicked in the world to come, because they had not observed the commandments of the law in this world. For the law is the tree of life. Whosoever observeth it shall live and subsist as the tree of life.[3] Paradise and hell were supposed to be contiguous, only separated—it was said, perhaps allegorically—by an handbreadth. But although we may here find some slight resemblance to the localisation of the history of the rich man and Lazarus (Luke 16:25, 26), only those acquainted with the theological thinking of the time can fully judge what infinite difference there is between the story in the Gospel and the pictures drawn in contemporary literature. Witness here the 22nd chapter of the book of Enoch, which, as so many other passages from pseudo-epigraphic and Rabbinical writings, has been mangled and misquoted by modern writers, for purposes hostile to Christianity.[4] The Rabbis seem to have believed in a multitude of heavens—most of them holding that there were *seven*, as there were also seven departments in paradise, and as many in hell. The pre-existence of the souls of all mankind before their actual appearance upon earth, and even the doctrine of the migration of souls, seem also to have been held—both probably, however, chiefly as speculative views, introduced from foreign, non-Judaean sources.

But all these are preliminary and outside questions, which only indirectly touch the great problems of the human soul concerning sin and salvation. And here we can, in this place, only state that the deeper and stronger our conviction that the language,

But Abraham replied, "Son, remember that in your lifetime you received your good things, while Lazarus received bad things, but now he is comforted here and you are in agony. And besides all this, between us and you a great chasm has been fixed, so that those who want to go from here to you cannot, nor can anyone cross over from there to us" (Luke 16:25–26).

---

[3] Other Rabbinical sayings have it, that seven things existed before the world—the law, repentance, paradise, hell, the throne of God, the name of the Messiah, and the Temple. At the same time the reader will observe that the quotation from the Targum given in the text attempts an allegorising, and therefore rationalistic interpretation of the narrative in Gen. 3:24.

[4] We must take this opportunity of referring to a book which has long served as chief storehouse to certain writers, and been too often carelessly accepted as absolute authority by those who should have ascertained for themselves the accuracy of quotations. We are alluding to Gfrörer, *Gesch. d. Urchrist.* where the passage from Enoch 22 is certainly misquoted.

surroundings, and whole atmosphere of the New Testament were those of Palestine at the time when our Lord trod its soil, the more startling appears the contrast between the doctrinal teaching of Christ and His apostles and that of the Rabbis. In general, it may be said that the New Testament teaching concerning original sin and its consequences finds no analogy in the Rabbinical writings of that period. As to the mode of salvation, their doctrine may be broadly summed up under the designation of work-righteousness.

In view of this there is, strictly speaking, logical inconsistency in the earnestness with which the Rabbis insist on universal and immediate repentance, and the need of confession of sin, and of preparation for another world. For, a paradise which *might* be entered by all on their own merits, and which yet is to be sought by all through repentance and similar means, or else can only be obtained after passing through a kind of purgatory, constitutes no mean moral charge against the religion of Rabbinism. Yet such inconsistencies may be hailed as bringing the Synagogue, in another direction, nearer to Biblical truth. Indeed, we come occasionally upon much that also appears, only in quite another setting, in the New Testament. Thus the teaching of our Lord about the immortality of the righteous was, of course, quite consonant with that of the Pharisees. In fact, their contention also was, that the departed saints were in Scripture called "living" (*Ber.* 18 *a*).[5] Similarly, it was their doctrine (*Ber.* 17 *a*, and in several other passages)—though not quite consistently held—as it was that of our Lord (Matt. 22:30), that "in the world to come there is neither eating nor drinking, neither

If someone forces you to go one mile, go with him two miles. Give to the one who asks you, and do not turn away from the one who wants to borrow from you (Matt. 5:41–42).

At the resurrection people will neither marry nor be given in marriage; they will be like the angels in heaven (Matt. 22:30).

[5] I would here take leave generally to refer to my article on "Sickness and Death," in *The Bible Educator*, vol. iv. pp. 330–333. In *Sanh.* 90 *b*, 91 *a* and *b*, we have long argumentations in which the doctrines of immortality and of the resurrection are proved in controversy, chiefly with the Sadducees, but also with heathens, from the law, the prophets, and the hagiographa. The passages quoted are (in *Mechilta*, Ex. 15:1, which is rendered: "Then Moses shall sing"): Deut. 31:6; 11:21; 4:4; Num. 18:28; Ex. 6:4; Num. 15:31; Ex. 15:1; Deut. 32:39; Isa. 26:19; 52:8; Cant. 7:9; Ps. 72:16; 84:7 (the tense being in this, as in other of the quotations, made *future*). Similar reasoning on the subject is found in *Abod. S.* 18 *a*; *Pes.* 68 *a*; *Sanh.* 92 *b*; and in many of the *Midrashim*.

Then he said to his servants, "The wedding banquet is ready, but those I invited did not deserve to come. Go to the street corners and invite to the banquet anyone you find." So the servants went out into the streets and gathered all the people they could find, both good and bad, and the wedding hall was filled with guests.

But when the king came in to see the guests, he noticed a man there who was not wearing wedding clothes. "Friend," he asked, "how did you get in here without wedding clothes?" The man was speechless.

Then the king told the attendants, "Tie him hand and foot, and throw him outside, into the darkness, where there will be weeping and gnashing of teeth."

For many are invited, but few are chosen (Matt. 22:8–14).

"There is no peace," says the LORD, *"for the wicked" (Isa. 48:22).*

fruitfulness nor increase, neither trade nor business, neither envy, hatred, nor strife; but the righteous sit with their crowns on their heads, and feast themselves on the splendour of the Shechinah, as it is written, 'They saw God, and did eat and drink' (Ex. 24:11)." The following is so similar in form and yet so different in spirit to the parable of the invited guests and him without the wedding garment (Matt. 22:1–14), that we give it in full. "R. Jochanan, son of Saccai, propounded a parable. A certain king prepared a banquet, to which he invited his servants, without however having fixed the time for it. Those among them who were wise adorned themselves, and sat down at the door of the king's palace, reasoning thus: Can there be anything awanting in the palace of a king? But those of them who were foolish went away to their work, saying: Is there ever a feast without labour? Suddenly the king called his servants to the banquet. The wise appeared adorned, but the foolish squalid. Then the king rejoiced over the wise, but was very wroth with the foolish, and said: Those who have adorned themselves shall sit down, eat, drink, and be merry; but those who have not adorned themselves shall stand by and see it, as it is written in Isa. 65:13." A somewhat similar parable, but even more Jewish in its dogmatic cast, is the following: "The matter (of the world to come) is like an earthly king who committed to his servants the royal robes. They who were wise folded and laid them up in the wardrobes, but they who were careless put them on, and did in them their work. After some days the king asked back his robes. Those who were wise restored them as they were, that is, still clean; those who were foolish also restored them as they were, that is, soiled. Then the king rejoiced over the wise, but was very wroth with the careless servants, and he said to the wise: Lay up the robes in the treasury, and go home in peace. But to the careless he commanded the robes to be given, that they might wash them, and that they themselves should be cast into prison, as it is written of the bodies of the just in Isa. 57:2; 1 Sam. 25:29, but of the bodies of the unjust in Isa. 48:22; 57:21; and in 1 Sam.

25:29." From the same tractate (*Shab.* 152 *a*), we may, in conclusion, quote the following: "R. Eliezer said, Repent on the day before thou diest. His disciples asked him: Can a man know the hour of his death? He replied: Therefore let him repent to-day, lest haply he die on the morrow."

Quotations on these, and discussions on kindred subjects might lead us far beyond our present scope. But the second of the parables above quoted will point the direction of the final conclusions at which Rabbinism arrived. It is not, as in the Gospel, pardon and peace, but labour with the "may be" of reward. As for the "after death," paradise, hell, the resurrection, and the judgment, voices are more discordant than ever, opinions more unscriptural, and descriptions more repulsively fabulous. This is not the place farther to trace the doctrinal views of the Rabbis, to attempt to arrange and to follow them up. Work-righteousness and study of the law are the surest key to heaven. There is a kind of purgation, if not of purgatory, after death. Some seem even to have held the annihilation of the wicked. Taking the widest and most generous views of the Rabbis, they may be thus summed up: All Israel have share in the world to come; the pious among the Gentiles also have part in it. Only the perfectly just enter at once into paradise; all the rest pass through a period of purification and perfection, variously lasting, up to one year. But notorious breakers of the law, and especially apostates from the Jewish faith, and heretics, have no hope whatever, either here or hereafter! Such is the last word which the Synagogue has to say to mankind.

Not thus are we taught by the Messiah, the King of the Jews. If we learn our loss, we also learn that "The Son of Man has come to seek and to save that which was lost." Our righteousness is that freely bestowed on us by Him "Who was wounded for our transgressions and bruised for our iniquities." "With His stripes we are healed." The law which we obey is that which He has put within our hearts, by which we become temples of the Holy Ghost. "The Dayspring from on high hath visited us" through the tender

For it is by grace you have been saved, through faith—and this not from yourselves, it is the gift of God—not by works, so that no one can boast (Eph. 2:8–9).

He himself bore our sins in his body on the tree, so that we might die to sins and live for righteousness; by his wounds you have been healed (1 Pet. 2:24).

mercy of our God. The Gospel hath brought life and immortality to light, for we know Whom we have believed; and "perfect love casteth out fear." Not even the problems of sickness, sorrow, suffering, and death are unnoticed. "Weeping may endure for a night, but joy cometh in the morning." The tears of earth's night hang as dewdrops on flower and tree, presently to sparkle like diamonds in the morning sun. For, in that night of nights has Christ mingled the sweat of human toil and sorrow with the precious blood of His agony, and made it drop on earth as sweet balsam to heal its wounds, to soothe its sorrows, and to take away its death.

11
JEWISH VIEWS ON TRADE, TRADESMEN, AND TRADES' GUILDS

We read in the Mishnah (*Kidd.* iv. 14) as follows: "Rabbi Meir said: Let a man always teach his son a cleanly and a light trade; and let him pray to Him whose are wealth and riches; for there is no trade which has not both poverty and riches, and neither does poverty come from the trade nor yet riches, but everything according to one's deserving (merit). Rabbi Simeon, the son of Eleazar, said: Hast thou all thy life long seen a beast or a bird which has a trade? Still they are nourished, and that without anxious care. And if they, who are created only to serve me, shall not I expect to be nourished without anxious care, who am created to serve my Maker? Only that if I have been evil in my deeds, I forfeit my support.[1] Abba Gurjan of Zadjan said, in name of Abba Gurja: Let not a man bring up his son to be a donkey-driver, nor a camel-driver, nor a barber, nor a sailor, nor a shepherd, nor a pedlar; for their occupations are those of thieves. In his name, Rabbi Jehudah said: Donkey-drivers are mostly wicked; camel-drivers mostly honest; sailors mostly pious; the best among physicians is for Gehenna, and the most honest of butchers a companion of Amalek. Rabbi Nehorai said: I let alone every trade of this world, and teach my son nothing but the Thorah;[2] for a man eats of the fruit of it in this world (as it were, lives upon earth on the interest), while the capital remaineth for the

Even youths grow tired and weary,
and young men stumble and fall;
but those who hope in the LORD
will renew their strength.
They will soar on wings like eagles;
they will run and not grow weary,
they will walk and not be faint
(Isa. 40:30–31).

---

[1] The Jerusalem Talmud on this Mishnah rather mars its beauty by details.
[2] The law of God.

Do not think that I have come to abolish the Law or the Prophets; I have not come to abolish them but to fulfill them. I tell you the truth, until heaven and earth disappear, not the smallest letter, not the least stroke of a pen, will by any means disappear from the Law until everything is accomplished (Matt. 5:17–18).

world to come. But what is left over (what remains) in every trade (or worldly employment) is not so. For, if a man fall into ill-health, or come to old age or into trouble (chastisement), and is no longer able to stick to his work, lo! he dies of hunger. But the Thorah is not so, for it keeps a man from evil in youth, and in old age gives him both a hereafter and the hopeful waiting for it. What does it say about youth? 'They that wait upon the Lord shall renew strength.' And what about old age? 'They shall still bring forth fruit in old age.' And this is what is said of Abraham our father: 'And Abraham was old, and Jehovah blessed Abraham in all things.' But we find that Abraham our father kept the whole Thorah—the whole, even to that which had not yet been given—as it is said, 'Because that Abraham obeyed My voice, and kept My charge, My commandments, My statutes, and My laws.' "

If this quotation has been long, it will in many respects prove instructive; for it not only affords a favourable specimen of Mishnic teaching, but gives insight into the principles, the reasoning, and the views of the Rabbis. At the outset, the saying of Rabbi Simeon—which, however, we should remember, was spoken nearly a century after the time when our Lord had been upon earth—reminds us of His own words (Matt. 6:26): "Behold the fowls of the air: for they sow not, neither do they reap, nor gather into barns; yet your heavenly Father feedeth them. Are ye not much better than they?" It would be a delightful thought, that our Lord had thus availed Himself of the better thinking and higher feeling in Israel; so to speak, polished the diamond and made it sparkle, as He held it up in the light of the kingdom of God. For here also it holds true, that the Saviour came not in any sense to "destroy," but to "establish the law." All around the scene of His earthly ministry the atmosphere was Jewish; and all that was pure, true, and good in the nation's life, teaching, and sayings He made His own. On every page of the gospels we come upon what seems to waken the echoes of Jewish voices; sayings which remind us of what we have heard among the sages of Israel. And this is just what we should have expected, and what gives no small confirmation of the trustworthiness of these narratives as the record of what had really taken place. It is not a strange scene upon which we are here introduced; nor among strange actors; nor are the surroundings foreign. Throughout we have a life-picture of the period, in which we recognise the speakers from the sketches of them drawn elsewhere, and whose mode of speaking we know from contemporary literature. The gospels could not have set aside, they could not even have left out, the Jewish element. Otherwise they would not have been true to the period, nor to the people, nor to the writers, nor yet to that law of growth and development which always marks the progress of the kingdom of God. In one respect only all is different. The gospels are most Jewish in form, but most anti-Jewish in spirit—the record of the manifestation among Israel of the Son of God, the Saviour of the world, as the "King of the Jews."[3]

What then is my reward? Just this: that in preaching the gospel I may offer it free of charge, and so not make use of my rights in preaching it (1 Cor. 9:18).

This influence of the Jewish surroundings upon the circumstances of the gospel history has a most important bearing. It helps us to realise what Jewish life had been at the time of Christ, and to comprehend what might seem peculiarities in the gospel narrative. Thus—to come to the subject of this chapter—we now understand how so many of the disciples and followers of the Lord gained their living by some craft; how in the same spirit the Master Himself condescended to the trade of His adoptive father; and how the greatest of His apostles throughout earned his bread by the labour of his hands, probably following, like the Lord Jesus, the trade of his father. For it was a principle, frequently expressed, if possible "not to forsake the trade of the father"—most likely not merely from worldly considerations, but because it might be learned in the house; perhaps even from considerations of respect for parents. And what in this respect Paul practised, that he also preached.

---

[3] The elaboration and proof of this must be left for a work entering fully on the life and times of our Lord.

Surely you remember, brothers, our toil and hardship; we worked night and day in order not to be a burden to anyone while we preached the gospel of God to you (1 Thess. 2:9).

Nowhere is the dignity of labour and the manly independence of honest work more clearly set forth than in his Epistles. At Corinth, his first search seems to have been for work (Acts 18:3); and through life he steadily forbore availing himself of his right to be supported by the Church, deeming it his great "reward" to "make the Gospel of Christ without charge" (1 Cor. 9:18). Nay, to quote his impassioned language, he would far rather have died of hard work than that any man should deprive him of this "glorying." And so presently at Ephesus "these hands" minister not only unto his own necessities, but also to them that were with him; and that for the twofold reason of supporting the weak, and of following the Master, however "afar off," and entering into this joy of His, "It is more blessed to give than to receive" (Acts 20:34, 35). Again, so to speak, it does one's heart good when coming in contact with that Church which seemed most in danger of dreamy contemplativeness, and of unpractical, if not dangerous, speculations about the future, to hear what a manly, earnest tone also prevailed there. Here is the preacher himself! Not a man-pleaser, but a God-server; not a flatterer, nor covetous, nor yet seeking glory, nor courting authority, like the Rabbis. What then? This is the sketch as drawn from life at Thessalonica, so that each who had known him must have recognised it: most loving, like a nursing mother, who cherisheth her own children, so in tenderness willing to impart not only the Gospel of God, but his own life. Yet, with it all, no mawkishness, no sentimentality; but all stern, genuine reality; and the preacher himself is "labouring night and day," because he would not be chargeable to any of them, while he preached unto them the Gospel of God (1 Thess. 2:9). "Night and day," hard, unremitting, uninteresting work, which some would have denounced or despised as secular! But to Paul that wretched distinction, the invention of modern superficialism and unreality, existed not. For to the spiritual nothing is secular, and to the secular nothing is spiritual. Work night and day, and then as his rest, joy, and reward, to preach in public and in private the unsearchable riches of Christ, Who had redeemed him with His precious blood. And so his preaching, although one of its main burdens seems to have been the second coming of the Lord, was in no way calculated to make the hearers apocalyptic dreamers, who discussed knotty points and visions of the future, while present duty lay unheeded as beneath them, on a lower platform. There is a ring of honest independence, of healthy, manly piety, of genuine, self-denying devotion to Christ, and also of a practical life of holiness, in this admonition (1 Thess. 4:11, 12): "Make it your ambition to be quiet, to do your own" (each one for himself, not meddling with others' affairs), "and to work with your hands, as we commanded you, that ye may walk decorously towards them without, and have no need of any one"[4] (be independent of all men). And, very significantly, this plain, practical religion is placed in immediate conjunction with the hope of the resurrection and of the coming again of our Lord (vers. 13–18). The same admonition, "to work, and eat their own bread," comes once again, only in stronger language, in the Second Epistle to the Thessalonians, reminding them in this of his own example, and of his command when with them, "that, if any would not work, neither should he eat;" at the same time sternly rebuking "some who are walking disorderly, who are not at all busy, but are busybodies."[5]

Now, we certainly do not pretend to find a parallel to St. Paul among even the best and the noblest of the Rabbis. Yet Saul of Tarsus was a Jew, not merely trained at the feet of the great Gamaliel, "that sun in Israel," but deeply imbued with the Jewish spirit and lore; insomuch that long afterwards, when he is writing of the deepest mysteries of Christianity, we catch again and again expressions that remind us of some that occur in the earliest record of that secret Jewish doctrine, which was only

Brothers, we do not want you to be ignorant about those who fall asleep, or to grieve like the rest of men, who have no hope. We believe that Jesus died and rose again and so we believe that God will bring with Jesus those who have fallen asleep in him (1 Thess. 4:13–14).

---

[4] So literally.
[5] We have here tried to reproduce the play on the words in the original.

*A wife of noble character
who can find?
She is worth far more
than rubies...
Her children arise and call
her blessed;
her husband also, and he
praises her
(Prov. 31:10, 28).*

communicated to the most select of the select sages.[6] And this same love of honest labour, the same spirit of manly independence, the same horror of trafficking with the law, and using it either "as a crown or as a spade," was certainly characteristic of the best Rabbis. Quite different in this respect also—far asunder as were the aims of their lives—were the feelings of Israel from those of the Gentiles around. The philosophers of Greece and Rome denounced manual labour as something degrading; indeed, as incompatible with the full exercise of the privileges of a citizen. Those Romans who allowed themselves not only to be bribed in their votes, but expected to be actually supported at the public expense, would not stoop to the defilement of work. The Jews had another aim in life, another pride and ambition. It is difficult to give an idea of the seeming contrasts united in them. Most aristocratic and exclusive, contemptuous of mere popular cries, yet at the same time most democratic and liberal; law-abiding, and with the profoundest reverence for authority and rank, and yet with this prevailing conviction at bottom, that all Israel were brethren, and as such stood on precisely the same level, the eventual differences arising only from this, that the mass failed to realise what Israel's real vocation was, and how it was to be attained, viz., by theoretical and practical engagement with the law, compared to which everything else was but secondary and unimportant.

But this combination of study with honest manual labour—the one to support the other—had not been always equally honoured in Israel. We distinguish here three periods. The law of Moses evidently recognised the dignity of labour, and this spirit of the Old Testament appeared in the best times of the Jewish nation. The book of Proverbs, which contains so many sketches of what a happy, holy home in Israel had been, is full of the praises of domestic industry. But the Apocrypha, notably Ecclesiasticus (xxxviii. 24–31),

---

[6]We mean the book Jezirah. It is curious that this should have never been noticed. The coincidences are not in substance, but in modes of expression.

Potter

"*R. Meir says:...A man should always teach his son a cleanly craft, and let him pray to him to whom riches and possessions belong, for there is no craft wherein there is not both poverty and wealth; for poverty comes not from a man's craft, nor riches from a man's craft, but all is according to his merit*" (*Mishnah*, Kiddushin *xiv.4*).

strike a very different key-note. Analysing one by one every trade, the contemptuous question is put, how such "can get wisdom?" This "Wisdom of Jesus the Son of Sirach" dates from about two centuries before the present era. It would not have been possible at the time of Christ or afterwards, to have written in such terms of "the carpenter and workmaster," of them "that cut and grave seals," of "the smith," or "the potter;" nor to have said of them: "They shall not be sought for in public counsel, nor sit high in the congregation; they shall not sit on the judges' seat, nor understand the sentence of judgment; they cannot declare justice and judgment; and they shall not be found where parables are spoken" (Ecclus. xxxviii. 33). For, in point of fact, with few exceptions, all the leading Rabbinical authorities were working at some trade, till at last it became quite an affectation to engage in hard bodily labour, so that one Rabbi would carry his own chair every day to college, while others would drag heavy rafters, or work in some such fashion.[7] Without cumbering these pages with names, it is worth mentioning, perhaps as an extreme instance, that on one occasion a man was actually summoned from his trade of stone-cutter to the high-priestly office. To be sure, that was in revolutionary times.

---

[7]Compare Professor Delitzsch's beautiful tractate, *Jüd. Handwerkerleben zur Zeit Jesu* (p. 75), to which we would here generally acknowledge our obligations.

Enjoy life with your wife, whom you love, all the days of this meaningless life that God has given you under the sun—all your meaningless days. For this is your lot in life and in your toilsome labor under the sun (Eccl. 9:9).

The high-priests under the Herodian dynasty were of only too different a class, and their history possesses a tragic interest, as bearing on the state and fate of the nation. Still, the great Hillel was a wood-cutter, his rival Shammai a carpenter; and among the celebrated Rabbis of after times we find shoemakers, tailors, carpenters, sandalmakers, smiths, potters, builders, etc.—in short, every variety of trade. Nor were they ashamed of their manual labour. Thus it is recorded of one of them, that he was in the habit of discoursing to his students from the top of a cask of his own making, which he carried every day to the academy.

We can scarcely wonder at this, since it was a Rabbinical principle, that "whoever does not teach his son a trade is as if he brought him up to be a robber" (*Kidd.* 4.14). The Midrash gives the following curious paraphrase of Eccles. 9:9, "Behold, the life with the wife whom thou lovest:"[8] Look out for a trade along with the Divine study which thou lovest. "How highly does the Maker of the world value trades," is another saying. Here are some more: "There is none whose trade God does not adorn with beauty." "Though there were seven years of famine, it will never come to the door of the tradesman." "There is not a trade to which both poverty and riches are not joined; for there is nothing more poor, and nothing more rich, than a trade." "No trade shall ever disappear from the world. Happy he whom his teacher has brought up to a good trade; alas for him who has been put into a bad one."[9] Perhaps these are comparatively later Rabbinical sayings. But let us turn to the Mishnah itself, and especially to that tractate which professedly embodies the wisdom and the sayings of the fathers (*Aboth*). Shemaajah, the teacher of Hillel, has this cynical saying (*Ab.* i. 10)—perhaps the outcome of his experience: "Love work, hate Rabbiship, and do not press on the notice of those in power." The views of the great Hillel himself have been quoted in a previous chapter. Rabbi Gamaliel,

---

[8] So literally in the Hebrew.
[9] Compare Hamburger, *Real. Encycl.* p. 497, where these sayings are collated.

the son of Jehudah the Nasi, said (*Ab.* ii. 2): "Fair is the study of the law, if accompanied by worldly occupation: to engage in them both is to keep away sin; while study which is not combined with work must in the end be interrupted, and only brings sin with it." Rabbi Eleazar, the son of Asarjah, says, among other things: "Where there is no worldly support (literally, no meal, no flour), there is no study of the law; and where there is no study of the law, worldly support is of no value" (*Ab.* iii. 21). It is worth while to add what immediately follows in the Mishnah. Its resemblance to the simile about the rock, and the building upon it, as employed by our Lord (Matt. 7:24; Luke 6:47), is so striking, that we quote it in illustration of previous remarks on this subject. We read as follows: "He whose knowledge exceeds his works, to whom is he like? He is like a tree, whose branches are many and its roots few, and the wind cometh, and uproots the tree and throws it upon its face, as it is said (Jer. 17:6)…But he whose works exceed his knowledge, to whom is he like? To a tree whose branches are few, but its roots many; and if even all the winds that are in the world came and set upon such a tree, they would not move it from its place, as it is written (Jer. 17:8)." We have given this saying in its earliest form. Even so, it should be remembered that it dates from after the destruction of Jerusalem. It occurs in a still later form in the Babylon Talmud (*Sanh.* 99 *a*). But what is most remarkable is, that it also appears in yet another work, and in a form almost identical with that in the New Testament, so far as the simile of the building is concerned. In this form it is attributed to a Rabbi who is stigmatised as an apostate, and as the type of apostasy, and who, as such, died under the ban. The inference seems to be, that if he did not profess some form of Christianity, he had at least derived this saying from his intercourse with Christians.[10] But irrespective of this, two things are

Therefore everyone who hears these words of mine and puts them into practice is like a wise man who built his house on the rock (Matt. 7:24).

He will be like a tree planted by the water that sends out its roots by the stream.
It does not fear when heat comes;
its leaves are always green.
It has no worries in a year of drought
and never fails to bear fruit (Jer. 17:8).

---

[10] Elisha ben Abbuja, called Acher, "the other," on account of his apostasy. The history of that Rabbi is altogether deeply interesting. We can only put the question: Was he a Christian, or merely tainted with Gnosticism? The latter seems to us the most probable. His errors are traced by the Jews to his study of the Kabbalah.

plain on comparison of the saying in its Rabbinical and in its Christian form. First, in the parable as employed by our Lord, everything is referred to Him; and the essential difference ultimately depends upon our relationship towards Him. The comparison here is not between much study and little work, or little Talmudical knowledge and much work; but between coming to Him and hearing these sayings of His, and then either doing or else not doing them. Secondly, such an alternative is never presented by Christianity as, on the one hand, much knowledge and few works, and on the other, little knowledge and many works. But in Christianity the vital difference lies between works and no works; between absolute life and absolute death; all depending upon this, whether a man has digged down to the right foundation, and built upon the rock which is Christ, or has tried to build up the walls of his life without such foundation. Thus the very similarity of the saying in its Rabbinical form brings out all the more clearly the essential difference and contrariety in spirit existing between Rabbinism, even in its purest form, and the teaching of our Lord.

A man can do nothing better than to eat and drink and find satisfaction in his work. This too, I see, is from the hand of God, for without him, who can eat or find enjoyment (Eccl. 2:24–25)?

The question of the relation between the best teaching of the Jewish sages and some of the sayings of our Lord is of such vital importance, that this digression will not seem out of place. A few further quotations bearing on the dignity of labour may be appropriate. The Talmud has a beautiful Haggadah, which tells how, when Adam heard this sentence of his Maker: "Thorns also and thistles shall it bring forth to thee," he burst into tears. "What!" he exclaimed; "Lord of the world, am I then to eat out of the same manger with the ass?" But when he heard these additional words: "In the sweat of thy face shalt thou eat bread," his heart was comforted. For herein lies (according to the Rabbis) the dignity of labour, that man is not forced to, nor unconscious in, his work; but that while becoming the servant of the soil, he wins from it the precious fruits of golden harvest. And so, albeit labour may be hard, and the result doubtful, as when Israel stood by the shores of the

Red Sea, yet a miracle will cleave these waters also. And still the dignity of labour is great in itself: it reflects honour; it nourisheth and cherisheth him that engageth in it. For this reason also did the law punish with fivefold restitution the theft of an ox, but only with fourfold that of a sheep; because the former was that with which a man worked.[11]

Assuredly St. Paul spoke also as a Jew when he admonished the Ephesians (Eph. 4:28): "Let him that stole steal no more: but rather let him labour, working with his hands the thing which is good, that he may have to give to him that needeth." "Make a working day of the Sabbath: only be not dependent upon people," was the Rabbinical saying (*Pes.* 112). "Skin dead animals by the wayside," we read, "and take thy payment for it, but do not say, I am a priest; I am a man of distinction, and work is objectionable to me!" And to this day the common Jewish proverb has it: "Labour is no *cherpah* (disgrace);" or again: "*Melachah* is *berachah* (labour is blessing)." With such views, we can understand how universal industrious pursuits were in the days of our Lord. Although it is no doubt true, as the Rabbinical proverb puts it, that every man thinks most of his own trade, yet public opinion attached a very different value to different kinds of trade. Some were

Cursed is the ground because of you; through painful toil you will eat of it all the days of your life. It will produce thorns and thistles for you, and you will eat the plants of the field. By the sweat of your brow you will eat your food until you return to the ground, since from it you were taken; for dust you are and to dust you will return (Gen. 3:17b–19).

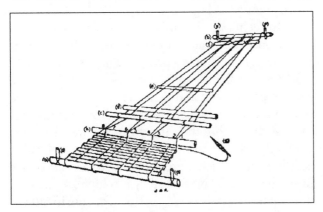

Loom

---

[11] All these are Rabbinical sayings. Compare the references in *Tendlau Sprüchw. u. Redensarten*, p. 263.

avoided on account of the unpleasantnesses connected with them, such as those of tanners, dyers, and miners. The Mishnah lays it down as a principle, that a man should not teach his son a trade which necessitates constant intercourse with the other sex (*Kidd.* iv. 14). Such would include, among others, jewellers, makers of handmills, perfumers, and weavers. The latter trade seems to have exposed to as many troubles as if the weavers of those days had been obliged to serve a modern fashionable lady. The saying was: "A weaver must be humble, or his life will be shortened by excommunication;" that is, he must submit to anything for a living. Or, as the common proverb put it (*Ab. S.* 26 *a*): "If a weaver is not humble, his life is shortened by a year." This other saying, of a similar kind, reminds us of the Scotch estimate of, or rather disrespect for, weavers: "Even a weaver is master in his own house." And this not only in his own opinion, but in that of his wife also. For as the Rabbinical proverb has it: "Though a man were only a comber of wool, his wife would call him up to the house-door, and sit down beside him," so proud is she of him. Perhaps in the view of the Rabbis there was a little of female self-consciousness in this regard for her husband's credit, for they have it: "Though a man were only the size of an ant, his wife would try to sit down among the big ones."

In general, the following sound views are expressed in the Talmud (*Ber.* 17 *a*): "The Rabbi of Jabne said: I am simply a being like my neighbour. He works in the field, and I in the town. We both rise early to go to work; and there is no cause for the one setting himself up above the other. Do not think that the one does more than the other; for we have been taught that there is as much merit in doing that which is little as that which is great, provided the state of our hearts be right." And so a story is told, how one who dug cisterns and made baths (for purification) accosted the great Rabbi Jochanan with the words: "I am as great a man as thou;" since, in his own sphere, he served the wants of the community quite as much as the most learned teacher in Israel. In the same

When a farmer plows for planting, does he plow continually?
Does he keep on breaking up and harrowing the soil?...
His God instructs him and teaches him the right way...
All this also comes from the LORD *Almighty, wonderful in counsel and magnificent in wisdom* (Isa. 28:24, 26, 29).

spirit another Rabbi admonished to strict conscientiousness, since in a sense all work, however humble, was really work for God. There can be no doubt that the Jewish tradesman who worked in such a spirit would be alike happy and skilful.

It must have been a great privilege to be engaged in any work connected with the Temple. A large number of workmen were kept constantly employed there, preparing what was necessary for the service. Perhaps it was only a piece of Jerusalem jealousy of the Alexandrians which prompted such Rabbinical traditions, as, that, when Alexandrians tried to compound the incense for the Temple, the column of smoke did not ascend quite straight; when they

Working in metal

repaired the large mortar in which the incense was bruised, and again, the great cymbal with which the signal for the commencement of the Temple music was given, in each case their work had to be undone by Jerusalem workmen, in order to produce a proper mixture, or to evoke the former sweet sounds. There can be no question, however, notwithstanding Palestinian prejudices, that there were excellent Jewish workmen in Alexandria; and plenty of them, too, as we know from their arrangement in guilds in their great synagogue. Any poor workman had only to apply to his guild, and he was supported till he found employment. The guild of coppersmiths there had, as we are informed, for their device a leathern apron; and when its members went abroad they used to carry with them a bed which could be taken to pieces. At Jerusalem, where this guild was organised under its Rabban, or chief, it possessed a synagogue and a burying-place of its own.[12] But the Palestinian workmen, though they kept by each other, had no exclusive guilds; the principles of "free trade," so to speak, prevailing among them. Bazaars and streets were named after them. The workmen of Jerusalem were specially distinguished for their artistic skill. A whole valley—that of the Tyropoeon—was occupied by dairies; hence its name, "valley of cheesemongers."

---

[12] See Delitzsch, *u.s.* p. 38.

Spindles, used in making the veil

And when Jesus had cried out again in a loud voice, he gave up his spirit.
At that moment the curtain of the temple was torn in two from top to bottom.
The earth shook and the rocks split
(Matt. 27:50–51).

Even in Isa. 7:3 we read of "the field of the fullers," which lay "at the end of the conduit of the upper pool in the highway" to Joppa. A whole set of sayings is expressly designated in the Talmud as "the proverbs of the fullers."

From their love of building and splendour the Herodian princes must have kept many tradesmen in constant work. At the re-erection of the Temple no less than eighteen thousand were so employed in various handicrafts, some of them implying great artistic skill. Even before that, Herod the Great is said to have employed a large number of the most experienced masters to teach the one thousand priests who were to construct the Holy Place itself. For, in the building of that part of the Temple no laymen were engaged. As we know, neither hammer, axe, chisel, nor any tool of iron was used within the sacred precincts. The reason of this is thus explained in the Mishnah, when describing how all the stones for the altar were dug out of virgin-earth, no iron tool being employed in their preparation: "Iron is created to cut short the life of man; but the altar to prolong it. Hence it is not becoming to use that which shortens for that which lengthens" (*Midd.* iii. 4). Those who know the magnificence and splendour of that holy house will be best able to judge what skill in workmanship its various parts must have required. An instance may be interesting on account of its connection with the most solemn fact of New Testament history. We read in the Mishnah (*Shek.* viii. 5): "Rabbi Simeon, the son of Gamaliel, said, in the name of Rabbi Simeon, the son of the (former) Sagan (assistant of the high-priest): The veil (of the Most Holy Place) was an handbreadth thick, and woven of seventy-two twisted plaits; each plait consisted of twenty-four threads" (according to the Talmud, six threads of each of the four Temple-colours—white, scarlet, blue, and gold). "It was forty cubits long, and twenty wide (sixty feet by thirty), and made of eighty-two myriads" (the meaning of this in the Mishnah is not plain). "Two of these veils were made every year, and it took three hundred priests to immerse one" (before use). These statements must of course be considered as dealing in "round numbers;" but they are most interesting as helping us to realise, not only how the great veil of the Temple was rent, when the Lord of that Temple died on the cross, but also how the occurrence could have been effectually concealed from the mass of the people.

To turn to quite another subject. It is curious to notice in how many respects times and circumstances have really not changed. The old Jewish employers of labour seem to have had similar trouble with their men to that of which so many in our own times loudly complain. We have an emphatic warning to this effect, to beware of eating fine bread and giving black bread to one's workmen or servants; not to sleep on feathers and give them straw pallets, more especially if they were co-religionists, for, as it is added, he who gets a Hebrew slave gets his master! Possibly something of this kind was on the mind of St. Paul when he wrote this most needful precept (1 Tim. 6:1, 2): "Let as many servants as are under the yoke count their own masters worthy of all honour, that the name of God and His doctrine be not blasphemed. And they that have believing masters, let them not despise them, because they are brethren; but rather do them service, because they are believing and beloved, partakers of the benefit." But really there is nothing "new under the sun!" Something like the provisions of a mutual assurance appear in the associations of muleteers and sailors, which undertook to replace a beast or a ship that had been lost without negligence on the part of the owner. Nay, we can even trace the spirit of trade-unionism in the express permission of the Talmud (*Bab. B.* 9) to tradesmen to combine to work only one or two days in the week, so as to give sufficient employment to every workman in a place. We close with another quotation in the same direction, which will also serve to illustrate the peculiar mode of Rabbinical comment on the words of Scripture: " 'He doeth no evil to his neighbour'— this refers to one tradesman not interfering with the trade of another!"

"What is written in the Law?" he replied. "How do you read it?"
He answered: " 'Love the LORD *your God with all your heart and with all your soul and with all your strength and with all your mind'; and, 'Love your neighbor as yourself.' "*
"You have answered correctly," Jesus replied. "Do this and you will live" (Luke 10:26–28).

12
COMMERCE

Coin of Macedonia

The remarkable change which we have noticed in the views of Jewish authorities, from contempt to almost affectation of manual labour, could certainly not have been arbitrary. But as we fail to discover here any religious motive, we can only account for it on the score of altered political and social circumstances. So long as the people were, at least nominally, independent, and in possession of their own land, constant engagement in a trade would probably mark an inferior social stage, and imply either voluntary or necessary preoccupation with the things of this world that perish with the using. It was otherwise when Judaea was in the hands of strangers. Then honest labour afforded the means, and the only means, of manly independence. To engage in it, just sufficient to secure this result, to "stand in need of no one;" to be able to hold up one's head before friend and foe; to make unto God moral sacrifice of natural inclination, strength and time, so as to be able freely and independently to devote oneself to the study of the Divine law, was a noble resolve. And it brought its own reward. If, on the one hand, the alternation of physical and mental labour was felt to be healthy, on the other—and this had been the main object in view—there never were men more fearlessly outspoken, more unconcerned as to mere personality or as to consequences, more independent in thought and word than these Rabbis. We can understand the withering scorn of St. Jude (Jude 16) towards those "having men's persons in admiration," literally, "admiring faces"—an expression by which the LXX. translate the "respect" or "regard," or "acceptance" of persons (the *nasa panim*) mentioned in Lev. 19:15; Deut. 10:17; Job 13:10; Prov. 18:5, and many other passages. In this respect also, as so often, St. Paul spoke as a true Jew when he wrote (Gal. 2:6): "But of these who seemed to be somewhat, whatsoever they were, it maketh no matter to me: the face of man God accepteth not."

Do not pervert justice; do not show partiality to the poor or favoritism to the great, but judge your neighbor fairly (Lev. 19:15).

The Mishnah, indeed, does not in so many words inform us how the change in public feeling, to which we have referred, was brought about. But there are plenty of hints to guide us in certain short caustic sentences which would be inexplicable, unless read in the light of the history of that time. Thus, as stated in the previous chapter, Shemaajah admonished: "Love work, hate Rabbiship, and do not press on the notice of those in power." Similarly, Avtaljon warned the sages to be cautious in their words, for fear of incurring banishment for themselves and their followers (*Ab.* i. 10, 11). And Rabbi Gamaliel II had it (ii. 3): "Be cautious with the powers that be, for they only seek intercourse with a person for their own advantage. They are as if they loved you, when it serves for their profit, but in the hour of his need they do not stand by a man." In the same category of sayings for the times we may rank this of Rabbi Matithja: "Meet every one with a salutation of peace, and prefer to be the tail of lions, but be not the head to foxes." It is needless to multiply similar quotations, all expressive of an earnest desire for honourable independence through personal exertion.

Abtalion said: Ye Sages, give heed to your words lest ye incur the penalty of exile and ye be exiled to a place of evil waters, and the disciples that come after you drink [of them] and die, and the name of Heaven be profaned (Mishnah, 'Abot i. 11).

Quite different from those as to trades were the Rabbinical views about commerce, as we shall immediately show. In fact, the general adoption of business, which has so often been made the subject of jeer against Israel, marks yet another social state, and a terrible social necessity. When Israel was scattered by units, hundreds, or even thousands, but still a miserable, vanquished, homeless, weak minority among the nations of the earth—avoided, downtrodden, and at the mercy of popular passion—no other course was open to them than to follow commerce. Even if Jewish talent could have identified itself with the pursuits of the Gentiles, would public life have been open to them—we shall not say, on equal, but, on any terms? Or, to descend a step lower—except in those crafts which might be peculiarly theirs, could Jewish tradesmen have competed with those around? Would they even have been allowed to enter the lists? Moreover, it was necessary for their self-defence—almost for their existence—that they should gain influence. And in their circumstances this could only be obtained by the possession of wealth, and the sole road to this was commerce.

There can be no question that, according to the Divine purpose, Israel was not intended to be a commercial people. The many restrictions to the intercourse between Jews and Gentiles, which the Mosaic law everywhere presents, would alone have sufficed to prevent it. Then there was the express enactment against taking interest upon loans (Lev. 25:36, 37), which must have rendered commercial transactions impossible, even though it was relaxed in reference to those who lived outside the boundaries of Palestine (Deut. 23:20). Again, the law of the Sabbatic and of the Jubilee year would have brought all extended commerce to a standstill. Nor was the land at all suited for the requirements of trade. True, it possessed ample seaboard, whatever the natural capabilities of its harbours may have been. But the whole of that coast, with the harbours of Joppa, Jamneh, Ascalon, Gaza, and Acco or Ptolemais, remained, with short intervals, in the possession of the Philistines and Phoenicians. Even when Herod the Great built the noble harbour of Caesarea, it was almost exclusively used by foreigners (Jos. *Jew. War*, 409–413). And the whole history of Israel in Palestine points to the same inference. Only on one occasion, during the reign of Solomon, do we find anything like attempts to engage in mercantile pursuits on a large scale. The reference to the "king's merchants" (1 Kings 10:28, 29; 2 Chron. 1:16), who imported horses and linen yarn, has been regarded as indicating

If one of your countrymen becomes poor and is unable to support himself among you, help him as you would an alien or a temporary resident, so he can continue to live among you. Do not take interest of any kind from him, but fear your God, so that your countryman may continue to live among you. You must not lend him money at interest or sell him food at a profit (Lev. 25:35–37).

Two of the legions also he placed Cesarea, that they might there take their winter quarters, as perceiving the city very fit for such a purpose; but he placed the tenth and the fifth at Scythopolis, that he might not distress Cesarea with the entire army (Jos. Jewish War 3.412).

Solomon's horses were imported from Egypt and from Kue—the royal merchants purchased them from Kue. They imported a chariot from Egypt for six hundred shekels of silver, and a horse for a hundred and fifty. They also exported them to all the kings of the Hittites and of the Arameans (1 Kgs. 10:28–29).

the existence of a sort of royal trading company, or of a royal monopoly. A still more curious inference would almost lead us to describe Solomon as the first great "Protectionist." The expressions in 1 Kings 10:15 point to duties paid by retail and wholesale importers, the words, literally rendered, indicating as a source of revenue that "from the traders and from the traffick of the merchants;" both words in their derivation pointing to foreign trade, and probably distinguishing them as retail and wholesale.[1] We may here remark that, besides these duties and the tributes from "protected" kings (1 Kings 9:15), Solomon's income is described (1 Kings 10:14) as having amounted, at any rate, in one year,[2] to the enormous sum of between two and three million sterling! Part of this may have been derived from the king's foreign trade. For we know (1 Kings 9:26, etc.; 2 Chron. 8:17, etc.) that King Solomon built a navy at Ezion-geber, on the Red Sea, which port David had taken. This navy traded to Ophir, in company with the Phoenicians. But as this tendency of King Solomon's policy was in opposition to the Divine purpose, so it was not lasting. The later attempt of King Jehoshaphat to revive the foreign trade signally failed; "for the ships were broken at Ezion-geber" (1 Kings 22:48; 2 Chron. 20:36, 37), and soon afterwards the port of Ezion-geber passed once more into the hands of Edom (2 Kings 8:20).

King Solomon also built ships at Ezion Geber, which is near Elath in Edom, on the shore of the Red Sea (1 Kgs. 9:26).

In the time of Jehoram, Edom rebelled against Judah and set up its own king (2 Kgs. 8:20).

With this closes the Biblical history of Jewish commerce in Palestine, in the strict sense of that term. But our reference to what may be called the Scriptural indications against the pursuit of commerce brings up a kindred subject, for which, although confessedly a digression, we claim a hearing, on account of its great importance. Those most superficially acquainted with modern theological controversy are aware, that certain opponents of the Bible have specially directed their attacks against the antiquity of the Pentateuch, although they have not

---

[1] See Leyrer in Herzog, *Real Encycl.* v. p. 509; and Keil's *Comment.* on the passage.
[2] The Vulgate renders, "Every year."

If a fellow Hebrew, a man or a woman, sells himself to you and serves you six years, in the seventh year you must let him go free...You must not sacrifice the Passover in any town the LORD your God gives you except in the place he will choose as a dwelling for his Name. There you must sacrifice the Passover in the evening, when the sun goes down, on the anniversary of your departure from Egypt (Deut. 15:12; 16:5–6).

yet arranged among themselves what parts of the Pentateuch were written by different authors, nor by how many, nor by whom, nor at what times, nor when or by whom they were ultimately collected into one book. Now what we contend for in this connection is, that the legislation of the Pentateuch affords evidence of its composition before the people were settled in Palestine. We arrive at this conclusion in the following manner. Supposing a code of laws and institutions to be drawn up by a practical legislator—for unquestionably they were in force in Israel—we maintain, that no human lawgiver could have ordered matters for a nation in a settled state as we find it done in the Pentateuch. The world has had many speculative constitutions of society drawn up by philosophers and theorists, from Plato to Rousseau and Owen. None of these would have suited, or even been possible in a settled state of society. But no philosopher would ever have imagined or thought of such laws as some of the provisions in the Pentateuch. To select only a few, almost at random. Let the reader think of applying, for example, to England, such provisions as that all males were to appear three times a year in the place which the Lord would choose, or those connected with the Sabbatic and the Jubilee years, or those regulating religious and charitable contributions, or those concerning the corners of fields, or those prohibiting the taking of interest, or those connected with the Levitical cities. Then let any one seriously ask himself, whether such institutions could have been for the first time propounded or introduced by a legislator at the time of David, or of Hezekiah, or of Ezra? The more we think of the spirit and of the details of the Mosaic legislation, the stronger grows our conviction, that such laws and institutions could have been only introduced before the people actually settled in the land. So far as we are aware, this line of argument has not before been proposed; and yet it seems necessary for our opponents to meet this preliminary and, as we think, insuperable difficulty of their theory, before we can be asked to discuss their critical objections.

But to return. Passing from Biblical, or, at least, from Old Testament to later times, we find the old popular feeling in Palestine on the subject of commerce still existing. For once Josephus here correctly expresses the views of his countrymen. "As for ourselves," he writes (*Ag. Apion,* 1.60–68), "we neither inhabit a maritime country, nor do we delight in merchandise, nor in such a mixture with other men as arises from it; but the cities we dwell in are remote from the sea, and having a fruitful country for our habitation, we take pains in cultivating that only." Nor were the opinions of the Rabbis different. We know in what low esteem pedlars were held by the Jewish authorities. But even commerce was not much more highly regarded. It has been rightly said that, "in the sixty-three tractates of which the Talmud is composed, scarcely a word occurs in honour of commerce, but much to point out the dangers attendant upon money-making." "Wisdom," says Rabbi Jochanan, in explanation of Deut. 30:12, " 'is not in heaven'—that is, it is not found with those who are proud; neither is it 'beyond the sea'—that is, it will not be found among traders nor among merchants" (*Er.* 55 *a*). Still more to the point are the provisions of the Jewish law as to those who lent money on interest, or took usury. "The following," we read in *Rosh Hash.* i. 8, "are unfit for witness-bearing: he who plays with dice (a gambler); he who lends on usury; they who train doves (either for betting purposes, or as decoys); they who trade in seventh year's products, and slaves." Even more pungent is this, almost reminding one of the Rabbinic gloss: "Of the calumniator God says, 'There is not room in the world for him and Me' "—"The usurer bites off a piece from a man, for he takes from him that which he has not given him" (*Bab. Mez.* 60 *b*). A few other kindred sayings may here find a place. "Rabbi Meir saith: Be sparing (doing little) in business, but busy in the Thorah" (*Ab.* iv. 2). Among the forty-eight qualifications for acquiring the Thorah, "little business" is mentioned (vi. 6). Lastly, we have this from Hillel, concluding with a very noble saying, worthy to be

It is not up in heaven, so that you have to ask, "Who will ascend into heaven to get it and proclaim it to us so we may obey it?" (Deut. 30:12).

preserved to all times and in all languages: "He who engages much in business cannot become a sage; and in a place where there are no men, strive thou to be a man."

Half-Shekel, Shekel

It will perhaps have been observed, that, with the changing circumstances of the people, the views as to commerce also underwent a slow process of modification, the main object now being to restrict such occupations, and especially to regulate them in accordance with religion. Inspectorships of weights and measures are of comparatively late date in our own country. The Rabbis in this, as in so many other matters, were long before us. They appointed regular inspectors, whose duty it was to go from market to market, and, more than that, to fix the current market prices (*Baba B.* 88). The prices for produce were ultimately determined by each community. Few merchants would submit to interference with what is called the law of supply and demand. But the Talmudical laws against buying up grain and withdrawing it from sale, especially at a time of scarcity, are exceedingly strict. Similarly, it was prohibited artificially to raise prices, especially of produce. Indeed, it was regarded as cheating to charge a higher profit than sixteen per cent. In general, some would have it that in Palestine no one should make profit out of the necessaries of life. Cheating was declared to involve heavier punishment than a breach of some of the other moral commandments. For the latter, it was argued, might be set right by repentance. But he who cheated took in not merely one or several persons, but every one; and how could that ever be set right? And all were admonished to remember, that "God punisheth even where the eye of an earthly judge cannot penetrate."[3]

We have spoken of a gradual modification of Rabbinical views with the changing circumstances of the nation. This probably comes out most clearly in the advice of the Talmud (*Baba M.* 42), to divide one's money into three parts—to lay out one in the

---

[3] Compare Hamburger, *Real-Encycl.* p. 494.

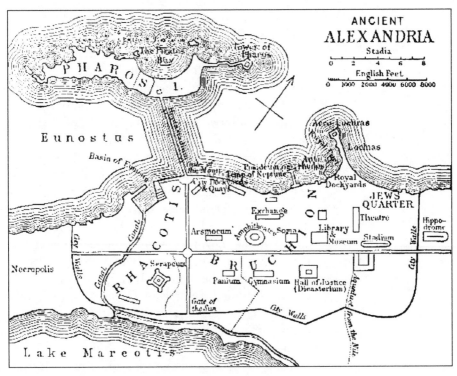

Ancient Alexandria

purchase of land, to invest the second in merchandise, and to keep the third in hand as cash. But there was always this comfort, which Rab enumerated among the blessings of the next world, that there was no commerce there (*Ber.* 17 *a*). And so far as this world was concerned, the advice was to engage in business, in order with the profit made to assist the sages in their pursuits, just as Sebua, one of the three wealthy men of Jerusalem, had assisted the great Hillel. From what has been said, it will be inferred that the views expressed as to Palestinian, or even Babylonian Jews, did not apply to those who were "dispersed abroad" among the various Gentile nations. To them, as already shown, commerce would be a necessity, and, in fact, the grand staple of their existence. If this may be said of all Jews of the dispersion, it applies specially to that community which was the richest and most influential among them—we mean the Jews of Alexandria.

Few phases, even in the ever-changeful history of the Jewish people, are more strange, more varied in interest, or more pathetic than those connected with the Jews of Alexandria. The immigration of Jews into Egypt commenced even before the Babylonish captivity. Naturally it received great increase from that event, and afterwards from the murder of Gedaliah. But the real exodus commenced under Alexander the Great. That monarch accorded to the Jews in Alexandria the same rights as its Greek inhabitants enjoyed, and so raised them to the rank of the privileged classes. Henceforth their numbers and their influence grew under successive rulers. We find them commanding Egyptian armies, largely influencing Egyptian thought and inquiry, and partially leavening it by the translation of the Holy Scriptures into Greek. Of the so-called Temple of Onias at Leontopolis, which rivalled that of Jerusalem, and of the magnificence of the great synagogue at Alexandria, we cannot speak in this place. There can be no doubt that, in the Providence of God, the location of so many Jews in Alexandria, and the mental influence which they acquired, were designed to have an important bearing on the later spread of the Gospel of Christ among the Greek-speaking and Grecian-thinking educated world. In this, the Greek translation of the Old Testament was also largely helpful. Indeed, humanly speaking, it would have scarcely been possible without it. At the time of Philo the number of Jews in Egypt amounted to no less than one million. In Alexandria they occupied two out of the five quarters of the town, which were called after the first five letters of the alphabet. They lived under rulers of their own, almost in a state of complete independence. Theirs was the quarter Delta, along the seashore. The supervision of navigation, both by sea and river, was wholly entrusted to them. In fact, the large export trade, especially in grain—and Egypt was the granary of the world—was entirely in their hands. The provisioning of Italy and of the world was the business of the Jews. It is a curious circumstance, as illustrating how little the history of the world changes, that during the troubles at Rome the Jewish bankers of Alexandria were able to obtain from their correspondents earlier and more trustworthy political tidings than any one else.[4] This enabled them to declare themselves in turn for Caesar and for Octavius, and to secure the full political and financial results flowing from such policy, just as the great Jewish banking houses at the beginning of this century were similarly able to profit by earlier and more trustworthy news of events than the general public could obtain.

Ancient Egyptian baskets

But no sketch of commerce among the early Jews, however brief, would be complete without some further notice both of the nature of the trade carried on, and of the legal regulations which guarded it. The business of the travelling hawker, of course, was restricted to negotiating an exchange of the products of one district for those of another, to buying and selling articles of home produce, or introducing among those who affected fashion or luxury in country districts specimens of the latest novelties from abroad. The foreign imports were, with the exception of wood and metals, chiefly articles of luxury. Fish from Spain, apples from Crete, cheese from Bithynia; lentils, beans, and gourds from Egypt and Greece; plates from Babylon, wine from Italy, beer from Media, household vessels from Sidon, baskets from Egypt, dresses from India, sandals from Laodicea, shirts from Cilicia, veils from Arabia—such were some of the goods imported. On the other hand, the exports from Palestine consisted of such produce as wheat, oil, balsam, honey, figs, etc., the value of exports and imports being nearly equal, and the balance, if any, in favour of Palestine.

Then, as to the laws regulating trade and commerce, they were so minute as almost to remind us of the Saviour's strictures on Pharisaic punctiliousness. Several Mishnic tractates are full of determinations on these points. "The dust of the balances" is a strictly Jewish idea and phrase. So far did the law interfere, as to order that a wholesale dealer must cleanse the

Sandals

---

[4] Hausrath, *Neutest. Zeitg.* vol. i. p. 57.

Egyptian balance

measures he used once every month, and a retail dealer twice a week; that all weights were to be washed once a week, and the balances wiped every time they had been used. By way of making assurance doubly sure, the seller had to give rather more than an ounce in addition to every ten pounds, if the article consisted of fluids, or half that if of solids (*Baba B.* v. 10, 11). Here are some of the principal ordinances relating to trade.[5] A bargain was not considered closed until both parties had taken possession of their respective properties. But after one of them had received the money, it was deemed dishonourable and sinful for the other to draw back. In case of overcharge, or a larger than the lawful profit, a purchaser had the right of returning the article, or claiming the balance in money, provided he applied for it after an interval not longer than was needful for showing the goods to another merchant or to a relative. Similarly, the seller was also protected. Money-changers were allowed to charge a fixed discount for light money, or to return it within a certain period, if below the weight at which they had taken it. A merchant might not be pressed to name the lowest price, unless the questioner seriously intended to purchase; nor might he be even reminded of a former overcharge to induce him to lower his prices. Goods of different qualities might not be mixed, even though the articles added were of superior value. For the protection of the public, agriculturists were forbidden to sell in Palestine wine diluted with water, unless in places where such was the known usage. Indeed, one of the Rabbis went so far as to blame merchants who gave little presents to children by way of attracting the custom of their parents. It is difficult to imagine what they would have said to the modern practice of giving discount to servants. All agreed in reprobating as deceit every attempt to give a better appearance to an article exposed for sale. Purchases of corn could not be concluded till the general market-price had been fixed.

---

[5] See my *History of the Jewish Nation,* p. 305, etc.

But beyond all this, every kind of speculation was regarded as akin to usury. With the delicacy characteristic of Rabbinical law, creditors were expressly prohibited from using anything belonging to a debtor without paying for it, from sending him on an errand, or even accepting a present from one who had solicited an advance. So punctilious were the Rabbis in avoiding the appearance of usury, that a woman who borrowed a loaf from her neighbour was told to fix its value at the time, lest a sudden rise in flour should make the loaf returned worth more than that borrowed! If a house or a field were rented, a somewhat higher charge might be made, if the money were not paid in advance, but not in the case of a purchase. It was regarded as an improper kind of speculation to promise a merchant one-half of the profit on the sales he effected, or to advance him money and then allow him one-half of the profits on his transactions. In either case, it was thought, a merchant would be exposed to more temptation. By law he was only entitled to a commission and to compensation for his time and trouble.

Do not deprive the alien or the fatherless of justice, or take the cloak of the widow as a pledge (Deut. 24:17).

Equally strict were the regulations affecting debtor and creditor. Advances were legally secured by regular documents, drawn out at the expense of the debtor, and attested by witnesses, about whose signature minute directions are given. To prevent mistakes, the sum lent was marked at the top, as well as in the body of the document. A person was not taken as security for another after the loan was actually contracted. In reference to interest (which among the Romans was calculated monthly), in regard to pledges, and in dealing with insolvent debtors, the mildness of the Jewish law has never been equalled. It was lawful, under certain restrictions, to take a pledge, and in the event of non-payment to sell it: but wearing apparel, bedding, the ploughshare, and all articles required for the preparation of food were excepted. Similarly, it was unlawful, under any circumstances, to take a pledge from a widow, or to sell that which belonged to her. These are only some of the provisions by which the interests of all parties were not only guarded, but a higher religious tone sought to be imparted to ordinary life. Those who are acquainted with the state of matters among the nations around, and the cruel exactions of the Roman law, will best appreciate the difference in this respect also between Israel and the Gentiles. The more the Rabbinical code is studied, the higher will be our admiration of its provisions, characterised as these are by wisdom, kindliness, and delicacy, we venture to say, far beyond any modern legislation. Not only the history of the past, the present privileges, and the hope connected with the promises, but the family, social, and public life which he found among his brethren would attach a Jew to his people. Only one thing was awanting—but that, alas! the "one thing needful." For, in the language of St. Paul (Rom. 10:2), "I bear them record that they have a zeal of God, but not according to knowledge."

13

AMONG THE PEOPLE, AND WITH THE PHARISEES

It would have been difficult to proceed far either in Galilee or in Judaea without coming into contact with an altogether peculiar and striking individuality, differing from all around, and which would at once arrest attention. This was the Pharisee. Courted or feared, shunned or flattered, reverently looked up to or laughed at, he was equally a power everywhere, both ecclesiastically and politically, as belonging to the most influential, the most zealous, and the most closely-connected religious fraternity, which in the pursuit of its objects spared neither time nor trouble, feared no danger, and shrunk from no consequences. Familiar as the name sounds to readers of the New Testament and students of Jewish history, there is no subject on which more crude or inaccurate notions prevail than that of Pharisaism, nor yet any which, rightly understood, gives fuller insight into the state of Judaism at the time of our Lord, or better illustrates His words and His deeds. Let us first view the Pharisee as, himself seemingly unmoved, he moves about among the crowd, which either respectfully gives way or curiously looks after him.

There was probably no town or village inhabited by Jews which had not its Pharisees, although they would, of course, gather in preference about Jerusalem with its Temple, and what, perhaps, would have been even dearer to the heart of a genuine Pharisee—its four hundred and eighty synagogues, its Sanhedrims (great and small), and its schools of study. There could be no difficulty in recognising

Two men went up to the temple to pray, one a Pharisee and the other a tax collector. The Pharisee stood up and prayed about himself: "God, I thank you that I am not like other men—robbers, evildoers, adulterers—or even like this tax collector. I fast twice a week and give a tenth of all I get."

But the tax collector stood at a distance. He would not even look up to heaven, but beat his breast and said, "God, have mercy on me, a sinner" (Luke 18:10–13).

Ruin of Jewish synagogue

such an one. Walking behind him, the chances were, he would soon halt to say his prescribed prayers. If the fixed time for them had come, he would stop short in the middle of the road, perhaps say one section of them, move on, again say another part, and so on, till, whatever else might be doubted, there could be no question of the conspicuousness of his devotions in market-place or corners of streets. There he would stand, as taught by the traditional law, would draw his feet well together, compose his body and clothes, and bend so low "that every vertebra in his back would stand out separate," or, at least, till "the skin over his heart would fall into folds" (*Ber.* 28 *b*). The workman would drop his tools, the burden-bearer his load; if a man had already one foot in the stirrup, he would withdraw it. The hour had come, and nothing could be suffered to interrupt or disturb him. The very salutation of a king, it was said, must remain unreturned; nay, the twisting of a serpent around one's heel must remain unheeded. Nor was it merely the prescribed daily seasons of prayer which so claimed his devotions. On entering a village, and again on leaving it, he must say one or two benedictions; the same in passing through a fortress, in encountering any danger, in meeting with anything new, strange, beautiful, or unexpected. And the longer he prayed the better. In the view of the Rabbis this had a twofold advantage; for "much prayer is sure to be heard," and "prolix prayer prolongeth life." At the same time, as each prayer expressed, and closed with a benediction of the Divine Name, there would be special religious merit attaching to mere number, and a hundred "benedictions" said in one day was a kind of measure of great piety.

But on meeting a Pharisee face to face his identity could still less be doubted. His self-satisfied, or else mock-modest or ostentatiously meek bearing would betray him, even irrespective of his superciliousness towards others, his avoidance of every touch of persons or things which he held unclean, and his extravagant religious displays. We are, of course, speaking of the class, or, rather, the party, as such, and of its tendencies, and not of *all* the individuals who composed it. Besides, there were, as we shall by-and-by see, various degrees among them, from the humblest Pharisee, who was simply a member of the fraternity, only initiated in its lowest degree, or perhaps even a novice, to the most advanced *chasid,* or "pietist." The latter would, for example, bring every day a trespass-offering, in case he had committed some offence of which he was doubtful. How far the punctiliousness of that class, in observing the laws of Levitical purity, would go, may be gathered from a Rabbi, who would not allow his son to remain in the room while he was in the hands of the surgeon, lest he might be defiled by contact with the amputated limb, which, of course, was thenceforth dead. Another *chasid* went so far in his zeal for Sabbath observance, that he would not build up again his house because he had thought about it on the Sabbath; and it was even declared by some improper to intrust a letter to a Gentile, lest he should deliver it on the holy day! These are real, but by no means extreme cases. For, a

Then some Pharisees and teachers of the law came to Jesus from Jerusalem and asked, "Why do your disciples break the tradition of the elders? They don't wash their hands before they eat!" Jesus replied, "And why do you break the command of God for the sake of your tradition?" (Matt. 15:1–3).

Rabbi, contemporary with the apostles, was actually
obliged to denounce, as incompatible with the continuance of society, the vagaries of the so-called
"Chasid Shoteh," or silly pietist. What was meant by
these will appear from such instances as the refusal to
save a woman from drowning for fear of touching
a female, or waiting to put off the phylacteries
before stretching out a hand to rescue a child from
the water!

Readers of the New Testament will remember
that the very dress of the Pharisees differed from that
of others. Simple as the garb of Orientals is, it must
not be thought that, in those days, wealth, rank, and
luxury were not recognisable quite as much, if not
more, than among ourselves. No doubt the polished
Grecian, the courtly Herodian, the wealthy Sadducee,
as well as many of the lady patronesses of the
Pharisees (Jos. *Ant.* 17.32–45), would have been easily
recognised. At any rate, Jewish writings give us such
descriptions of their toilette, that we can almost
transport ourselves among the fashionable society
of Tiberias, Caesarea, Jerusalem, or that of "the
dispersed," who were residents of Alexandria or of
the wealthy towns of Babylonia.

Altogether, it seems, eighteen garments were
supposed to complete an elegant toilette. The material,
the colour, and the cut distinguished the wearer.
While the poor used the upper garment for a covering at night, the fashionable wore the finest white,
embroidered, or even purple garments, with curiously-
wrought silk girdles. It was around this upper
garment that "the borders" were worn which the
Pharisees "enlarged" (Matt. 23:5). Of these we shall
speak presently. Meantime we continue our description. The inner garment went down to the heels. The
head-dress consisted of a pointed cap, or kind of
turban, of more or less exquisite material, and curiously wound, the ends often hanging gracefully
behind. Gloves were generally used only for protection. As for ladies, besides differences in dress, the
early charge of Isaiah (3:16–24) against the daughters
of Jerusalem might have been repeated with tenfold

*...for there was a certain
sect of men that were Jews,
who valued themselves
highly upon the exact skill
they had in the law of their
fathers, and made men
believe they were highly
favored by God, by whom
this set of women were
inveigled. These are those
that are called the sect of
the Pharisees, who were in
a capacity of greatly opposing kings. A cunning sect
they were, and soon elevated
to a pitch of open fighting
and doing mischief (Jos.
Antiquities 17.41).*

*Everything they do is done
for men to see: They make
their phylacteries wide and
the tassels on their garments
long (Matt. 23:5).*

The LORD *says,
"The women of Zion are
    haughty,
walking along with
    outstretched necks,
flirting with their eyes,
tripping along with
    mincing steps,
    with ornaments jingling
    on their ankles"
(Isa. 3:16).*

Veils

emphasis in New Testament times. We read of three
kinds of veils. The Arabian hung down from the
head, leaving the wearer free to see all around; the
veil-dress was a kind of mantilla, thrown gracefully
about the whole person, and covering the head; while
the Egyptian resembled the veil of modern Orientals,
covering breast, neck, chin, and face, and leaving only
the eyes free. The girdle, which was fastened lower
than by men, was often of very costly fabric, and studded
with precious stones. Sandals consisted merely of
soles strapped to the feet; but ladies wore also costly
slippers, sometimes embroidered, or adorned with
gems, and so arranged that the pressure of the foot
emitted a delicate perfume. It is well known that
scents and "ointments" were greatly in vogue, and
often most expensive (Matt. 26:7). The latter were
prepared of oil and of home or foreign perfumes, the
dearest being kept in costly alabaster boxes. The trade
of perfumer was, however, looked down upon, not
only among the Jews, but even among heathen
nations. But in general society anointing was combined with washing, as tending to comfort and
refreshment. The hair, the beard, the forehead, and
the face, even garlands worn at feasts, were anointed.
But luxury went much farther than all this. Some

Beards of various nationalities

Does not the very nature of things teach you that if a man has long hair, it is a disgrace to him (1 Cor. 11:14).

Nose-rings

ladies used cosmetics, painting their cheeks and blackening their eyebrows with a mixture of antimony, zinc, and oil. The hair, which was considered a chief point of beauty, was the object of special care. Young people wore it long; but in men this would have been regarded as a token of effeminacy (1 Cor. 11:14). The beard was carefully trimmed, anointed, and perfumed. Slaves were not allowed to wear beards. Peasant girls tied their hair in a simple knot; but the fashionable Jewesses curled and plaited theirs, adorning the tresses with gold ornaments and pearls. The favourite colour was a kind of auburn, to produce which the hair was either dyed or sprinkled with gold-dust. We read even of false hair (*Shab.* vi. 3), just as false teeth also were worn in Judaea. Indeed, as in this respect also there is nothing new under the sun, we are not astonished to find mention of hair-pins and elegant combs, nor to read that some Jewish dandies had their hair regularly dressed! However, the business of hairdresser was not regarded as very respectable, any more than that of perfumer.[1] As for ornaments, gentlemen generally wore a seal, either on the ring-finger or suspended round the neck. Some of them had also bracelets above the wrist (commonly of the right arm), made of ivory, gold, or precious stones strung together. Of course, the fashionable

---

[1] The learned Lightfoot (*Horae Hebr.* pp. 498 and 1081) has expressed a doubt whether the name "Magdalene" is to be rendered "from Magdala" or "the hairdresser." We have noted in a previous chapter, that the inhabitants of Magdala engaged in such and similar business. But the Rabbinical passages to which Lightfoot refers are not satisfactory, since they are evidently dictated by a special animus against Christ and Christianity.

lady was similarly adorned, adding to the bracelets finger-rings, ankle-rings, nose-rings, ear-rings, gorgeous head-dresses, necklaces, chains, and what are nowadays called "charms." As it may interest some, we shall add a few sentences of description. The earring was either plain, or had a drop, a pendant, or a little bell inserted. The nose-ring, which the traditional law ordered to be put aside on the Sabbath, hung gracefully over the upper lip, yet so as not to interfere with the salute of the privileged friend. Two kinds of necklaces were worn—one close-fitting, the other often consisting of precious stones or pearls, and hanging down over the chest, often as low as the girdle. The fashionable lady would wear two or three such chains, to which smelling-bottles and various ornaments, even heathen "charms," were attached. Gold pendants descended from the head-ornament, which sometimes rose like a tower, or was wreathed in graceful snake-like coils. The anklets were generally so wrought as in walking to make a sound like little bells. Sometimes the two ankle-rings were fastened together, which would oblige the fair wearer to walk with small, mincing steps. If to all this we add gold and diamond pins, and say that our very brief description is strictly based upon contemporary notices, the reader will have some idea of the appearance of fashionable society.[2]

The sketch just given will be of some practical use if it helps us more fully to realise the contrast presented by the appearance of the Pharisee. Whether sternly severe, blandly meek, or zealously earnest, he would carefully avoid all contact with one who was not of the fraternity, or even occupied an inferior degree in it, as we shall by-and-by show. He would also be recognisable by his very garb. For, in the language of our Lord, the Pharisees made "broad their phylacteries," and "enlarged the borders of their garments." The latter observance, at least so far as concerned the wearing of memorial fringes on the borders of the garments—not the conspicuous

The LORD said to Moses, "Speak to the Israelites and say to them: 'Throughout the generations to come you are to make tassels on the corners of your garments, with a blue cord on each tassel' " (Num. 15:37–38).

---

[2] Compare my *History of the Jewish Nation,* pp. 315–318.

Every man who prays or prophesies with his head covered dishonors his head (1 Cor. 11:4).

Fix these words of mine in your hearts and minds; tie them as symbols on your hands and bind them on your foreheads (Deut. 11:18).

Let love and faithfulness never leave you; bind them around your neck, write them on the tablet of your heart (Prov. 3:3).

enlargement of these borders—rested really on a Divine ordinance (Num. 15:37; Deut. 22:12). In Scripture these fringes are prescribed to be of blue, the symbolical colour of the covenant; but the Mishnah allows them also to be white (*Men.* iv. 1). They are not unfrequently referred to in the New Testament (Matt. 9:20; 14:36; 23:5; Mark 6:56; Luke 8:44). As already stated, they were worn on the border of the outer garment—no doubt by every pious Israelite. Later Jewish mysticism found in this fringed border deep references to the manner in which the *Shechinah* enwrapped itself in creation, and called the attention of each Israelite to the fact that, if in Num. 15:39 we read (in the Hebrew), "Ye shall look upon him" [not "it," as in our Authorised Version] "and remember," this change of gender (for the Hebrew word for "fringes" is feminine) indicated—"that, if thou doest so, it is as much as if thou sawest the throne of the Glory, which is like unto blue." And thus believing, the pious Jew would cover in prayer his head with this mysterious fringed garment; in marked contrast to which St. Paul declares all such superstitious practices as dishonouring (1 Cor. 11:4).[3]

If the practice of wearing borders with fringes had Scriptural authority, we are well convinced that no such plea could be urged for the so-called "phylacteries." The observance arose from a literal interpretation of Exod. 13:9, to which even the later injunction in Deut. 6:8 gives no countenance. This appears even from its repetition in Deut. 11:18, where the spiritual meaning and purport of the direction is immediately indicated, and from a comparison with kindred expressions, which evidently could not be taken literally—such as Prov. 3:3; 6:21; 7:3; Cant. 8:6; Isa. 49:16. The very term used by the Rabbis for phylacteries—"tephillin," prayer-fillets—is of com-

---

[3] The practice of modern Jews is somewhat different from that of ancient times. Without entering into details, it is sufficient here to say that they wear underneath their garments a small square, with fringes, called the little tallith (from "talal," to overshadow or cover), or the "arbah canphoth" (four "corners"); while during prayer they wrap themselves in the great tallith, or so-called prayer-cloak.

paratively modern origin, in so far as it does not occur in the Hebrew Old Testament. The Samaritans did not acknowledge them as of Mosaic obligation, any more than do the Karaite Jews, and there is, what seems to us, sufficient evidence, even from Rabbinical writings, that in the time of Christ phylacteries were not universally worn, nor yet by the priests while officiating in the Temple. Although the words of our Lord seem only expressly to condemn the making broad of the phylacteries, for purposes of religious ostentation, it is difficult to believe that He Himself had worn them. At any rate, while any ordinary Israelite would only put them on at prayer or on solemn occasions, the members of the Pharisaic confraternity wore them all day long. The practice itself, and the views and ordinances connected with it, are so characteristic of the party, that we shall add a few further particulars.

Phylacteries for head and arm

The "tephillin" were worn on the left arm, towards the heart, and on the forehead. They consisted —to describe them roughly—of capsules, containing, on parchment (that for the forehead on four distinct parchments), these four passages of Scripture: Exod. 13:1–10; 13:11–16; Deut. 6:4–9; and 11:13–21. The capsules were fastened on by black leather straps, which were wound round the arm and hand (seven times round the former, and three times round the latter), or else fitted to the forehead in a prescribed and mystically significant manner. The wearer of them could not be mistaken. But as for their value and importance in the eyes of the Rabbis, it were impossible to exaggerate it. They were reverenced as highly as the Scriptures, and, like them, might be rescued from the flames on a Sabbath, although not worn, as constituting "a burden!" It was said that Moses had received the law of their observance from God on Mount Sinai; that the "tephillin" were more sacred than the golden plate on the forehead of the high-priest, since its inscription embodied only once the sacred name of Jehovah, while the writing inside the "tephillin" contained it not less than twenty-three times; that the command of wearing them equalled all other commands put together, with many other similar extravagances.[4] How far the profanity of the Rabbis in this respect would go, appears from the circumstance, that they supposed God Himself as wearing phylacteries (*Ber.* 6 *a*). The fact is deduced from Isa. 62:8, where the "right hand" by which Jehovah swears is supposed to refer to the law, according to the last clause of Deut. 33:2; while the expression "strength of His arm" was applied to the "tephillin," since the term "strength" appeared in Ps. 29:11 in connection with God's people, and was in turn explained by a reference to Deut. 28:10. For "the strength" of God's people (Ps. 29:11) is that which would cause all to "be afraid" of Israel (Deut. 28:10); and this latter would be due to their *seeing* that Israel was "called by the name of Jehovah," this ocular demonstration being afforded through the "tephillin." Such was the evidence which traditionalism offered for such a monstrous proposition.

The LORD gives strength to his people; the LORD blesses his people with peace (Ps. 29:11).

Then all the peoples on earth will see that you are called by the name of the LORD, and they will fear you (Deut. 28:10).

The above may serve as a specimen alike of Rabbinical exegesis and theological inferences. It will also help us to understand, how in such a system inconvenient objections, arising from the plain meaning of Scripture, would be summarily set aside by exalting the interpretations of men above the teaching of the Bible. This brings us straight to the charge of our Lord against the Pharisees (Mark 7:13), that they made "the Word of God of none effect" through their "traditions." The fact, terrible as it is, nowhere, perhaps, comes out more strongly than in connection with these very "tephillin." We read in the Mishnah (*Sanh.* xi. 3), literally, as follows: "It is more punishable to act against the words of the Scribes than against those of Scripture. If a man were to say, 'There is no such thing as "tephillin," ' in order thereby

They worship me in vain; their teachings are but rules taught by men. You have let go of the commands of God and are holding on to the traditions of men (Mark 7:7–8).

---

[4] We can recommend nothing better, to those who have heard that the teaching of the New Testament has been derived from that of the Rabbis, than to collate the revolting details on this subject, as well as those connected with prayer, in *Ber.* 23 *a* to 25 *b*; or else to study their interpretations of dreams, or such details as *Ber.* 62 *a, b*. To those who have been told that Hillel might be compared with Jesus, we recommend the perusal of what at times engaged that great Jewish Rabbi's teaching; for example, in *Ber.* 23 *a*.

to act contrary to the words of Scripture, he is not to be treated as a rebel. But if he should say, 'There are five divisions in the prayer-fillets' (instead of four in those for the forehead, as the Rabbis taught), in order to add to the words of the Scribes, he is guilty." Assuredly, a more signal instance could scarcely be found of "teaching for doctrines the commandments of men," and of, even on their own showing, "laying aside the commandment of God," in order to "hold the tradition of men" (Mark 7:7, 8).

Before passing from this subject, it may be convenient to explain the meaning of the Greek term "phylacteries" for these "tephillin," and to illustrate its aptness. It is now almost generally admitted, that the real meaning of phylacteries is equivalent to amulets or charms. And as such the Rabbinists really regarded and treated them, however much they might otherwise have disclaimed all connection with heathen views. In this connection we are not going to enter into the unsavoury subject of their heathen superstitions, such as where to find, how to detect, and by what means to get rid of evil spirits, or how to conjure up demons—as these are indicated in the Talmud. Considering the state of civilisation at the time, and the general prevalence of superstition, we should perhaps have scarcely wondered at all this, had it not been for the claims which the Rabbis set up to Divine authority, and the terrible contrast exhibited between their teaching and that—we will not say of the New, but—of the Old Testament. In reference to the "phylacteries," even the language of Josephus (*Ant.* 4.212–213) savours of belief in their magical efficacy; although in this matter also he is true to himself, showing us, at the same time, that certain proverbial views of gratitude were already in vogue in his time. For, writing of the phylacteries, which, he maintains, the Jews wore in remembrance of their past deliverance, he observes, that this expression of their gratitude "served not only by way of return for past, but also by way of invitation of future favours!" Many instances of the magical ideas attaching to these "amulets" might be quoted; but the following will

They are also to inscribe the principal blessings they have received from God upon their doors, and show the same remembrance of them upon their arms; as also they are to bear on their forehead and their arm those wonders which declare the power of God, and his good will towards them, that God's readiness to bless them may appear everywhere conspicuous about them (Jos. Antiquities 4.213).

"You mean he has deceived you also?" the Pharisees retorted. "Has any of the rulers or of the Pharisees believed in him? No! But this mob that knows nothing of the law—there is a curse on them" (John 7:47–49).

suffice. It is said that, when a certain Rabbi left the audience of some king, he had turned his back upon the monarch. Upon this, the courtiers would have killed the Rabbi, but were deterred by seeing that the straps of his "tephillin" shone like bands of fire about him; thus verifying the promise in Deut. 28:10 (*Jer. Ber.* v. 1). Indeed, we have it expressly stated in an ancient Jewish Targum (that on Cant. 8:3), that the "tephillin" prevented all hostile demons from doing injury to any Israelite.

What has been said will in some measure prepare the reader for investigating the history and influence of the Pharisees at the time of Christ. Let it be borne in mind, that patriotism and religion equally combined to raise them in popular esteem. What made Palestine a land separate and distinct from the heathen nations around, among whom the ruling families would fain have merged them, was that Jewish element which the Pharisees represented. Their very origin as a party stretched back to the great national struggle which had freed the soil of Palestine from Syrian domination. In turn, the Pharisees had deserted those Maccabees whom formerly they had supported, and dared persecution and death, when the descendants of the Maccabees declined into worldly pomp and Grecian ways, and would combine the royal crown of David with the high-priest's mitre. And now, whoever might fear Herod or his family, the Pharisees at least would not compromise their principles. Again, were they not the representatives of the Divine law—not only of that given to Israel on Mount Sinai, but also of those more secret ordinances which were only verbally communicated to Moses, in explanation of, and addition to the law? If they had made "a hedge" around the law, it was only for the safety of Israel, and for their better separation from all that was impure, as well as from the Gentiles. As for themselves, they were bound by vows and obligations of the strictest kind. Their dealings with the world outside their fraternity, their occupations, their practices, their bearing, their very dress and appearance among that motley crowd—either careless, gay, and Grecianising, or self-condemned by a practice in sad discord with their Jewish profession and principles —would gain for them the distinction of uppermost rooms at feasts, and chief seats in the synagogues, and greetings in the markets, and to be called of men, Rabbi, Rabbi ("my great one, my great one"), in which their hearts so much delighted.

In very truth they mostly did represent, in some one or other degree of their order, what of earnestness and religious zeal there was in the land. Their name—probably in the first instance not chosen by themselves—had become to some a byword, to others a party title. And sadly they had declined from their original tendency—at least in most cases. They were not necessarily "scribes," nor "lawyers," nor yet "teachers of the law." Nor were they a sect, in the ordinary sense of the term. But they were a fraternity, which consisted of various degrees, to which there was a regular novitiate, and which was bound by special vows and obligations. This fraternity was, so to speak, hereditary; so that St. Paul could in very truth speak of himself as "a Pharisee of the Pharisees"—"a Pharisee the son of a Pharisee." That their general principles became dominant, and that they gave its distinctiveness alike to the teaching and the practices of the Synagogue, is sufficiently known. But what tremendous influence they must have wielded to attain this position will best appear from the single fact, which has apparently been too much overlooked, of their almost incredibly small numbers. According to Josephus (*Ant.* 17.32–45), the number of the fraternity amounted at the time of Herod only to about six thousand. Yet this inconsiderable minority could cast Judaism in its mould, and for such terrible evil give its final direction to the nation! Surely the springs of such a movement must have reached down to the very heart of Jewish religious life. What these were, and how they affected the whole community, deserves and requires not merely passing notice, but special and careful attention.

Accordingly, when all the people of the Jews gave assurance of their good will to Caesar, and to the king's government, these very men did not swear, being above six thousand; and when the king imposed a fine upon them, Pheroras's wife paid their fine for them (Jos. Antiquities 17.42).

14
THE "FRATERNITY" OF PHARISEES

The next morning the Jews formed a conspiracy and bound themselves with an oath not to eat or drink until they had killed Paul... But when the son of Paul's sister heard of this plot, he went into the barracks and told Paul (Acts 23:12, 16).

To realise the state of religious society at the time of our Lord, the fact that the Pharisees were a regular "order," and that there were many such "fraternities," in great measure the outcome of the original Pharisees, must always be kept in view. For the New Testament simply transports us among contemporary scenes and actors, taking the then existent state of things, so to speak, for granted. But the fact referred to explains many seemingly strange circumstances, and casts fresh light upon all. Thus, if, to choose an illustration, we should wonder how so early as the morning after the long discussion in the Sanhedrim, which must have occupied a considerable part of the day, "more than forty men" should have been found "banded together" under an anathema, neither to eat nor to drink "till they had killed Paul" (Acts 23:12, 21); and, still more, how such "a conspiracy," or rather "conjuration," which, in the nature of it, would be kept a profound secret, should have become known to "Paul's sister's son" (ver. 16), the circumstances of the case furnish a sufficient explanation. The Pharisees were avowedly a "Chabura" —that is, a fraternity or "guild"—and they, or some of their kindred fraternities, would furnish the ready material for such a "band," to whom this additional "vow" would be nothing new nor strange, and, murderous though it sounded, only seem a farther carrying out of the principles of their "order." Again, since the wife and all the children of a "chaber," or member, were *ipso facto* members of the "Chabura," and Paul's father had been a "Pharisee" (ver. 6), Paul's sister also would by virtue of her birth belong to the fraternity, even irrespective of the probability that, in accordance with the principles of the party, she would have married into a Pharisaical family. Nor need we wonder that the rage of the whole "order" against Paul should have gone to an extreme, for which ordinary Jewish zeal would scarcely account. The day before, the excitement of discussion in the Sanhedrim had engrossed their attention, and in a measure diverted it from Paul. The apologetic remark then made (ver. 9), "If a spirit or an angel hath spoken to him, let us not fight against God," coming immediately after the notice (ver. 8) that the Sadducees said, there was "neither angel nor spirit," may indicate, that the Pharisees were quite as anxious for a dogmatic victory over their opponents as to throw the shield of the "fraternity" over one of its professed members. But with the night other and cooler thoughts came. It might be well enough to defend one of their order against the Sadducees, but it was intolerable to have such a member in the fraternity. A grosser outrage on every principle and vow—nay, on the very reason of being of the whole "Chabura"—could scarcely be conceived than the conduct of St. Paul and the views which he avowed. Even regarding him as a simple Israelite, the multitude which thronged the Temple had, on the day before, been only restrained by the heathens from executing the summary vengeance of "death by the rebel's beating." How much truer was it as the deliberate conviction of the party, and not merely the cry of an excited populace, "Away with such a fellow from the earth; for it is not fit that he should live!" But while we thus understand the conduct of the Pharisees, we need be under no apprehension as to the consequences to those "more than forty men" of their rash vow. The Jerusalem Talmud (*Avod. Sar. 40 a*) here furnishes the following curious illustration, which almost reads like a commentary: "If a man makes a vow to abstain from food, Woe to him if he eateth, and, Woe to him if he does not eat! If he eateth, he sinneth against his vow; if he does not

Then Paul, knowing that some of them were Sadducees and the others Pharisees, called out in the Sanhedrin, "My brothers, I am a Pharisee, the son of a Pharisee. I stand on trial because of my hope in the resurrection of the dead" (Acts 23:6).

As they were shouting and throwing off their cloaks and flinging dust into the air, the commander ordered Paul to be taken into the barracks. He directed that he be flogged and questioned in order to find out why the people were shouting at him like this (Acts 22:23–24).

Now make confession to the LORD, the God of your fathers, and do his will. Separate yourselves from the peoples around you and from your foreign wives (Ezra. 10:11).

eat, he sins against his life. What then must he do? Let him go before 'the sages,' and they will absolve him from his vow." In connection with the whole of this matter it is, to say the least, a very curious coincidence that, at the very time when the party so acted against St. Paul, or immediately afterwards, three new enactments should have been passed by Simeon, the son of Gamaliel (Paul's teacher), which would exactly meet the case of St. Paul. The first of these ordained, that in future the children of a "Chaber" should not be necessarily such, but themselves require special and individual reception into the "order;" the second, that the previous conduct of the candidate should be considered before admitting him into the fraternity; while the third enjoined, that any member who had left the "order," or become a publican, should never afterwards be received back again.

Three words of modern significance, with which of late we have all become too familiar, will probably better help us to understand the whole state of matters than more elaborate explanations. They are connected with that ecclesiastical system which in so many respects seems the counterpart of Rabbinism. Ultramontanism is a direction of religious thought; the Ultramontanes are a party; and the Jesuits not only its fullest embodiment, but an "order," which, originating in a revival of the spirit of the Papacy, gave rise to the Ultramontanes as a party, and, in the wider diffusion of their principles, to Ultramontanism as a tendency. Now, all this applies equally to the Pharisees and to Pharisaism. To make the analogy complete, the order of the Jesuits also consists of four degrees[1]—curiously enough, the exact number of those in the fraternity of "the Pharisees!" Like that of the Jesuits, the order of the Pharisees originated in a period of great religious reaction. They themselves delighted in tracing their history up to the time of

---

[1]When speaking of the four degrees in the order of Jesuits, we refer to those which are professed. We are, of course, aware of the existence of the so-called "*professi trium votorum*" of whom nothing definite is really known by the outside world, and whom we may regard as "the secret Jesuits," and of that of lay and clerical "coadjutors," whose services and vows are merely temporary.

Ezra, and there may have been substantial, though not literal truth in their claim. For we read in Ezra 6:21; 9:1; 10:11; and Neh. 9:2 of the "Nivdalim," or those who had "separated" themselves "from the filthiness of the heathen;" while in Neh. 10:29 we find, that they entered into a "solemn league and covenant," with definite vows and obligations. Now, it is quite true that the Aramaean word "Perishuth" also means "separation," and that the "Perushim," or Pharisees, of the Mishnah are, so far as the meaning of the term is concerned, "the separated," or the "Nivdalim" of their period. But although they could thus, not only linguistically but historically, trace their origin to those who had "separated" themselves at the time of Ezra and Nehemiah, they were not their successors in spirit; and the difference between the designations "Nivdalim" and "Perushim" marks also the widest possible internal difference, albeit it may have been gradually brought about in the course of historical development. All this will become immediately more plain.

At the time of Ezra, as already noted, there was a great religious revival among those who had returned to the land of their fathers. The profession which had of old only characterised individuals in Israel (Ps. 30:4; 31:23; 37:28) was now taken up by the covenanted people as a whole: they became the "Chasidim" or "pious" (rendered in the Authorised Version, "saints"). As "Chasidim," they resolved to be "Nivdalim," or "separated from all filthiness of heathenism" around. The one represented, so to speak, the positive; the other, the negative element in their religion. It is deeply interesting to notice, how the former Pharisee (or "separated one"), Paul, had this in view in tracing the Christian life as that of the true "chasid," and therefore "Nivdal"—in opposition to the Pharisees of externalism—in such passages as 2 Cor. 6:14–7:1, closing with this admonition to "cleanse ourselves from all filthiness[2] of the flesh and

...all these now join their brothers the nobles, and bind themselves with a curse and an oath to follow the Law of God given through Moses the servant of God and to obey carefully all the commands, regulations and decrees of the LORD our LORD (Neh. 10:29).

For the LORD loves the just and will not forsake his faithful ones. They will be protected forever, but the offspring of the wicked will be cut off (Ps. 37:28)

---

[2] The Greek word for "filthiness" occurs in this passage only, but the verb from which it is derived seems to have a ceremonial allusion attaching to it in the three passages in which it is used: 1 Cor. 8:7; Rev. 3:4; 14:4.

spirit, perfecting holiness in the fear of God." And so St. Paul's former life and thinking seem ever to have served him as the type of the spiritual realities of his new state.[3]

Therefore come out from them and be separate, says the LORD. *Touch no unclean thing, and I will receive you. I will be a Father to you, and you will be my sons and daughters, says the* LORD *Almighty (2 Cor. 6:17–18).*

Two points in Jewish history here claim our special attention, without attempting to unravel the whole somewhat tangled web of events. The first is the period immediately after Alexander the Great. It was one of the objects of the empire which he founded to Grecianise the world; and that object was fully prosecuted by his successors. Accordingly, we find a circle of Grecian cities creeping up along the coast, from Anthedon and Gaza in the south, northwards to Tyre and Seleucia, and eastwards to Damascus, Gadara, Pella, and Philadelphia, wholly belting the land of Israel. Thence the movement advanced into the interior, taking foothold in Galilee and Samaria, and gathering a party with increasing influence and spreading numbers among the people. Now it was under these circumstances, that the "Chasidim" as a party stood out to stem the torrent, which threatened to overwhelm alike the religion and the nationality of Israel. The actual contest soon came, and with it the second grand period in the history of Judaism. Alexander the Great had died in July 323 B.C. About a century and a half later, the "Chasidim" had gathered round the Maccabees for Israel's God and for Israel. But the zeal of the Maccabees soon gave place to worldly ambition and projects. When these leaders united in their person the high-priestly with the royal dignity, the party of the "Chasidim" not only deserted them, but went into open opposition. They called on them to resign the high-priesthood, and were ready to suffer martyrdom, as many of them did, for their outspoken convictions. Thenceforth the "Chasidim" of the early type disappear as a class. They had, as a party, already given place to the

---

[3] If St. Paul was originally a Pharisee, the accounts given by the earliest tradition (Euseb. *H. E.* ii. 23), compared with that of Josephus (*Ant.* 20.197–203), would almost lead us to infer that St. James was a "Chasid." All the more significant would then be the part he took in removing the yoke of the law from the Gentile converts (Acts 15:13–21).

Alexander the Great mosaic

Pharisees—the modern "Nivdalim;" and when we meet them again they are only a higher order or branch of the Pharisees—"the pious" of old having, so to speak, become "pietists." Tradition (*Men.* 40) expressly distinguishes "the early Chasidim" (harishonim) from "the later" (acheronim). No doubt, those are some of their principles, although tinged with later colouring, which are handed down as the characteristics of the "chasid" in such sayings of the Mishnah as: "What is mine is thine, and what is thine

At this time there were three sects among the Jews, who had different opinions concerning human actions; the one was called the sect of the Pharisees, another the sect of the Sadducees, and the other the sect of the Essenes (Jos. Antiquities 13.171).

remains thine as well" (*P. Ab. V.* 10); "Hard to make angry, but easy to reconcile" (11); "Giving alms, and inducing others to do likewise" (13); "Going to the house of learning, and at the same time doing good works" (14).

The earliest mention of the Pharisees occurs at the time of the Maccabees. As a "fraternity" we meet them first under the rule of John Hyrcanus, the fourth of the Maccabees from Mattathias (135–105 B.C.); although Josephus speaks of them already two reigns earlier, at the time of Jonathan (*Ant.* 13.171–173). He may have done so by anticipation, or applying later terms to earlier circumstances, since there can be little doubt that the Essenes, whom he names at the same time, had not then any corporate existence. Without questioning that, to use a modern term, "the direction" existed at the time of Jonathan,[4] we can put our finger on a definite event with which the origin of "the fraternity" of the Pharisees is connected. From Jewish writings we learn, that at the time of Hyrcanus a commission was appointed to inquire throughout the land, how the Divine law of religious contributions was observed by the people.[5] The result showed that, while the "therumah,"[6] or priestly "heave-offerings," was regularly given, neither the first or Levitical tithe, nor yet the so-called "second" or "poor's tithe," was paid, as the law enjoined. But such transgression involved mortal sin, since it implied the personal use of what really belonged to the Lord. Then it was that the following arrangements were made. All that the "country people" (*'am ha-aretz*) sold was to be considered "demai"—a word derived from the Greek for "people," and so betraying the time of its introduction, but really implying that it was "doubtful" whether or nor it had been tithed.

---

[4] In proof of this, it may be stated that before the formal institution of the "order," R. Jose, the son of Joezer, declared all foreign glass vessels, and indeed the whole soil of heathen lands, "unclean," thus "separating" Israel from all possible intercourse with Gentiles.

[5] It may be to the decrees then enacted by Hyrcanus that Josephus refers (*Ant.* 13.293–298), when he speaks of their "abolition" after Hyrcanus broke with the Pharisaical party.

[6] I cannot here enter into explanations of the therumah, but must refer the reader to my book on *The Temple and its Service*.

In such cases the buyer had to regard the "therumah," and the "poor's tithe" as still due on what he had purchased. On the other hand, the Pharisees formed a "Chabura," or fraternity, of which each member— "Chaber," or "companion"—bound himself to pay these tithes before use or sale. Each "Chaber" was regarded as "neeman," or "credited"—his produce being freely bought and sold by the rest of the "Chaberim."[7] Of course, the burden of additional expense which this involved to each non-"chaber" was very great, since he had to pay "therumah" and tithe on all that he purchased or used, while the Pharisee who bought from another Pharisee was free. One cannot help suspecting that this, in connection with kindred enactments, which bore very hard upon the mass of the people, while they left "the Pharisee" untouched, may underlie the charge of our Lord (Matt. 23:4): "They bind heavy burdens and grievous to be borne, and lay them on men's shoulders; but they themselves will not move them with one of their fingers."

The rich are not to give more than a half shekel and the poor are not to give less when you make the offering to the LORD to atone for your lives (Exod. 30:15).

But the rigorous discharge of tithes was only one part of the obligations of a "Chaber." The other part consisted in an equally rigorous submission to all the laws of Levitical purity as then understood. Indeed, the varied questions as to what was, or what made "clean," divided the one "order" of Pharisees into members of various degrees. Four such degrees, according to increasing strictness in "making clean," are mentioned. It would take too long to explain this fourfold gradation in its details. Suffice it, that, generally speaking, a member of the first degree was called a "Chaber," or "Ben hacheneseth," "son of the

---

[7] It is with very great reluctance that I dissent from such an authority as Canon Lightfoot. But I cannot regard the reference to *Niddah*, 33 *b*, in his admirable essay on the Essenes (*Commentary on the Epistle to the Colossians*, p. 130), as conclusive of the fact that a Sadducee and even a Samaritan might be a "Chaber." Of course, there is a general application of the term "Chaber" to any kind of association. But the whole passage *Niddah*, 33 *b*, originating in a prandial discussion on which R. Papah is very reluctant to enter, shows that neither the term "Samaritan" nor yet that of "Chaber" can be pressed in its primary meaning. If anything, the statement that, under given circumstances, "all Israel are to be regarded as *Chaberim*," would be decisive, that strict historical value must not be attached to the expressions of Rabbi Papah.

Woe to you, teachers of the law and Pharisees, you hypocrites! You clean the outside of the cup and dish, but inside they are full of greed and self-indulgence. Blind Pharisee! First clean the inside of the cup and dish, and then the outside also will be clean (Matt. 23:25–26).

He that undertakes to be an Associate may not sell to an Am-haaretz [foodstuff that is] wet or dry, or buy from him [foodstuff that is] wet; and he may not be the guest of an Am-haaretz nor may he receive him as a guest in his own raiment (Mishnah, Demai ii. 3).

union"—an ordinary Pharisee; while the other three degrees were ranked together under the generic name of "Teharoth" (purifications). These latter were probably the "Chasidim" of the later period. The "Chaber," or ordinary Pharisee, only bound himself to tithing and avoidance of all Levitical uncleanness. The higher degrees, on the other hand, took increasingly strict vows. Any one might enter "the order" if he took, before three members, the solemn vow of observing the obligations of the fraternity. A novitiate of a year (which was afterwards shortened) was, however, necessary. The wife or widow of a "Chaber," and his children, were regarded as members of the fraternity. Those who entered the family of a "Pharisee" had also to seek admission into the "order." The general obligations of a "Chaber" towards those that were "without" the fraternity were as follows. He was neither to buy from, nor to sell to him anything, either in a dry or fluid state; he was neither to eat at his table (as he might thus partake of what had not been tithed), nor to admit him to his table, unless he had put on the garments of a "Chaber" (as his own old ones might else have carried defilement); nor to go into any burying-place; nor to give "therumah" or tithes to any priest who was not a member of the fraternity; nor to do anything in presence of an "am ha-aretz," or non-"Chaber," which brought up points connected with the laws of purification, etc. To these, other ordinances, partly of an ascetic character, were added at a later period. But what is specially remarkable is that not only was a novitiate required for the higher grades, similar to that on first entering the order; but that, just as the garment of a non-"chaber" defiled a "Chaber" of the first degree, that of the latter equally defiled him of the second degree, and so on.[8]

To sum up then: the fraternity of the Pharisees were bound by these two vows—that of tithing and that in regard to purifications. As the most varied

[8]It is impossible here to reproduce the Talmudical passages in evidence. But the two obligations of "making clean" and of "tithing," together with the arrangement of the Pharisees into various grades, are even referred to in the Mishnah (*Chag.* ii. 5, 6, and *Demai* ii. 2, 3).

Mount Sinai and adjacent valleys

questions would here arise in practice, which certainly were not answered in the law of Moses, the "traditions," which were supposed to explain and supplement the Divine law, became necessary. In point of fact, the Rabbis speak of them in that sense, and describe them as "a hedge" around Israel and its law. That these traditions should have been traced up to oral communications made to Moses on Mount Sinai, and also deduced by ingenious methods from the letter of Scripture, was only a further necessity of the case. The result was a system of pure externalism, which often contravened the spirit of those very ordinances, the letter of which was slavishly worshipped. To what arrant hypocrisy it often gave rise, appears from Rabbinical writings almost as much as from the New Testament. We can understand how those "blind guides" would often be as great a trouble to their own party as to others. "The plague of

Woe to you, teachers of the law and Pharisees, you hypocrites! You give a tenth of your spices—mint, dill and cummin. But you have neglected the more important matters of the law—justice, mercy and faithfulness. You should have practiced the latter, without neglecting the former (Matt. 23:23).

Pharisaism" was not an uncommon expression; and this religious sore is ranked with "a silly pietist, a cunning sinner, and a woman Pharisee," as constituting "the troubles of life" (*Sot.* iii. 4). "Shall we stop to explain the opinions of Pharisees?" asks a Rabbi, in supreme contempt for "the order" as such. "It is as a tradition among the Pharisees," we read (*Ab. de R. Nathan,* 5), "to torment themselves in this world, and yet they will not get anything in the next." It was suggested by the Sadducees, that "the Pharisees would by-and-by subject the globe of the sun itself to their purifications." On the other hand, almost Epicurean sentences are quoted among their utterances, such as, "Make haste, eat and drink, for the world in which we are is like a wedding feast;" "If thou possessest anything, make good cheer of it; for there is no pleasure underneath the sod, and death gives no respite…Men are like the flowers of the field; some flourish, while others fade away."

"Like the flowers of the field!" What far other teaching of another Rabbi, Whom these rejected with scorn, do the words recall! And when from their words we turn to the kingdom which He came to found, we can quite understand the essential antagonism of nature between the two. Assuredly, it has been a bold stretch of assertion to connect in any way the origin or characteristics of Christianity with the Rabbis. Yet, when we bring the picture of Pharisaism, as drawn in Rabbinical writings, side by side with the sketch of it given by our Lord, we are struck not only with the life-likeness, but with the selection of the distinctive features of Pharisaism presented in His reproofs. Indeed, we might almost index the history of Pharisaism by passages from the New Testament. The "tithing of mint and anise," to the neglect of the weightier matters of the law, and "the cleansing" of the outside—these twofold obligations of the Pharisees, "hedged around," as they were, by a traditionalism which made void the spirit of the law, and which manifested itself in gross hypocrisy and religious boasting—are they not what we have just traced in the history of "the order?"

15

RELATION OF THE PHARISEES TO THE SADDUCEES AND ESSENES, AND TO THE GOSPEL OF CHRIST

On taking a retrospective view of Pharisaism, as we have described it, there is a saying of our Lord which at first sight seems almost unaccountable. Yet it is clear and emphatic. "All therefore whatsoever they bid you observe, that observe and do" (Matt. 23:3). But if the early disciples were not to break at once and for ever with the Jewish community, such a direction was absolutely needful. For, though the Pharisees were only "an order," Pharisaism, like modern Ultramontanism, had not only become the leading direction of theological thought, but its principles were solemnly proclaimed, and universally acted upon—and the latter, even by their opponents the Sadducees. A Sadducee in the Temple or on the seat of judgment would be obliged to act and decide precisely like a Pharisee. Not that the party had not attempted to give dominance to their peculiar views. But they were fairly vanquished, and it is said that they themselves destroyed the book of Sadducean ordinances, which they had at one time drawn up. And the Pharisees celebrated each dogmatic victory by a feast! What is perhaps the oldest post-Biblical Hebrew book—the "Megillath Taanith," or roll of fasts —is chiefly a Pharisaic calendar of self-glorification, in which dogmatic victories are made days when fasting, and sometimes even mourning, is prohibited. Whatever, therefore, the dogmatic views of the Sadducees were, and however they might, where possible, indulge personal bias, yet in office both parties acted as Pharisees. They were well matched

So you must obey them and do everything they tell you. But do not do what they do, for they do not practice what they preach (Matt. 23:3).

The LORD said to Moses, "Say to the Israelites: 'On the fifteenth day of the seventh month the LORD's Feast of Tabernacles begins, and it lasts for seven days' " (Lev. 23:33–34).

The LORD said to Moses, "Speak to the Israelites and say to them: 'When you enter the land I am going to give you and you reap its harvest, bring to the priest a sheaf of the first grain you harvest' " (Lev. 23:9–10).

indeed. When a Sadducean high-priest, on the Feast of Tabernacles, poured out the water on the ground instead of into the silver funnel of the altar, Maccabean king though he was, he scarce escaped with his life, and ever afterwards the shout resounded from all parts of the Temple, "Hold up thy hand," as the priest yearly performed this part of the service. The Sadducees held, that on the Day of Atonement the high-priest should light the incense before he actually entered the Most Holy Place. As this was contrary to the views of the Pharisees, they took care to bind him by an oath to observe their ritual customs before allowing him to officiate at all. It was in vain that the Sadducees argued, that the daily sacrifices should not be defrayed from the public treasury, but from special contributions. They had to submit, and besides to join in the kind of half-holiday which the jubilant majority inscribed in their calendar to perpetuate the memory of the decision. The Pharisees held, that the time between Easter and Pentecost should be counted from the second day of the feast; the Sadducees insisted that it should commence with the literal "Sabbath" after the festive day.[1] But, despite argument, the Sadducees had to join when the solemn procession went on the afternoon of the feast to cut down the "first sheaf," and to reckon Pentecost as did their opponents.

We have here referred to only a few of the differences in ritual between the views of the Sadducees and those of the Pharisees. The essential principle of them lay in this, that the Sadducees would hold by the simple letter of the law—do neither more nor less, whether the consequences were to make decisions more severe or more easy. The same principle they applied in their juridical and also in their doctrinal views. It would take us too much into detail to explain the former. But the reader will understand how this literality would, as a rule, make their judicial decisions (or rather such as they had proposed) far

---

[1] I would here refer the reader who wishes further details to the accounts of the feasts and services in the Temple, given in my volume on *The Temple*.

more strict than those of the Pharisees, by a rigidly literal application of the principle, "an eye for an eye; a tooth for a tooth." The same holds true in regard to the laws of purification, and to those which regulated inheritance. The doctrinal views of the Sadducees are sufficiently known from the New Testament. It is quite true that, in opposition to Sadducean views as to the non-existence of another world and the resurrection, the Pharisees altered the former Temple-formula into "Blessed be God from world to world" (from generation to generation; or, "world without end"), to show that after the present there was another life of blessing and punishment, of joy and sorrow. But the Talmud expressly states that the real principle of the Sadducees was not, that there was no resurrection, but only that it could not be proved from the Thorah, or Law. From this there was, of course, but a short step to the entire denial of the doctrine; and no doubt it was taken by the vast majority of the party. But here also it was again their principle of strict literality, which underlay even the most extreme of their errors.

"How is it you don't understand that I was not talking to you about bread? But be on your guard against the yeast of the Pharisees and Sadducees." Then they understood that he was not telling them to guard against the yeast used in bread, but against the teaching of the Pharisees and Sadducees (Matt. 16:11–12).

This principle was indeed absolutely necessary to their very existence. We have traced the Pharisees not only to a definite period, but to a special event; and we have been able perfectly to explain their name as "the separated." Not that we presume they gave it to themselves, for no sect or party ever takes a name; they all pretend to require no distinctive title, because they alone genuinely and faithfully represent the truth itself. But when they were called Pharisees, the "Chaberim," no doubt, took kindly to the popular designation. It was to them—to use an illustration—what the name "Puritans" was to a far different and opposite party in the Church. But the name "Sadducee" is involved in quite as much obscurity as the origin of the party. Let us try to cast some fresh light upon both—only premising that the common derivations of their name, whether from the high-priest Zadok, or from a Rabbi called Zadok, whose fundamental principle of not seeking reward in religion they were thought to have misunderstood

And if we are careful to
obey all this law before the
LORD our God, as he has
commanded us, that will
be our righteousness
(Deut. 6:25).

and misapplied, or from the Hebrew word "zaddikim"
—the righteous—are all unsatisfactory, and yet may
all contain elements of truth.

There can be no question that the "sect" of the
Sadducees originated in a reaction against the
Pharisees. If the latter added to the law their own
glosses, interpretations, and traditions, the Sadducee
took his stand upon the bare letter of the law. He
would have none of their additions and superer-
ogations; he would not be righteous overmuch.
Suffice it for him to have to practise "zedakah,"
"righteousness." We can understand how this
shibboleth of theirs became, in the mouth of the people,
the byname of a party—some using it ironically,
some approvingly. By-and-by the party no doubt
took as kindly to the name as the Pharisees did to
theirs. Thus far, then, we agree with those who derive
the title of Sadducees from "zaddikim." But why
the grammatically-unaccountable change from
"zaddikim" to "zaddukim?" May it not be that the
simple but significant alteration of a letter had, after a
not uncommon fashion, originated with their opponents, as if they would have said: "You are 'zaddikim?'
Nay, rather, 'zaddukim' " from the Aramaean word
"zadu" (wasting or desolation)—meaning, you are
not upholders but destroyers of righteousness? This
origin of the name would in no way be inconsistent
with the later attempts of the party to trace up their
history either to the high-priest Zadok, or to one of
the fathers of Jewish traditionalism, whose motto
they ostentatiously adopted. History records not a
few similar instances of attempts to trace up the origin
of a religious party. Be this as it may, we can understand how the adherents of Saducean opinions
belonged chiefly to the rich, luxurious, and aristocratic party, including the wealthy families of priests;
while, according to the testimony of Josephus, which
is corroborated by the New Testament, the mass of
the people, and especially the women, venerated and
supported the Pharisaical party. Thus the "order" of
the "Chaberim" gradually became a popular party,
like the Ultramontanes. Finally, as from the nature of

it Pharisaism was dependent upon traditional lore, it became not only the prevailing direction of Jewish theological study, but the "Chaber" by-and-by merged into the Rabbi, the "sage," or "disciple of the sages;" while the non-"chaber," or "am ha-aretz," became the designation for ignorance of traditional lore, and neglect of its ordinances. This was specially the case when the dissolution of the Jewish commonwealth rendered the obligations of the "fraternity" necessarily impossible. Under such altered circumstances the old historical Pharisee would often be no small plague to the leaders of the party, as is frequently the case with the original adherents and sticklers of a sect in which the irresistible progress of time has necessarily produced changes.

Now for the Pharisees, they say that some actions, but not all, are the work of fate, and some of them are in our own power, and that they are liable to fate, but are not caused by fate. But the sect of the Essenes affirm, that fate governs all things, and that nothing befalls men but what is according to its determination (Jos. Antiquities 13.172).

The course of our investigations has shown, that neither Pharisees nor Sadducees were a sect, in the sense of separating from Temple or Synagogue; and also that the Jewish people as such were not divided between Pharisees and Sadducees. The small number of professed Pharisees (six thousand) at the time of Herod, the representations of the New Testament, and even the curious circumstance that Philo never once mentions the name of Pharisee, confirm the result of our historical inquiries, that the Pharisees were first an "order," then gave the name to a party, and finally represented a direction of theological thought. The New Testament speaks of no other than these two parties. But Josephus and Philo also mention the "Essenes." It is beyond our present scope either to describe their tenets and practices, or even to discuss the complex question of the origin of their name. From the nature of it, the party exercised no great influence, and was but short-lived. They seem to have combined a kind of higher grade Pharisaism with devotional views, and even practices, derived from Eastern mysticism, and more particularly from the Medo-Persian religion. Of the former, the fact that the one object of all their institutions was a higher purity, may here be regarded as sufficient evidence. The latter is apparent from a careful study of their views, as these have been preserved to us, and from

These Essenes reject plea-sures as an evil, but esteem continence, and the con-quest over our passions, to be virtue. They neglect wedlock, but choose out other persons' children, while the are pliable, and fit for learning; and esteem them to be of their kindred, and form them according to their own manners (Jos. Jewish War 2.120).

their comparison with the Zoroastrian system. And of the fact that "Palestine was surrounded by Persian influences," there are abundant indications.[2]

As a sect the Essenes never attained a larger number than four thousand; and as they lived apart from the rest, neither mingling in their society nor in their worship, and—as a general rule—abstained from marriage, they soon became extinct. Indeed, Rabbinical writings allude to quite a number of what may probably be described as sectaries, all of them more or less distinctly belonging to the mystical and ascetic branch of Pharisaism. We here name, first, the "Vathikin," or "strong ones," who performed their prayers with the first dawn; secondly, the "Toble Shachrith," or "morning baptists," who immersed before morning prayer, so as to utter the Divine Name only in a state of purity; thirdly, the "Kehala Kadisha," or "holy congregation," who spent a third of the day in prayer, a third in study, and a third in labour; fourthly, the "Banaim," or "builders," who, besides aiming after highest purity, occupied them-selves with mystical studies about God and the world; fifthly, the "Zenuim," or "secret pious," who besides kept their views and writings secret; sixthly, the "Nekije hadaath," "men of a pure mind," who were really separatists from their brethren; seventhly, the "Chashaim," or "mysterious ones;" and lastly, the "Assiim," "helpers" or "healers," who professed to possess the right pronunciation of the sacred Name of Jehovah, with all that this implied.[3]

---

[2]Canon Lightfoot, *Comm. on Coloss.* p. 151. The masterly discussion of Professor Lightfoot on the Essenes, so full of most solid learning, and so calm in its judicial summing up, may be said to have almost opened a new era in the study of the sect of the Essenes, taking it beyond often wild speculation into the domain of historical investigation. It is not within the scope of this book either to discuss in a scientific manner the distinctive doctrinal views of the Pharisees and Sadducees, or to enter on those of the Essenes. This must be reserved for another occasion. But in view of Professor Lightfoot's results I may be allowed to refer, not without sat-isfaction, to the circumstance that I had arrived at conclusions somewhat similar to his in my *History of the Jewish Nation.* See my treatment of the Essenes and abstract of the *Kabbalah,* pp. 433–461.

[3]Compare Hamburger *Real-Enc. für Bibel u. Talmud,* vol. ii. p. 173. Hegesippus (in Eus. *H. E.* ii.) speaks of seven Hebrew sects; but his information is evidently second-hand.

If in any of the towns of Judaea one had met the strange apparition of a man dressed wholly in white, whose sandals and garments perhaps bore signs of age—for they might not be put away till quite worn out—but who was scrupulously clean, this man was an Essene. The passers would stop short and look after him with mingled reverence and curiosity. For he was but rarely seen in town or village—the community separating from the rest of the people, and inhabiting desert places, specially the neighbourhood of the Dead Sea; and the character of the "order" for asceticism and self-denial, as well as for purity, was universally known. However strictly they observed the Sabbath, it was in their own synagogues; and although they sent gifts to the altar, they attended not the Temple nor offered sacrifices, partly because they regarded their arrangements as not sufficiently Levitically clean, and partly because they came to consider their own table an altar, and their common meals a sacrifice. They formed an "order," bound by the strictest vows, taken under terrible oaths, and subject to the most rigorous discipline. The members abstained from wine, meat, and oil, and most of them also from marriage. They had community of goods; were bound to poverty, chastity, and obedience to their superiors. Purity of morals was enjoined, especially in regard to speaking the truth. To take an oath was prohibited, as also the keeping of slaves. The order consisted of four grades; contact with one of a lower always defiling him of the higher grade. The novitiate lasted two years, though at the end of the first the candidate was taken into closer fellowship. The rule was in the hands of "elders," who had the power of admission and expulsion—the latter being almost equivalent to death by starvation, as the Essene had bound himself by a terrible oath not to associate with others. Their day began with sunrise, when they went to prayer. Before that, nothing secular might be spoken. After prayer, they betook themselves to agricultural labour—for they were not allowed to keep herds and flocks—or else to works of charity, specially the healing of the sick. At eleven

They [the Essenes] think that oil is a defilement; and if any one of them be anointed without his own approbation, it is wiped off his body; for they think to be sweaty is a good thing, as they do also to be clothed in white garments. They also have stewards appointed to take care of their common affairs, who every one of them have no separate business for any, but what is for the use of them all (Jos. Jewish War 2.123).

o'clock they bathed, changed their dress, and then gathered for the common meal. A priest opened and closed it with prayer. They sat according to age and dignity; the eldest engaging in serious conversation, but in so quiet a tone as not to be heard outside. The young men served. Each had bread and salt handed him, also another dish; the elders being allowed the condiment of hyssop and the luxury of warm water. After the meal they put off their clothes, and returned to work till the evening, when there was another common meal, followed by mystical hymns and dances, to symbolise the rapt, ecstatic state of mind.

It is needless to follow the subject farther. Even what has been said—irrespective of their separation from the world, their punctilious Sabbath-observance, and views on purification; their opposition to sacrifices, and notably their rejection of the doctrine of the resurrection—is surely sufficient to prove that they had no connection with the origin of Christianity. Assertions of this kind are equally astonishing to the calm historical student and painful to the Christian. Yet there can be no doubt that among these mystical sects were preserved views of the Divine Being, of the Messiah and His kingdom, and of kindred doctrines, which afterwards appeared in the so-called "secret tradition" of the Synagogue, and which, as derived from the study of the prophetic writings, contain marvellous echoes of Christian truth. On this point, however, we may not here enter.

Christ and the Gospel among Pharisees, Sadducees, and Essenes! We can now realise the scene, and understand the mutual relations. The existing communities, the religious tendencies, the spirit of the age, assuredly offered no point of attachment— only absolute and essential contrariety to the kingdom of heaven. The "preparer of the way" could appeal to neither of them; his voice only cried "in the wilderness." Far, far beyond the origin of Pharisees, Sadducees, and Essenes, he had to point back to the original Paschal consecration of Israel as that which was to be now exhibited in its reality: "Behold the Lamb of God, which taketh away the sin of the

The doctrine of the Essenes is this: That all things are best ascribed to God. They teach the immortality of souls, and esteem that the rewards of righteousness are to be earnestly striven for; and when they send what they have dedicated to God into the temple, they do not offer sacrifices, because they have more pure lustrations of their own; on which account they are excluded from the common court of the temple, but offer their sacrifices themselves; yet is their course of life better than that of other men; and they entirely addict themselves to husbandry (Jos. Antiquities 18.18–19).

He grew up before him like a tender shoot,
and like a root out of dry ground.
He had no beauty or majesty to attract us to him,
nothing in his appearance that we should desire him.
He was despised and rejected by men,
a man of sorrows, and familiar with suffering.
Like one from whom men hide their faces
he was despised, and we esteemed him not (Isa. 53:2–3).

world." If the first great miracle of Christianity was the breaking down of the middle wall of partition, the second—perhaps we should have rather put it first, to realise the symbolism of the two miracles in Cana— was that it found nothing analogous in the religious communities around, nothing sympathetic, absolutely no stem on which to graft the new plant, but was literally "as a root out of a dry ground," of which alike Pharisee, Sadducee, and Essene would say: "He hath no form nor comeliness; and when we shall see Him, there is no beauty that we should desire Him."

16
SYNAGOGUES: THEIR ORIGIN, STRUCTURE, AND OUTWARD ARRANGEMENTS

Ancient synagogue at Capernaum

It was a beautiful saying of Rabbi Jochanan (*Jer. Ber.* v. 1), that he who prays in his house surrounds and fortifies it, so to speak, with a wall of iron. Nevertheless, it seems immediately contradicted by what follows. For it is explained that this only holds good where a man is alone, but that where there is a community prayer should be offered in the synagogue. We can readily understand how, after the destruction of the Temple, and the cessation of its symbolical worship, the excessive value attached to mere attendance at the synagogue would rapidly grow in public estimation, till it exceeded all bounds of moderation or reason. Thus, such Scriptural sayings as Isa. 66:20; 55:6, and Ps. 82:1 were applied to it. The Babylon Talmud goes even farther. There we are told (*Ber.* 6 *a*), that the prayer which a man addresses to God has only its proper effect if offered in the synagogue; that if an individual, accustomed to frequent every day the synagogue, misses it for once, God will demand an account of him; that if the Eternal finds fewer than ten persons there gathered, His anger is kindled, as it is written in Isa. 50:2 (*Ber.* 6 *b*); that if a person has a synagogue in his own town, and does not enter it for prayer, he is to be called an evil neighbour, and provokes exile alike upon himself and his children, as it is written in Jer. 12:4; while, on the other hand, the practice of early resorting to the synagogue would account for the longevity of people (*Ber.* 8 *a*). Putting aside these extravagances, there cannot, however, be doubt that, long before the Talmudical period, the institution of synagogues had spread, not only among the Palestinian, but among the Jews of the dispersion, and that it was felt a growing necessity, alike from internal and external causes.

Readers of the New Testament know, that at the time of our Lord synagogues were dotted all over the land; that in them "from of old" Moses had been read (Acts 15:21); that they were under the rule of certain authorities, who also exercised discipline; that the services were definitely regulated, although considerable liberty obtained, and that part of them consisted in reading the prophets, which was generally followed by an "exhortation" (Acts 13:15) or an address (Luke 4:17). The word "synagogue" is, of course, of Greek derivation, and means "gathering together"—for religious purposes. The corresponding Rabbinical terms, "chenisah," "cheneseth," etc., "zibbur," "vaad," and "kahal," may be generally characterised as equivalents. But it is interesting to notice, that both the Old Testament and the Rabbis have shades of distinction, well known in modern theological discussions. To begin with the former. Two terms are used for Israel

"And they will bring all your brothers, from all the nations, to my holy mountain in Jerusalem as an offering to the LORD—on horses, in chariots and wagons, and on mules and camels," says the LORD. "They will bring them, as the Israelites bring their grain offerings, to the temple of the LORD in ceremonially clean vessels" (Isa. 66:20).

When I came, why was there no one? When I called, why was there no one to answer? Was my arm too short to ransom you? Do I lack the strength to rescue you? By a mere rebuke I dry up the sea, I turn rivers into a desert; their fish rot for lack of water and die of thirst (Isa. 50:2).

For Moses has been preached in every city from the earliest times and is read in the synagogues on every Sabbath (Acts 15:21).

They said in their hearts, "We will crush them completely!" They burned every place where God was worshiped in the land (Ps. 74:8).

as a congregation: "edah" and "kahal;" of which the former seems to refer to Israel chiefly in their outward organisation as a congregation—what moderns would call the visible Church—while "kahal" rather indicates their inner or spiritual connection. Even the LXX. seem to have seen this distinction. The word "edah" occurs one hundred and thirty times, and is always rendered in the LXX. by "synagogue," never by "ecclesia" (church); while "kahal" is translated in seventy places by "ecclesia," and only in thirty-seven by "synagogue." Similarly, the Mishnah employs the term "kahal" only to denote Israel as a whole; while the term "zibbur," for example, is used alike for churches and for the Church—that is, for individual congregations, and for Israel as a whole.

The origin of the synagogue is lost in the obscurity of tradition. Of course, like so many other institutions, it is traced by the Rabbis to the patriarchs. Thus, both the Targum Jonathan and the Jerusalem Targum represent Jacob as an attendant in the synagogue, and Rebekah as resorting thither for advice when feeling within her the unnatural contest of her two sons. There can be no occasion for seriously discussing such statements. For when in 2 Kings 22:8 we read that "the book of the law" was discovered by Shaphan the scribe in "the house of the Lord," this implies that during the reign of King Josiah there could have been no synagogues in the land, since it was their main object to secure the weekly reading, and of course the preservation, of the books of Moses (Acts 15:21). Our Authorised Version, indeed, renders Ps. 74:8, "They have burned up all the synagogues of God in the land." But there is good authority for questioning this translation; and, even if admitted, it would not settle the question of the exact time when synagogues originated. On the other hand, there is not a hint of synagogue-worship either in the law or the prophets; and this of itself would be decisive, considering the importance of the subject. Besides, it may be said that there was no room for such meetings under the Old Testament dispensation. There the whole worship was typical—the sacrificial services alike constituting the manner in which Israel approached unto God, and being the way by which He communicated blessings to His people. Gatherings for prayer and for fellowship with the Father belong, so far as the Church as a whole is concerned, to the dispensation of the Holy Spirit. It is quite in accordance with this general principle, that when men filled with the Spirit of God were raised up from time to time, those who longed for deeper knowledge and closer converse with the Lord should have gathered around them on Sabbaths and new moons, as the pious Shunammite resorted to Elisha (2 Kings 4:23), and as others were no doubt wont to do, if within reach of "prophets" or their disciples. But quite a different state of matters ensued during the Babylonish captivity. Deprived of the Temple services, some kind of religious meetings would become an absolute necessity, if the people were not to lapse into practical heathenism—a danger, indeed, which, despite the admonitions of the prophets, and the prospect of deliverance held out, was not quite avoided. For the preservation, also, of the national bond which connected Israel, as well as for their continued religious existence, the institution of synagogues seemed alike needful and desirable. In point of fact, the attentive reader of the books of Ezra and Nehemiah will discover in the period after the return from Babylon the beginnings of the synagogue. Only quite rudimentary as yet, and chiefly for the purposes of instructing those who had come back ignorant and semi-heathenish—still, they formed a starting-point. Then came the time of terrible Syrian oppression and persecutions, and of the Maccabean rising. We can understand, how under such circumstances the institution of the synagogue would develop, and gradually assume the proportions and the meaning which it afterwards attained. For it must be borne in mind, that, in proportion as the spiritual import of the Temple services was lost to view, and Judaism became a matter of outward ordinances, nice distinctions, and logical discussion, the synagogue would grow in importance. And so it came to pass, that at

She called her husband and said, "Please send me one of the servants and a donkey so I can go to the man of God quickly and return."
"Why go to him today?" he asked. "It's not the New Moon or the Sabbath."
"It's all right," she said (2 Kgs. 4:22–23).

So on the first day of the seventh month Ezra the priest brought the Law before the assembly, which was made up of men and women and all who were able to understand. He read it aloud from daybreak till noon as he faced the square before the Water Gate in the presence of the men, women and others who could understand. And all the people listened attentively to the Book of the Law (Neh. 8:2–3).

What is deemed a large town? Any in which are ten unoccupied men. If there are fewer than this, it is a village (Mishnah, Megillah i. 3).

How long will this wicked community grumble against me? I have heard the complaints of these grumbling Israelites (Num. 14:27).

the time of Christ there was not a foreign settlement of Jews without one or more synagogues—that of Alexandria, of which both the Talmuds speak in such exaggerated language, being specially gorgeous— while throughout Palestine they were thickly planted. It is to these latter only that we can for the present direct attention.

Not a town, nor a village, if it numbered only ten men, who could or would wholly give themselves to Divine things,[1] but had one or more synagogues. If it be asked, why the number ten was thus fixed upon as the smallest that could form a congregation, the reply is that, according to Num. 14:27, the "evil con- gregation" consisted of the spies who had brought a bad report, and whose number was ten—after deducting, of course, Joshua and Caleb. Larger cities had several, some of them many, synagogues. From Acts 6:9 we know that such was the case in Jerusalem, tradition having also left us an account of the synagogue of "the Alexandrians," to which class of Jews Stephen may have belonged by birth or educa- tion, on which ground also he would chiefly address himself to them. The Rabbis have it that, at the time of the destruction of Jerusalem, that city had not fewer than 480, or at least 460, synagogues. Unless the number 480 was fixed upon simply as the multiple of symbolical numbers (4 x 10 x 12), or with a kindred mystical purpose in view, it would, of course, be a gross exaggeration. But, as a stranger entered a town or village, it could never be difficult to find out the synagogue. If it had not, like our churches, its spire, pointing men, as it were, heavenward, the highest ground in the place was at least selected for it, to symbolise that its engagements overtopped all things else, and in remembrance of the prophetic saying, that the Lord's house should "be established in the top of the mountains," and "exalted above the hills" (Isa. 2:2). If such a situation could not be secured, it was sought to place it "in the corners of streets," or at

---

[1] The so-called "Batlanim." The exact meaning of the term has given rise to much learned discussion.

the entrance to the chief squares, according to what was regarded as a significant direction in Prov. 1:21. Possibly our Lord may have had this also in view when He spoke of those who loved "to pray standing in the synagogues and in the corners of the streets" (Matt. 6:5), it being a very common practice at the time to offer prayer on entering a synagogue. But if no prominent site could be obtained, a pole should at least be attached to the roof, to reach up beyond the highest house. A city whose synagogue was lower than the other dwellings was regarded as in danger of destruction.

Of the architecture of ordinary synagogues, not only the oldest still in existence, but the recent excavations in Palestine, enable us to form a correct idea. Internally they were simply rectangular or round buildings, with a single or double colonnade, and more or less adorned by carvings. Externally they had generally some sacred symbol carved on the lintels—commonly the seven-branched candlestick, or perhaps the pot of manna.[2] There is one remarkable instance of the use of the latter emblem, too important to be passed over.[3] In Capernaum, our Lord's "own city" (Matthew 9:1), there was but one synagogue—that built at the cost of the pious centurion. For, although our Authorised Version renders the commendation of the Jewish elders, "He loveth our nation, and has built us *a* synagogue" (Luke 7:5), in the original the article is definite: "he hath built us *the* synagogue"—just as in a similar manner we infer that Nazareth had

In the last days the mountain of the LORD's temple will be established as chief among the mountains; it will be raised above the hills, and all nations will stream to it (Isa. 2:2).

And when you pray, do not be like the hypocrites, for they love to pray standing in the synagogues and on the street corners to be seen by men. I tell you the truth, they have received their reward in full (Matt. 6:5).

So Moses said to Aaron, "Take a jar and put an omer of manna in it. Then place it before the LORD to be kept for the generations to come" (Exod. 16:33).

---

[2] "Of the tabernacle in which the ark rested at Shiloh, from the time of Joshua to that of Samuel, no trace, of course, remains. But on the summit of a little knoll we find the remains of what was once a Jewish synagogue, afterwards used as a church, and subsequently as a mosque. On the lintel over the doorway, between two wreaths of flowers, is carved a vessel, shaped like a Roman amphora. It so closely resembles the conventional type of the 'pot of manna,' as found on coins and in the ruins of the synagogue at Capernaum, that it doubtless formed part of the original building. It is a not improbable conjecture that the synagogue may have been erected on the sacred spot which for so many generations formed the centre of Jewish worship."—*Those Holy Fields.*

[3] Pointed out by Canon Williams, the learned author of *The Holy City.* See *The Bible, as Illustrated by Modern Science and Travel; Papers read before the Church Congress at Dublin* (1868), pp. 31, 32.

only one synagogue (Matt. 13:54). The site of the ancient Capernaum had till comparatively recently been unknown. But its identification with the modern Tell Hum is now so satisfactory, that few would care to question it. What is even more interesting, the very ruins of that synagogue which the good centurion built have been brought to light; and, as if to make doubt impossible, its architecture is evidently that of the Herodian period. And here comes in the incidental but complete confirmation of the gospel narrative. We remember how, before, the Lord Jesus had by His word of blessing multiplied the scanty provision, brought, it might be accidentally, by a lad in the company of those five thousand who had thronged to hear Him, so that there was not only sufficient for their wants, but enough for each of the twelve apostles to fill his basket with the fragments of what the Saviour had dispensed. That day of miraculous provision had been followed by a night of equally wondrous deliverance. His disciples were crossing the lake, now tossed by one of those sudden storms which so frequently sweep down upon it from the mountains. All at once, in their perplexity, it was the Master Whom they saw, walking on the sea, and nearing the ship. As the light of the moon fell upon that well-known form, and, as He drew nigh, cast His shadow in increasing proportions upon the waters which, obedient, bore His feet, they feared. It was a marvellous vision—too marvellous almost to believe it a reality, and too awful to bear it, if a reality. And so they seem to have hesitated about receiving Him into the ship.[4] But His presence and voice soon reassured them, and "immediately the ship was at the land." That "land" was the seashore of Capernaum. The next morning broke with the usual calm and beauty of spring on the lake. Presently white sails were spreading over its tranquil waters; marking the approach of many from the other side, who, missing "the Prophet," Whom, with the characteristic enthusiasm

Lintel stones

Coming to his hometown, he began teaching the people in their synagogue, and they were amazed. "Where did this man get this wisdom and these miraculous powers?" they asked (Matt. 13:54).

When they had rowed three or three and a half miles, they saw Jesus approaching the boat, walking on the water; and they were terrified. But he said to them, "It is I; don't be afraid." Then they were willing to take him into the boat, and immediately the boat reached the shore where they were heading (John 6:19–21).

---

[4]Such, at least, is the impression conveyed to my mind by John 6:21, as compared with vers. 19 and 20.

of the inhabitants of that district, they would fain have made a king, now followed Him across the water. There could be no difficulty in "finding Him" in "His own city," the home of Peter and Andrew (Mark 1:21, 29). But no ordinary dwelling would have held such a concourse as now thronged around Him. So, we imagine, the multitude made their way towards the synagogue. On the road, we suppose, the question and answers passed, of which we have an account in John 6:25–28. They had now reached the entrance to the synagogue; and the following discourse was pronounced by the Lord in the synagogue itself, as we are expressly told in ver. 59: "These things said He in the synagogue, as He taught in Capernaum." But what is so remarkable is, that the very lintel of this synagogue has been found, and that the device upon it bears such close reference to the question which the Jews put to Jesus, that we can almost imagine them pointing up to it, as they entered the synagogue, and said: "Our fathers did eat manna in the desert; as it is written, He gave them bread from heaven to eat" (John 6:31). For, in the words of Canon Williams, "The lintel lying among the ruins of the good centurion's synagogue at Capernaum has carved on it the device of the pot of manna. What is further remarkable, this lintel is ornamented besides with a flowing pattern of vine leaves and clusters of grapes, another emblem of the mystery of which our Lord discoursed so largely in this synagogue."

Before parting from this most interesting subject, we may place beside the Master, as it were, the two representatives of His Church, a Gentile and a Jew, both connected with this synagogue. Of its builder, the good centurion, Canon Williams thus writes: "In what spirit the large-hearted Roman soldier had made his offering, the rich and elaborate carvings of cornices and entablatures, of columns and capitals, and niches, still attest." As for the ruler of that same synagogue, we know that it was Jairus, whose cry of anguish and of faith brought Jesus to his house to speak the life-giving "Talitha cumi" over the

When they found him on the other side of the lake, they asked him, "Rabbi, when did you get here?"

Jesus answered, "I tell you the truth, you are looking for me, not because you saw miraculous signs but because you ate the loaves and had your fill. Do not work for food that spoils, but for food that endures to eternal life, which the Son of Man will give you. On him God the Father has placed his seal of approval."

Then they asked him, "What must we do to do the works God requires?" (John 6:25–28).

one only daughter, just bursting into womanhood, who lay dead in that chamber, while the crowd outside and the hired minstrels made shrill, discordant mourning.

Thus far as to the external appearance of synagogues. Their internal arrangement appears to have been originally upon the plan of the Temple, or, perhaps, even of the Tabernacle. At least, the oldest still standing synagogue, that of the Cyrenian Jews, in the island of Gerbe, is, according to the description of a missionary, Dr. Ewald, tripartite, after the model of the Court, the Holy, and the Most Holy Place. And in all synagogues the body of the building, with the space around, set apart for women, represents the Court of the Women, while the innermost and highest place, with the Ark behind, containing the rolls of the law, represents the sanctuary itself. In turn the synagogue seems to have been adopted as the model for the earliest Christian churches. Hence not only the structure of the "basilica," but the very term "bema," is incorporated in Rabbinical language.[5] This is only what might have been expected, considering that the earliest Christians were Jews by nationality, and that heathenism could offer no type for Christian worship. To return. As concerned the worshippers, it was deemed wrong to pray behind a synagogue without turning the face to it; and a story is told (*Ber.* 6 *b*) of Elijah appearing in the form of an Arab merchant, and punishing one guilty of this sin. "Thou standest before thy Master as if there were two Powers [or Gods]," said the seeming Arab; and with these words "he drew his sword and killed him." A still more curious idea prevailed, that it was requisite to advance the length of at least "two doors" within a synagogue before settling to prayer, which was justified by a reference to Prov. 8:34 (*Ber.* 8 *a*). The inference is peculiar, but not more so, perhaps, than those of some modern critics, and certainly not more strange than that of the Talmud itself, which, on a preceding page, when discussing the precise duration of the

Then one of the synagogue rulers, named Jairus, came there. Seeing Jesus, he fell at his feet and pleaded earnestly with him, "My little daughter is dying. Please come and put your hands on her so that she will be healed and live."… He took her by the hand and said to her, "Talitha koum!" (which means, "Little girl, I say to you, get up!"). Immediately the girl stood up and walked around (she was twelve years old). At this they were completely astonished (Mark 5:22–23, 41–42).

---

[5] This subject is fully discussed in Vitringa, *Synag.* pp. 444–456.

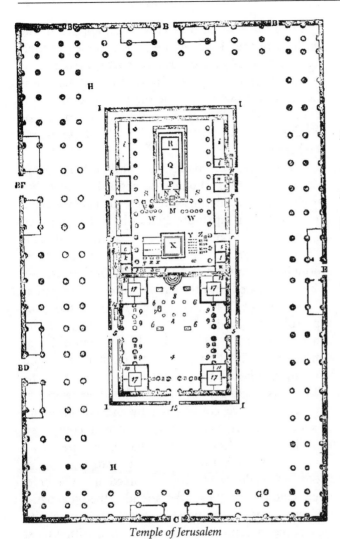

Temple of Jerusalem

Let us acknowledge the
  LORD;
 let us press on to
  acknowledge him.
As surely as the sun rises,
  he will appear;
he will come to us like the
  winter rains,
 like the spring rains that
  water the earth
(Hos. 6:3).

wrath of the Almighty, concludes that Balaam had been the only person who knew it exactly, since it is written of him (Num. 24:16), that he "knew the thoughts of the Most High!" Another direction of the Talmud was to leave the synagogue with slow steps, but to hasten to it as rapidly as possible, since it was written (Hos. 6:3, as the Rabbis arranged the verse), "Let us pursue to know the Lord." Rabbi Seira tells us how, at one time, he had been scandalised by seeing the Rabbis running on the Sabbath—when bodily rest was enjoined—to attend a sermon; but that, when he understood how Hos. 11:10 applied to the teaching of the Halachah, he himself joined in their race. And so Rabbi Seira, as it seems to us, somewhat caustically concludes: "The reward of a discourse is the haste" with which people run to it—no matter, it would appear, whether they get in to hear it, or whether there is anything in the discourse worth the hearing.

They will follow the LORD; he will roar like a lion. When he roars, his children will come trembling from the west (Hos. 11:10).

As a rule, synagogues were built at the expense of the congregation, though perhaps assisted by richer neighbours. Sometimes, as we know, they were erected at the cost of private individuals, which was supposed to involve special merit. In other cases, more particularly when the number of Jews was small, a large room in a private house was set apart for the purpose. This also passed into the early Church, as we gather from Acts 2:46; 5:42. Accordingly we understand the apostolic expression, "Church in the house" (Rom. 16:3, 5; 1 Cor. 16:19; Col. 4:15; Philemon 2), as implying that in all these and other instances a room in a private house had been set apart, in which the Christians regularly assembled for their worship. Synagogues were consecrated by prayer, although, even thus, the ceremony was not deemed completed till after the ordinary prayers had been offered by some one, though it were a passing stranger. Rules of decorum, analogous to those enforced in the Temple, were enjoined on those who attended the synagogue. Decency and cleanliness in dress, quietness and reverence in demeanour, are prescribed with almost wearisome details and distinctions. Money collections were only to be made for the poor or for the redemption of captives. If the building were in a dangerous condition, the synagogue might be broken down, provided another were built as rapidly as possible in its place. But even so, the sanctity of the place remained, and synagogue-ruins might not be converted into mourning places, nor used as thoroughfares, nor might ropes be hung up in them, nor nets spread, nor fruits laid out for drying. The principle of sanctity applied, of course, to all analogous uses to which such ruins might have been put. Money

They devoted themselves to the apostles' teaching and to the fellowship, to the breaking of bread and to prayer (Acts 2:42).

...to Apphia our sister, to Archippus our fellow soldier and to the church that meets in your home (Philm. 2).

collected for building a synagogue might, if absolute necessity arose, be employed by the congregation for other purposes; but if stones, beams, etc., had been purchased for the building, these could not be resold, but were regarded as dedicated. A town synagogue was considered absolutely inalienable; those in villages might be disposed of under the direction of the local Sanhedrim, provided the *locale* were not afterwards to be used as a public bath, a wash-house, a tannery, or a pool. The money realised was to be devoted to something more sacred than the mere stone and mortar of a synagogue—say, the ark in which the copies of the law were kept. Different from synagogues, though devoted to kindred purposes, were the so-called "oratories" or "places where prayer was wont to be made" (Acts 16:13). These were generally placed outside towns and in the vicinity of running water or of the sea (Jos. *Ant.* 14.256–258), for the purpose of the customary lustrations connected with prayer (Philo. ii. 535).

...we have decreed, that as many men and women of the Jews as are willing so to do, may celebrate their Sabbaths, and perform their holy offices, according to the Jewish laws; and may make their proseuchae at the seaside ...
(Jos. Antiquities *14.258).*

The separation of the sexes, which was observed even in the Temple at the time of Christ, was strictly carried out in the synagogues, such division being made effectual by a partition, boarded off and provided with gratings, to which there was separate access. The practice seems simply in accordance with Eastern manners and modes of thinking. But the Rabbis, who seek Scripture authority for every arrangement, however trivial, find in this case their warrant in Zech. 12:11–14, where "the wives" are no less than five times spoken of as "apart," while engaged in their prayerful mourning. The synagogue was so placed that, on entering it, the worshippers would face towards Jerusalem—mere "orientation," as it is now called, having no meaning in Jewish worship. Beyond the middle of the synagogue rose the platform or "bima," as it was anciently, or "almmeor," as it is presently named. Those who were called up to it for reading ascended by the side nearest, and descended by that most remote from their seats in the synagogue. On this "bima" stood the pulpit, or rather lectern, the "migdal ez," "wooden

The land will mourn, each clan by itself, with their wives by themselves: the clan of the house of David and their wives, the clan of the house of Nathan and their wives, the clan of the house of Levi and their wives, the clan of Shimei and their wives (Zech. 12:12–13).

tower" of Neh. 8:4, whence the prescribed portions of the law and of the prophets were read, and addresses delivered. The reader stood; the preacher sat. Thus we find (Luke 4:20) that, after reading a portion from the prophet Isaiah, our Lord "closed the book, and He gave it again to the minister, and sat down," before delivering His discourse in the synagogue of Nazareth. Prayer also was offered standing, although in the Temple the worshippers prostrated themselves, a practice still continued in certain of the most solemn litanies. The pulpit or lectern—"migdal" (tower), "chisse" and "churseja" (chair or throne), or "pergulah" (the Latin "pergula," probably elevation) —stood in the middle of the "bima," and in front of "the ark." The latter, which occupied the innermost place in the synagogue, as already noticed, corresponded to the Most Holy Place in the Temple, and formed the most important part. It was called the "aron" (ark), the "tevah," or "tevutha" (chest, like that in which Noah and Moses were saved), or the "hechal" (little temple). In reality, it consisted of a press or chest, in which the rolls of the law were deposited. This "ark" was made movable (*Taan.* ii. 1, 2), so as to lift out on occasions of public fasting and prayer, in order to have it placed in the street or market-place where the people gathered. Sometimes there was also a second press for the rolls of the prophets, in which the disused or damaged rolls of the law were likewise deposited. In front of the ark hung the "vilon" ("velum," veil), in imitation of that before the Holy Place. Above it was suspended the "ner olam," or ever-burning lamp, and near to it stood the eight-branched candlestick, lit during the eight days of the feast of the dedication of the Temple (John 10:22), or Candlemas. The practice of lighting candles and lamps, not merely for use, but in honour of the day or feast, is not unknown in the synagogues. Of course, in regard to this, as to other practices, it is impossible to determine what was the exact custom at the time of our Lord, although the reader may be able to infer how much and what special practices may have been gradually introduced. It would lead beyond

Candlestick

our present scope to describe the various directions to be observed in copying out the synagogue-rolls, which embodied the five books of Moses, or to detail what would render them unfit for use. No less than twenty such causes are mentioned by the Rabbis. At present the vellum, on which the Pentateuch is written, is affixed to two rollers, and as each portion of the law is read it is unrolled from the right, and rolled on to the left roller. The roll itself was fastened together by linen wrappers or cloths ("mitpachoth"), and then placed in a "case" ("tik," the Greek "theke"). All these articles are already mentioned in the Mishnah. Later practices need not here occupy our attention. Lastly, it should be noted, that at first the people probably stood in the synagogues or sat on the ground. But as the services became more protracted, sitting accommodation had to be provided. The congregation sat facing the ark. On the other hand, "the rulers of the synagogue," Rabbis, distinguished Pharisees, and others, who sought honour of men, claimed "the chief seats," which were placed with their backs to the ark, and facing the worshippers. These seats, which bear the same name as in the New Testament, were made objects of special ambition (Matt. 23:6), and rank, dignity, or seniority entitled a Rabbi or other influential man to priority. Our Lord expressly refers to this (Matt. 23:6) as one of the characteristic manifestations of Pharisaical pride. That both the same spirit and practice had crept into some of the early churches, appears from the warning of St. James (Jas. 2:2, 3) against an un-Christ-like "respect of persons," which would assign a place high up in "synagogues" of Christians to the mere possession of "goodly apparel" or the wearing of the "gold ring."

Hitherto we have chiefly described the outward arrangements of synagogues. It will now be necessary, however rapidly in this place, to sketch their various uses, their worship, and their officials, most of which are also referred to in various parts of the New Testament.

…[the teachers of the Law and the Pharisees] love the place of honor at banquets and the most important seats in the synagogues (Matt. 23:6).

Suppose a man comes into your meeting wearing a gold ring and fine clothes, and a poor man in shabby clothes also comes in. If you show special attention to the man wearing fine clothes and say, "Here's a good seat for you," but say to the poor man, "You stand there" or "Sit on the floor by my feet," have you not discriminated among yourselves and become judges with evil thoughts (Jas. 2:2–4)?

17
THE WORSHIP OF THE SYNAGOGUE

Synagogue at Kefr Berim

One of the most difficult questions in Jewish history is that connected with the existence of a synagogue within the Temple. That such a "synagogue" existed, and that its meeting-place was in "the hall of hewn stones," at the south-eastern angle of the court of the priests, cannot be called in question, in face of the clear testimony of contemporary witnesses. Considering that "the hall of hewn stones" was also the meeting-place for the great Sanhedrim, and that not only legal decisions, but lectures and theological discussions formed part of their occupation, we might be tempted to conjecture that the term "synagogue" had been employed in its wider sense, since such buildings were generally used throughout the country for this two-fold purpose as well as for worship. Of theological lectures and discussions in the Temple, we have an instance on the occasion when our Lord was found by His parents "sitting in the midst of the doctors, both hearing them, and asking them questions" (Luke 2:46). And it can scarcely be doubted, that this also explains how the scribes and Pharisees could so frequently "come upon Him," while He taught in the Temple, with their difficult and entangling questions, up to that rejoinder about the nature of the Messiah, with which He finally silenced them: "If David then call Him Lord, how is He his Son?" (Matt. 22:45). But in reference to the so-called "Temple-synagogue," there is this difficulty, that certain prayers and rites seem to have been connected with it, which formed no part of the regular Temple services, and yet were somehow engrafted upon them. We can therefore only conclude that the growing change in the theological views of Israel, before and about the time of Christ, made the Temple services alone appear insufficient. The symbolical and typical elements which constituted the life and centre of Temple worship had lost their spiritual meaning and attraction to the majority of that generation, and their place was becoming occupied by so-called teaching and outward performances. Thus the worship of the letter took the place of that of the spirit, and Israel was preparing to reject Christ for Pharisaism. The synagogue was substituted for the Temple, and overshadowed it, even within its walls, by an incongruous mixture of man-devised worship with the God-ordained typical rites of the sanctuary. Thus, so far from the "Temple-synagogue" being the model for those throughout the country, as some

After three days they found him in the temple courts, sitting among the teachers, listening to them and asking them questions (Luke 2:46).

He has made us competent as ministers of a new covenant—not of the letter but of the Spirit; for the letter kills, but the Spirit gives life (2 Cor. 3:6).

writers maintain, it seems to us of later origin, and to have borrowed many rites from the country synagogues, in which the people had become accustomed to them.[1]

Jesus went throughout Galilee, teaching in their synagogues, preaching the good news of the kingdom, and healing every disease and sickness among the people (Matt. 4:23).

The subject has a far deeper than merely historical interest. For the presence of a synagogue within the Temple, or rather, as we prefer to put it, the addition of synagogue-worship to that of the Temple, is sadly symbolical. It is, so to speak, one of those terribly significant utterances (by deed), in which Israel, all unconsciously, pronounced its own doom, just as was this: "His blood be upon us and our children," or the cry for the release of Barabbas (the son of the father), who had been condemned "for sedition" and "murder" —no doubt in connection with a pseudo-Messianic rising against the Roman power—instead of the true Son of the Father, who would indeed have "restored the kingdom to Israel." And yet there was nothing in the worship itself of the synagogue which could have prevented either the Lord, or His apostles and early followers, from attending it till the time of final separation had come. Readers of the New Testament know what precious opportunities it offered for making known the Gospel. Its services were, indeed, singularly elastic. For the main object of the synagogue was the teaching of the people. The very idea of its institution, before and at the time of Ezra, explains and conveys this, and it is confirmed by the testimony of Josephus (*Ag. Apion*, 2.157–172). But perhaps the ordinary reader of the New Testament may have failed to notice, how prominently this element in the synagogue is brought out in the gospel history. Yet the word "teaching" is used so frequently in connection with our Lord's appearance in the synagogue, that its lesson is obvious (see Matt. 4:23; Mark 1:21; 6:2; Luke 4:15; 6:6; 13:10; John 6:59; 18:20). The "teaching" part of the service consisted mainly in reading a section from the law, with which the reading of a portion from the prophets, and a sermon, or address, were conjoined. Of course, the liturgical element

---

[1] This is substantially admitted by Herzfeld, *Gesch. d. Volkes Jisr.* vol. iii. pp. 131, 132.

could in such services never have been quite wanting, and it soon acquired considerable importance. It consisted of prayer and the pronouncing of the Aaronic blessing (Num. 6:24–26) by priests—that is, of course, not by Rabbis, who were merely teachers or doctors, but by lineal descendants of the house of Aaron. There was no service of "praise" in the synagogues.

The Lord bless you and keep you; the Lord make his face shine upon you and be gracious to you; the Lord turn his face toward you and give you peace (Num. 6:24–26).

Public worship[2] commenced on ordinary occasions with the so-called "Shema," which was preceded in the morning and evening by two "benedictions," and succeeded in the morning by one, and in the evening by two, benedictions; the second being, strictly speaking, an evening prayer. The "Shema" was a kind of "belief," or "creed," composed of these three passages of Scripture: Deut. 6:4–9; 11:13–21; Num. 15:37–41. It obtained its name from the initial word "shema": "Hear, O Israel," in Deut. 6:4. From the Mishnah (*Ber.* i. 3) we learn, that this part of the service existed already before the time of our Lord; and we are told (*Ber.* iii. 3), that all males were bound to repeat this belief twice every day; children and slaves, as well as women, being exempted from the obligation. There can be no reasonable doubt on the subject, as the Mishnah expressly mentions the three Scriptural sections of the "Shema," the number of benedictions before and after it, and even the initial words of the closing benediction (*Ber.* ii. 2; i. 4; *Tamid,* v. 1). We have, therefore, here certain prayers which our Lord Himself had not only heard, but in which He must have shared—to what extent will appear in the sequel. These prayers still exist in the synagogue, although with later additions, which, happily, it is not difficult to eliminate. Before transcribing them, it may be quoted as a mark of the value attached to them, that it was lawful to say this and the other daily prayers—to which we shall hereafter refer—and the "grace at meat," not only in the Hebrew,

Hear, O Israel: The Lord our God, the Lord is one. Love the Lord your God with all your heart and with all your soul and with all your strength (Deut. 6:4–5).

---

[2]Our description here applies to the worship of the *ancient,* not of the modern synagogue; and we have thought it best to confine ourselves to the testimony of the Mishnah, so as to avoid the danger of bringing in practices of a later date.

These may be said in any language: the paragraph of the Suspected Adulteress, the Avowal concerning the [Second] Tithe, the recital of the Shemà, the Tefillah, the Benediction over food, the oath of testimony, and the oath concerning a deposit (Mishnah, Soṭa vii. 1).

but in any other language, in order to secure a general understanding of the service (*Sotah,* vii. 1). At the same time, expressions are used which lead us to suppose that, while the liturgical formulae connected with the "Shema" were fixed, there were local variations, in the way of lengthening or shortening (*Ber.* i. 4). The following are the "benedictions" before the "Shema," in their original form:

1. "Blessed be Thou, O Lord, King of the world, Who formest the light and createst the darkness, Who makest peace and createst everything; Who, in mercy, givest light to the earth and to those who dwell upon it, and in Thy goodness day by day and every day renewest the works of creation. Blessed be the Lord our God for the glory of His handiwork and for the light-giving lights which He has made for His praise. Selah! Blessed be the Lord our God, Who hath formed the lights."[3]

2. "With great love hast Thou loved us, O Lord our God, and with much overflowing pity hast Thou pitied us, our Father and our King. For the sake of our fathers who trusted in Thee, and Thou taughtest them the statutes of life, have mercy upon us and teach us. Enlighten our eyes in Thy law; cause our hearts to cleave to Thy commandments; unite our hearts to love and fear Thy name, and we shall not be put to shame, world without end. For Thou art a God Who preparest salvation, and us hast Thou chosen from among all nations and tongues, and hast in truth brought us near to Thy great Name—Selah—that we may lovingly praise Thee and Thy Oneness. Blessed be the Lord Who in love chose His people Israel."[4]

After this followed the "Shema." The Mishnah gives the following beautiful explanation of the order in which the portions of Scripture of which it is composed are arranged (*Ber.* ii. 2). The section Deut.

---

[3]This "benediction," while acknowledging the Creator, has such frequent reference to God in connection with the "lights," that it reads like a confession of Israel against the idolatries of Babylon. This circumstance may help to fix the time of its origination.

[4]This reads peculiarly like the thanksgiving of Israel as God's covenant people.

6:4–9 is said to precede that in 11:13–21, so that we might "take upon ourselves the yoke of the kingdom of heaven, and only after that the yoke of the commandments." Again: Deut. 11:13–21 precedes Num. 15:37–41, because the former applies, as it were, both night and day; the latter only by day. The reader cannot fail to observe the light cast by the teaching of the Mishnah upon the gracious invitation of our Lord: "Come unto Me, all ye that labour and are heavy laden, and I will give you rest. Take My yoke upon you, and learn of Me; for I am meek and lowly in heart: and ye shall find rest unto your souls. For My yoke is easy, and My burden is light" (Matt. 11:28–30). These words must indeed have had a special significance to those who remembered the Rabbinic lesson as to the relation between the kingdom of heaven and the commandments, and they would now understand how by coming to the Saviour they would first take upon them "the yoke of the kingdom of heaven," and then that of "the commandments," finding this "yoke easy" and the "burden light."

So if you faithfully obey the commands I am giving you today—to love the LORD your God and to serve him with all your heart and with all your soul—then I will send rain on your land in its season, both autumn and spring rains, so that you may gather in your grain, new wine and oil. I will provide grass in the fields for your cattle, and you will eat and be satisfied (Deut. 11:13–15).

The prayer after the "Shema" was as follows:[5]

"True it is, that Thou art Jehovah our God and the God of our fathers, our King and the King of our fathers, our Saviour and the Saviour of our fathers, our Creator, the Rock of our salvation, our Help and our Deliverer. Thy Name is from everlasting, and there is no God beside Thee. A new song did they that were delivered sing to Thy Name by the seashore; together did all praise and own Thee King, and say, Jehovah shall reign world without end! Blessed be the Lord Who saveth Israel!

The anti-Sadducean views expressed in this prayer will strike the student of that period, while he will also be much impressed with its suitableness and beauty. The special prayer for the evening is of not quite so old a date as the three just quoted. But as it is referred to in the Mishnah, and is so apt and simple, we reproduce it, as follows:

---

[5] In the form here given it is older than even the prayer referred to in the Mishnah (*Ber.* ii. 2).

"O Lord our God! cause us to lie down in peace, and raise us up again to life, O our King! Spread over us the tabernacle of Thy peace; strengthen us before Thee in Thy good counsel, and deliver us for Thy Name's sake. Be Thou for protection round about us; keep far from us the enemy, the pestilence, the sword, famine, and affliction. Keep Satan from before and from behind us, and hide us in the shadow of Thy wings, for Thou art a God Who helpest and deliverest us; and Thou, O God, art a gracious and merciful King. Keep Thou our going out and our coming in, for life and for peace, from henceforth and for ever!"[6]

The "Shema" and its accompanying "benedictions" seem to have been said in the synagogue at the lectern; whereas for the next series of prayers the leader of the devotions went forward and stood before "the ark." Hence the expression, "to go up before the ark," for leading in prayer. This difference in position seems implied in many passages of the Mishnah (specially *Megillah*, iv.), which makes a distinction between saying the "Shema" and "going up before the ark." The prayers offered before the ark consisted of the so-called eighteen eulogies, or benedictions, and formed the "tephillah," or supplication, in the strictest sense of the term. These eighteen, or rather, as they are now, nineteen, eulogies are of various dates—the earliest being the first three and the last three. There can be no reasonable doubt that these were said at worship in the synagogues, when our Lord was present. Next in date are eulogies 4, 5, 6, 7, 9, and 16. Eulogy 7, which in its present position seems somewhat incongruous, dates from a period of great national calamity—perhaps the time of Pompey. The other eulogies, and some insertions in the older benedictions, were added after the fall of the Jewish commonwealth—eulogy 12 especially being intended against the early Jewish converts to Christianity. In all likelihood it had been the practice originally to insert prayers of private composition

If there are less than ten present they may not recite the Shemà with its Benedictions, nor may one go before the Ark, nor may they lift up their hands, nor may they read the [prescribed portion of] the Law or the reading from the Prophets, nor may they observe the Stations [when burying the dead] or say the Benediction of the Mourners or the mourners' consolation, or the Benediction over the newly wed, nor may they make mention of the name of God in the Common Grace (Mishnah, Megillah iv. 3).

---

[6]To this prayer a further addition was made at a later period. On the whole, compare Zunz, *Gottesd. Vortr.* p. 367, etc.

between the (present) first three and last three eulogies; and out of these the later eulogies were gradually formulated. At any rate, we know that on Sabbaths and on other festive occasions only the first three and the last three eulogies were repeated, other petitions being inserted between them. There was thus room for the endless repetitions and "long prayers" which the Saviour condemned (Mark 12:40; Luke 20:47). Besides, it must be borne in mind that, both on entering and leaving the synagogue, it was customary to offer prayer, and that it was a current Rabbinical saying, "Prolix prayer prolongeth life." But as we are sure that, on the Sabbaths when our Lord attended the synagogues at Nazareth and Capernaum, the first three and the last three of the eulogies were repeated, we produce them here, as follows:

They devour widows' houses and for a show make lengthy prayers. Such men will be punished most severely (Mark 12:40).

1. "Blessed be the Lord our God and the God of our fathers, the God of Abraham, the God of Isaac, and the God of Jacob; the great, the mighty, and the terrible God; the Most High God, Who showeth mercy and kindness, Who createth all things, Who remembereth the gracious promises to the fathers, and bringeth a Saviour to their children's children, for His own Name's sake, in love. O King, Helper, Saviour, and Shield! Blessed art Thou, O Jehovah, the Shield of Abraham."

2. "Thou, O Lord, art mighty for ever; Thou, Who quickenest the dead, art mighty to save. In Thy mercy Thou preservest the living; Thou quickenest the dead; in Thine abundant pity Thou bearest up those who fall, and healest those who are diseased, and loosest those who are bound, and fulfillest Thy faithful word to those who sleep in the dust. Who is like unto Thee, Lord of strength, and who can be compared to Thee, Who killest and makest alive, and causest salvation to spring forth? And faithful art Thou to give life unto the dead. Blessed be Thou, Jehovah, Who quickenest the dead!"

3. "Thou art holy, and Thy Name is holy; and the holy ones praise Thee every day. Selah! Blessed art Thou, Jehovah God, the Holy One!"

It is impossible not to feel the solemnity of these prayers. They breathe the deepest hopes of Israel in simple, Scriptural language. But who can fully realise their sacred import as uttered not only in the Presence, but by the very lips of the Lord Jesus Christ, Who Himself was their answer?

The three concluding eulogies were as follows:

17. "Take gracious pleasure, O Jehovah our God, in Thy people Israel, and in their prayers. Accept the burnt-offerings of Israel, and their prayers, with Thy good pleasure; and may the services of Thy people Israel be ever acceptable unto Thee. And oh that our eyes may see it, as Thou turnest in mercy to Zion! Blessed be Thou, O Jehovah, Who restoreth His Shechinah to Zion!"

High-priest in robes

18. "We praise Thee, because Thou art Jehovah our God, and the God of our fathers, for ever and ever. Thou art the Rock of our life, the Shield of our salvation, from generation to generation. We laud Thee, and declare Thy praise for our lives which are kept within Thine hand, and for our souls which are committed unto Thee, and for Thy wonders which are with us every day, and Thy wondrous deeds and Thy goodnesses, which are at all seasons—evening, morning, and mid-day. Thou gracious One, Whose compassions never end; Thou pitying One, Whose grace never ceaseth—for ever do we put our trust in Thee! And for all this Thy Name, O our King, be blessed and extolled always, for ever and ever! And all living bless Thee—Selah—and praise Thy Name in truth, O God, our Salvation and our Help. Blessed art Thou, Jehovah; Thy Name is the gracious One, to Whom praise is due."

19.[7] "Oh bestow on Thy people Israel great peace, for ever; for Thou art King and Lord of all peace, and it is good in Thine eyes to bless Thy people Israel with praise at all times and in every hour. Blessed art Thou, Jehovah, Who blesseth His people Israel with peace."

---

[7] We give this eulogy in its shorter form, as it is at present used in evening prayer.

Another fact, hitherto, so far as we know, unnoticed, requires here to be mentioned. It invests the prayers just quoted with a new and almost unparalleled interest. According to the Mishnah (*Megillah,* iv. 5), the person who read in the synagogue the portion from the prophets was also expected to say the "Shema," and to offer the prayers which have just been quoted. It follows that, in all likelihood, our Lord Himself had led the devotions in the synagogue of Capernaum on that Sabbath when He read the portion from the prophecies of Isaiah which was that day "fulfilled in their hearing" (Luke 4:16–21). Nor is it possible to withstand the impression, how specially suitable to the occasion would have been the words of these prayers, particularly those of eulogies 2 and 17.

The prayers were conducted or repeated aloud by one individual, specially deputed for the occasion, the congregation responding by an "Amen." The liturgical service concluded with the priestly benediction (Num. 6:23, 24), spoken by the descendants of Aaron. In case none such were present, "the legate of the Church," as the leader of the devotions was called, repeated the words from the Scriptures in their connection. In giving the benediction, the priests elevated their hands up to the shoulders (*Sotah,* vii. 6); in the Temple, up to the forehead. Hence this rite is designated by the expression, "the lifting up of the hands."[8] According to the present practice, the fingers of the two hands are so joined together and separated as to form five interstices; and a mystic meaning attaches to this. It was a later superstition to forbid looking at the priests' hands, as involving physical danger. But the Mishnah already directs that priests having blemishes on their hands, or their fingers dyed, were not to pronounce the benediction, lest the attention of the people should be attracted. Of the attitude to be observed in prayer, this is perhaps scarcely the place to speak in detail. Suffice it, that the body was to

"The Spirit of the LORD is on me, because he has anointed me to preach good news to the poor. He has sent me to proclaim freedom for the prisoners and recovery of sight for the blind, to release the oppressed, to proclaim the year of the LORD's favor." Then he rolled up the scroll, gave it back to the attendant and sat down. The eyes of everyone in the synagogue were fastened on him, and he began by saying to them, "Today this scripture is fulfilled in your hearing" (Luke 4:18–21).

---

[8]The apostle may have had this in his mind when, in directing the order of public ministration, he spoke of "the men...lifting up holy hands, without wrath or doubting" (1 Tim. 2:8). At any rate, the expression is precisely the same as that used by the Rabbis.

be fully bent, yet so, that care was taken never to make it appear as if the service had been burdensome. One of the Rabbis tells us, that, with this object in view, he bent down as does a branch; while, in lifting himself up again, he did it like a serpent—beginning with the head! Any one deputed by the rulers of a congregation might say prayers, except a minor. This, however, applies only to the "Shema." The eulogies or "tephillah" proper, as well as the priestly benediction, could not be pronounced by those who were not properly clothed, nor by those who were so blind as not to be able to discern daylight. If any one introduced into the prayers heretical views, or what were regarded as such, he was immediately stopped; and, if any impropriety had been committed, was put under the ban for a week. One of the most interesting and diffi-cult questions relates to certain modes of dress and appearance, and certain expressions used in prayer, which the Mishnah (*Megillah*, iv. 8, 9) declares either to mark heresy or to indicate that a man was not to be allowed to lead prayers in the synagogue. It may be, that some of these statements refer not only to certain Jewish "heretics," but also to the early Jewish Christians. If so, they may indicate certain peculiarities with which they were popularly credited.[9]

If a man said, "I will not go before the Ark in coloured raiment", he may not even go before it in white raiment. [If he said,] "I will not go before it in sandals", he may not even go before it barefoot (Mishnah, Megillah iv. 8).

Of the services hitherto noticed, the most important were the repetition of the eulogies and the priestly benediction. What now followed was regarded as quite as solemn, if, indeed, not more so. It has already been pointed out, that the main object of the synagogue was the teaching of the people. This was specially accomplished by the reading of the law. At present the Pentateuch is for this purpose arranged into fifty-four sections, of which one is read on each successive Sabbath of the year, beginning immediately after the feast of Tabernacles. But anciently the lectionary, at least in Palestine, seems to have been differently arranged, and the Pentateuch so divided that its reading occupied three, or, according to

---

[9]The Gemara (*Ber.* 33 *b*, 34 *a*) adds little to our understanding of this important question.

some, three and a-half years (half a Jubilee-period).[10]
The section for the day was subdivided, so that every
Sabbath at least seven persons were called up to read,
each a portion, which was to consist of not less than
three verses. The first reader began, and the last
closed, with a benediction. As the Hebrew had given
place to the Aramaic, a "meturgeman," or interpreter,
stood by the side of the reader, and translated verse by
verse into the vernacular. It was customary to have
service in the synagogues, not only on Sabbaths and
feast-days, but also on the second and fifth days of the
week (Monday and Thursday), when the country-
people came to market, and when the local
Sanhedrim also sat for the adjudication of minor
causes. At such week-day services only three persons
were called up to read in the law; on new moon's day
and on the intermediate days of a festive week, four;
on festive days—when a section from the prophets
was also read—five; and on the day of atonement, six.
Even a minor was allowed to read, and, if qualified, to
act as "meturgeman." The section describing the sin
of Reuben, and that giving a second account of the sin
of the golden calf, were read, but not interpreted;
those recounting the priestly blessing, and, again, the
sin of David and of Amnon, were neither read nor
interpreted. The reading of the law was followed by a
lesson from the prophets. At present there is a regular lectionary, in which these lessons are so selected as
to suit the sections from the law appointed for the
day. This arrangement has been traced to the time of
the Syrian persecutions, when all copies of the law
were sought for and destroyed; and the Jewish
authorities are supposed to have selected portions
from the prophets to replace those from the law
which might not be produced in public. But it is
evident that, if these persecuting measures had been
rigidly enforced, the sacred rolls of the prophets
would not have escaped destruction any more than
those of the law. Besides, it is quite certain that such

Priest in robes

---

[10]For these reasons I cannot adopt the views and inferences so ably stated by Mr. Basil
Cooper in his papers on "The Synagogue," in the *Sunday at Home* for 1876, however interesting.

He that reads in the Law may not read less than three verses; he may not read to the interpreter more than one verse, or, in [a reading from] the Prophets, three verses; but if these three are three separate paragraphs, he must read them out singly. They may leave out verses in the Prophets, but not in the Law. How much may they leave out? Only so much that he leaves no time for the interpreter to make a pause (Mishnah, Megillah iv. 4).

His horses will be so many that they will cover you with dust. Your walls will tremble at the noise of the war horses, wagons and chariots when he enters your gates as men enter a city whose walls have been broken through (Ezek. 26:10).

a lectionary of the prophets as that presently in use did not exist at the time of our Lord, nor even when the Mishnah was collated. Considerable liberty seems to have been left to individuals; and the expression used by St. Luke in reference to our Lord in the synagogue at Capernaum (Luke 4:17), "And when He had opened the book, He found the place where it was written," most accurately describes the state of matters. For, from *Megillah* iv. 4, we gather that, in reading from the prophets, it was lawful to pass over one or more verses, provided there were no pause between the reading and the translation of the "meturgeman." For here also the services of a "meturgeman" were employed; only that he did not, as in reading the law, translate verse by verse, but after every three verses. It is a remarkable fact that the Rabbis exclude from public reading the section in the prophecies of Ezekiel which describes "the chariot and wheels." Rabbi Elieser would also have excluded that in Ezek. 16:2.

The reading of the prophets was often followed by a sermon or address, with which the service concluded. The preacher was called "darshan," and his address a "derashah" (homily, sermon, from "darash," to ask, inquire, or discuss). When the address was a learned theological discussion—especially in academies —it was not delivered to the people directly, but whispered into the ear of an "amora," or speaker, who explained to the multitude in popular language the weighty sayings which the Rabbi had briefly communicated to him. A more popular sermon, on the other hand, was called a "meamar," literally, a "speech, or talk." These addresses would be either Rabbinical expositions of Scripture, or else doctrinal discussions, in which appeal would be made to tradition and to the authority of certain great teachers. For it was laid down as a principle (*Eduj.* i. 3), that "every one is bound to teach in the very language of his teacher." In view of this two-fold fact, we can in some measure understand the deep impression which the words of our Lord produced, even on those who remained permanently uninfluenced by them. The substance of His addresses was far other than they had ever heard of, or conceived possible. It seemed as if they opened quite a new world of thought, hope, duty, and comfort. No wonder that even in contemptuous Capernaum "all bare Him witness, and wondered at the gracious words which proceeded out of His mouth;" and that the very Temple-guard sent to make Him prisoner were overawed, and before the council could only give this account of their strange negligence: "Never man spake like this man" (John 7:46). Similarly, the form also of His teaching was so different from the constant appeal of the Rabbis to mere tradition; it seemed all to come so quite fresh and direct from heaven, like the living waters of the Holy Spirit, that "the people were astonished at His doctrine: for He taught them as one having authority, and not as the scribes" (Matt. 7:28, 29).

18
BRIEF OUTLINE OF ANCIENT JEWISH THEOLOGICAL LITERATURE

After the reading from the Law and the Prophets, the synagogue rulers sent word to them, saying, "Brothers, if you have a message of encouragement for the people, please speak" (Acts 13:15).

The arrangements of the synagogue, as hitherto described, combined in a remarkable manner fixedness of order with liberty of the individual. Alike the seasons and the time of public services, their order, the prayers to be offered, and the portions of the law to be read were fixed. On the other hand, between the eighteen "benedictions" said on ordinary days, and the seven repeated on the Sabbaths, free prayer might be inserted; the selection from the prophets, with which the public reading concluded—the "Haphtarah" (from "patar," to "conclude")—seems to have been originally left to individual choice; while the determination who was to read, or to conduct the prayers, or to address the people, was in the hands of the "rulers of the synagogue" (Acts 13:15). The latter, who were probably also the members of the local Sanhedrim, had naturally charge of the conduct of public worship, as well as of the government and discipline of the synagogues. They were men learned in the law and of good repute, whom the popular voice designated, but who were regularly set apart by "the laying on of hands," or the "Semichah," which was done by at least three, who had themselves received ordination, upon which the candidate had the formal title of Rabbi bestowed on him, and was declared qualified to administer the law (*Sanh.* 13 *b*). The Divine Majesty was supposed to be in the midst of each Sanhedrim, on account of which even that consisting of only three members might be designated as "Elohim." Perhaps this may have been said in explanation and application of Ps. 82:6: "I have said, Ye are Elohim; and all of you children of the Most High."

The special qualifications for the office of Sanhedrist, mentioned in Rabbinical writings, are such as to remind us of the directions of St. Paul to Timothy (1 Tim. 3:1–10). A member of the Sanhedrim must be wise, modest, God-fearing, truthful, not greedy of filthy lucre, given to hospitality, kindly, not a gambler, nor a usurer, nor one who traded in the produce of Sabbatical years, nor yet one who indulged in unlawful games (*Sanh.* iii. 3). They were called "Sekenim," "elders" (Luke 7:3), "Memunim," "rulers" (Mark 5:22), "Parnasin," "feeders, overseers, shepherds of the flock" (Acts 20:28; 1 Pet. 5:2), and "Manhigei," "guides" (Heb. 13:7). They were under the presidency and supreme rule of an "Archisynagogos," or "Rosh-ha-Cheneseth," "head of the synagogue" (*Yom.* vii. 1; *Sot.* vii. 7), who sometimes seems to have even exercised sole authority. The designation occurs frequently in the New Testament (Matt. 9:18; Mark 5:35, 36, 38; Luke 8:41, 49; 13:14; Acts 18:8, 17). The inferior functions in the synagogue devolved on the "chassan," or "minister" (Luke 4:20). In course of time, however, the "chassanim" combined with their original duties the office of schoolmaster; and at present they lead both the singing and the devotions of the synagogue. This duty originally devolved not on any fixed person, but whoever was chosen might for the time being act as "Sheliach Zibbur," or "legate of the congregation." Most modern writers have imagined, that the expression "angel of the Church," in the epistles to the seven churches in the book of Revelation, was used in allusion to this ancient arrangement of the synagogue. But the fact that the "Sheliach Zibbur" represented not an office but a function, renders this view untenable. Besides, in that case, the corresponding Greek expression would rather have been "apostle" than "angel of the Church." Possibly, however, the writer of the Epistle to the Hebrews may refer to it, when he designates the Lord Jesus "the Apostle and High-Priest of our profession" (Heb. 3:1). Besides these functionaries,

Here is a trustworthy saying: If anyone sets his heart on being an overseer, he desires a noble task. Now the overseer must be above reproach, the husband of but one wife, temperate, self-controlled, respectable, hospitable, able to teach, not given to drunkenness, not violent but gentle, not quarrelsome, not a lover of money. He must manage his own family well and see that his children obey him with proper respect. (If anyone does not know how to manage his own family, how can he take care of God's church?) (1 Tim. 3:1–5).

Therefore, holy brothers, who share in the heavenly calling, fix your thoughts on Jesus, the apostle and high priest whom we confess (Heb. 3:1).

Those who are wise will shine like the brightness of the heavens, and those who lead many to righteousness, like the stars for ever and ever (Dan. 12:3).

I am the LORD your God, who brought you out of Egypt, out of the land of slavery. You shall have no other gods before me. You shall not make for yourself an idol in the form of anything in heaven above or on the earth beneath or in the waters below...
You shall not misuse the name of the LORD your God, for the LORD will not hold anyone guiltless who misuses his name. Remember the Sabbath day by keeping it holy... Honor your father and your mother, so that you may live long in the land the LORD your God is giving you (Exod. 20:2–3, 4, 7, 8, 12).

we also read of "Gabaei Zedakah," or collectors of charity, to whom the Talmud (*B. Bathra*, 8 *b*) by a *jeu de mots*[1] applies the promise that they "shall be as the stars for ever and ever" (Dan. 12:3), since they lead many to "righteousness." Alms were collected at regular times every week, either in money or in victuals. At least two were employed in collecting, and three in distributing charity, so as to avoid the suspicion of dishonesty or partiality. These collectors of charity, who required to be "men of good repute, and faithful," are thought by many to have been the model for the institution of the Diaconate in the early Church. But the analogy scarcely holds good; nor, indeed, were such collectors employed in every synagogue.

In describing the conduct of public worship in the synagogues, reference was made to the "meturgeman," who translated into the vernacular dialect what was read out of the Hebrew Scriptures, and also to the "darshan," who expounded the Scriptures or else the traditional law in an address, delivered after the reading of the "Haphtarah," or section from the prophets. These two terms will have suggested names which often occur in writings on Jewish subjects, and may fitly lead to some remarks on Jewish theology at the time of our Lord. Now the work of the "meturgeman"[2] was perpetuated in the Targum, and that of the "darshan" in the Midrash. Primarily the Targum, then, was intended as a translation of the Hebrew Scriptures into the vernacular Aramaean. Of course, such translations might be either literal, or else more or less paraphrastic. Every Targum would also naturally represent the special views of the translator, and be interesting as affording an insight into the ideas prevalent at the time, and the manner in which Scripture was understood. But some Targumim are much more paraphrastic than others, and indeed become a kind of commentary, showing us the popular theology of the time. Strictly speaking, we have really no Targum dating from the time of our Lord, nor

[1] Zedakah means righteousness, but is also used for "charity."
[2] Hence also the term "dragoman."

even from the first century of our era. There can be no doubt, however, that such a Targum did exist, although it has been lost. Still, the Targumim preserved to us, although collated, and having received their present form at later periods, contain very much that dates from the Temple-period, and even before that. Mentioning them in the order of their comparative antiquity, we have the Targum of Onkelos, on the five books of Moses; the Targum of Jonathan, on the prophets (inclusive of Joshua, Judges, and the books of Samuel and of the Kings); the so-called (or pseudo) Jonathan on the Pentateuch; and the Jerusalem Targum, which is but a fragment. Probably the latter two were intended to be supplemental to the Targum Onkelos. Late criticism has thrown doubt even on the existence of such a person as Onkelos. Whoever may have been the author, this Targum, in its present form, dates probably from the third, that of Jonathan on the prophets from the fourth century.

You shall not murder. You shall not commit adultery. You shall not steal. You shall not give false testimony against your neighbor. You shall not covet your neighbor's house. You shall not covet your neighbor's wife, or his manservant or maidservant, his ox or donkey, or anything that belongs to your neighbor (Exod. 20: 13–17).

In some respects more interesting than the Targumim are the Midrashim, of which we possess three, dating probably, in their present form, from the first or second century of our era, but embodying many parts much older. These are—mentioning them again in the order of their antiquity—"Siphra" (the book), a commentary on Leviticus; "Siphri," a commentary on Numbers and Deuteronomy; and "Mechiltha," a commentary on certain portions of Exodus. But we have even a monument more interesting than these, of the views of the ancient Pharisees, and of their Scriptural interpretations. Some of the fathers referred to a work called "Lesser Genesis," or the "Book of Jubilees." This had been lost to theological literature, till again discovered within the present century, although not in the original Hebrew, nor even in its first or Greek translation, but in an Ethiopic rendering from the latter. The work, which no doubt dates from the era of our Lord, covers the same ground as the first book of Moses, whence the name of "Lesser Genesis." It gives the Biblical narrative from the creation of the world to the institution

High-priest in robes on Day of Atonement

of the Passover, in the spirit in which the Judaism of that period would view it. The legendary additions, the Rabbinical ideas expressed, the interpretations furnished, are just such as one would expect to find in such a work. One of the main objects of the writer seems to have been the chronology of the book of Genesis, which it is attempted to settle. All events are recorded according to Jubilee-periods of forty-nine years, whence the name "Book of Jubilees," given to the work. These "Jubilees" are again arranged into "weeks," each of seven years (a day for a year); and events are classified as having taken place in a certain month of a certain year, of a certain "week" of years, of a certain "Jubilee"-period. Another tendency of the book, which, however, it has in common with all similar productions, is to trace up all later institutions to the patriarchal period.[3]

Besides these works, another class of theological literature has been preserved to us, around which of late much and most serious controversy has gathered. Most readers, of course, know about the Apocrypha; but these works are called the "pseudo-epigraphic writings." Their subject-matter may be described as mainly dealing with unfulfilled prophecy; and they are couched in language and figures borrowed, among others, from the book of Daniel. In fact, they read like attempts at imitating certain portions of that prophecy—only that their scope is sometimes wider. This class of literature is larger than those not acquainted with the period might have expected. Yet when remembering the troubles of the time, the feverish expectations of a coming deliverance, and the peculiar cast of mind and training of those who wrote them, they scarcely seem more numerous, nor perhaps even more extravagant, than a certain kind of prophetic literature, abundant among us not long ago, which the fear of Napoleon or other political events from time to time called forth. To that kind of

---

[3] Although the "Book of Jubilees" seems most likely of Pharisaic authorship, the views expressed in it are not always those of the Pharisees. Thus the resurrection is denied, although the immortality of the soul is maintained.

production, they seem, at least to us, to bear an essential likeness—only that, unlike the Western, the Oriental expounder of unfulfilled prophecy assumes rather the language of the prophet than that of the commentator, and clothes his views in mystic emblematic language. In general, this kind of literature may be arranged into Greek and Hebrew—according as the writers were either Egyptian (Hellenistic) or Palestinian Jews. Considerable difficulty exists as to the precise date of some of these writings—whether previous or subsequent to the time of Christ. These difficulties are, of course, increased when it is sought to fix the precise period when each of them was composed. Still, late historical investigations have led to much accord on general points. Without referring to the use which opponents of Christianity have of late attempted to make of these books, it may be safely asserted that their proper study and interpretation will yet be made very helpful, not only in casting light upon the period, but in showing the essential difference between the teaching of the men of that age and that of the New Testament.[4] For each branch and department of sacred study, the more carefully, diligently, and impartially it is pursued, affords only fresh testimony to that truth which is most certainly, and on the best and surest grounds, believed among us.

This is The Account of the Division of Days of the Law and the Testimony for Annual Observance according to their Weeks *(of years)* and their Jubilees throughout all the Years of the World *just as the* LORD *told it to Moses on Mount Sinai when he went up to receive the tablets of the Law and the commandment by the word of the* LORD, *as he said to him,* "Come up to the top of the mountain." *(Title to the Book of Jubilees, from* Old Testament Pseudepigrapha *ed. Charlesworth).*

It were, however, a mistake to suppose that the Rabbinical views, extravagant as they so often are, were propounded quite independently of Scripture. On the contrary, every traditional ordinance, every Rabbinical institution, nay, every legend and saying, is somehow foisted upon the text of the Old Testament. To explain this, even in the briefest manner, it is necessary to state that, in general, Jewish traditionalism is distinguished into the "Halachah" and the "Haggadah." The "Halachah" (from "halach," to "walk") indicates the settled legal determinations, which constituted the "oral law," or "Thorah shebeal peh." Nothing could here be altered, nor was any

---

[4]This most important and interesting subject is one of those which must be specially reserved for full elaboration in a larger work.

He declared to you his covenant, the Ten Commandments, which he commanded you to follow and then wrote them on two stone tablets (Deut. 4:13).

freedom left to the individual teacher, save that of explanation and illustration. The object of the "Halachah" was to state in detail, and to apply to all possible cases, the principles laid down in the law of Moses; as also to surround it, as it were, with "a hedge," in order to render every unwitting transgression impossible. The "Halachah" enjoyed not only the same authority with the law of Moses, but, as being explanatory, in some respects was even more highly esteemed. Indeed, strictly speaking, it was regarded as equally with the Pentateuch the revelation of God to Moses; only the form or manner of revelation was regarded as different—the one being committed to writing, the other handed down by word of mouth. According to tradition, Moses explained the traditional law successively to Aaron, to his sons, to the seventy elders, and to the people—care being taken that each class heard it four times (Maimonides' *Preface to Seraim,* 1 *a*). The Talmud itself attempts to prove that the whole traditional law, as well as the writings of the prophets and the Hagiographa, had been communicated to Moses, by quoting Ex. 24:12: "I will give thee tables of stone, and a law, and commandments which I have written; that thou mayest teach them." "The 'tables of stone,' " argues Rabbi Levi (*Ber.* 5 *a*), "are the ten commandments; the 'law' is the written law (in the Pentateuch); the 'commandments' are the Mishnah; 'which I have written,' refers to the prophets and the Hagiographa; while the words, 'that thou mayest teach them,' point to the Gemara. From this we learn, that all this was given to Moses on Sinai."

If such was the "Halachah," it is not so easy to define the limits of the "Haggadah." The term, which is derived from the verb "higgid," to "discuss," or "tell about," covers all that possessed not the authority of strict legal determinations. It was legend, or story, or moral, or exposition, or discussion, or application—in short, whatever the fancy or predilections of a teacher might choose to make it, so that he could somehow connect it either with Scripture or with a "Halachah." For this purpose some definite rules were necessary to preserve, if not from extravagance, at least from utter absurdity. Originally there were four such canons for connecting the "Haggadah" with Scripture. Contracting, after the favourite manner of the Jews, the initial letters, these four canons were designated by the word *"Pardes"*[5] (Paradise). They were—1. To ascertain the plain meaning of a passage (the "Peshat"); 2. To take the single letters of a word as an indication or hint ("Remes") of other words, or even of whole sentences; 3. The "Derush," or practical exposition of a passage; and 4. To find out the "Sod" (mystery), or mystical meaning of a verse or word. These four canons were gradually enlarged into thirty-two rules, which gave free vent to every kind of fancifulness. Thus one of these rules—the "Gematria" (geometry, calculation)—allowed the interpreter to find out the numerical value of the letters in a word—the Hebrew letters, like the Roman, being also numerals—and to substitute for a word one or more which had the same numerical value. Thus, if in Num. 12:1 we read that Moses was married to an "Ethiopian woman" (in the original, "Cushith"), Onkelos substitutes instead of this, by "gematria," the words, "of fair appearance"—the numerical value both of Cushith and of the words "of fair appearance" being equally 736. By this substitution the objectionable idea of Moses' marrying an Ethiopian was at the same time removed. Similarly, the Mishnah maintains that those who loved God were to inherit each 310 worlds, the numerical value of the word "substance" ("Yesh") in Prov. 8:21 being 310.[6] On the other hand, the canons for the deduction of a "Halachah" from the text of Scripture were much more strict and logical. Seven such rules are ascribed to Hillel, which were afterwards enlarged to thirteen.[7] Little objection can be taken to them; but

The four canons for correcting the "Haggadah" with Scripture:
1. *Peshat*
2. *Remes*
3. *Derush*
4. *Sod*

---

[5] Of course the vowels are not marked in the Hebrew.

[6] Compare Gfrörer, *Jahrh. d. Heils,* i. p. 244, etc.

[7] It would be beyond the scope of this volume to explain these "middoth," or "measurements," and to illustrate them by examples. Those who are interested in the matter are referred to the very full discussion on Rabbinical exegesis in my *History of the Jewish Nation,* pp. 570-580.

unfortunately their practical application was generally almost as fanciful, and certainly as erroneous, as in the case of the "Haggadah."

Probably most readers would wish to know something more of those "traditions" to which our Lord so often referred in His teaching. We have here to distinguish, in the first place, between the Mishnah and the Gemara. The former was, so to speak, the text, the latter its extended commentary. At the same time, the Mishnah contains also a good deal of commentary, and much that is not either legal determination or the discussion thereof; while the Gemara, on the other hand, also contains what we would call "text." The word Mishnah (from the verb "shanah") means "repetition"—the term referring to the supposed repetition of the traditional law, which has been above described. The Gemara, as the very word shows, means "discussion," and embodies the discussions, opinions, and sayings of the Rabbis upon, or *à propos* of, the Mishnah. Accordingly, the text of the Mishnah is always given in the pages of the Talmud, which reproduce those discussions thereon of the Jewish theological parliament or academy, which constitute the Gemara. The authorities introduced in the Mishnah and the Gemara range from about the year 180 B.C. to 430 A.D. (in the Babylon Talmud). The Mishnah is, of course, the oldest work, and dates, in its present form and as a written compilation, from the close of the second century of our era. Its contents are chiefly "Halachah," there being only one Tractate (Aboth) in which there is no "Halachah" at all, and another (on the measurements of the Temple) in which it but very rarely occurs. Yet these two Tractates are of the greatest historical value and interest. On the other hand, there are thirteen whole Tractates in the Mishnah which have no "Haggadah" at all, and other twenty-two in which it is but of rare occurrence. Very much of the Mishnah must be looked upon as dating before, and especially from the time of Christ, and its importance for the elucidation of the New Testament is very great, though it requires to be most judiciously used. The Gemara, or book of

Miriam and Aaron began to talk against Moses because of his Cushite wife, for he had married a Cushite (Num. 12:1).

discussions on the Mishnah, forms the two Talmuds —the Jerusalem and the Babylon Talmud. The former is so called because it is the product of the Palestinian academies; the latter is that of the Babylonian school. The completion of the Jerusalem or Palestinian Talmud ("Talmud" = doctrine, lore) dates from the middle of the fourth, that of the Babylonian from the middle of the sixth century of our era. It need scarcely be said that the former is of much greater historical value than the latter. Neither of these two Gemaras, as we now possess them, is quite complete—that is, there are Tractates in the Mishnah for which we have no Gemara, either in the Jerusalem or in the Babylon Talmud. Lastly, the Babylon Talmud is more than four times the size of that of Jerusalem. Obviously this is not the place for giving even the briefest outline of the contents of the Mishnah.[8] Suffice it here to state that it consists of six books ("sedarim," "orders"), which are subdivided into Tractates ("Massichthoth"), and these again into chapters ("Perakim"), and single determinations or traditions ("Mishnaioth"). In quoting the Mishnah it is customary to mention not the Book (or "Seder") but the special Tractate, the Perek (or chapter), and the Mishnah. The names of these Tractates (not those of the books) give a sufficient idea of their contents, which cover every conceivable, and well-nigh every inconceivable case, with full discussions thereon. Altogether the Mishnah contains sixty-three Tractates, consisting of 525 chapters, and 4,187 "Mishnaioth."

There is yet another branch of Jewish theology, which in some respects is the most interesting to the Christian student. There can be no doubt, that so early as the time of our Lord a series of doctrines and speculations prevailed which were kept secret from the multitude, and even from ordinary students, probably from fear of leading them into heresy. This class of study bears the general name of the "Kabbalah," and, as even the term (from "kabal," to

Like the appearance of a rainbow in the clouds on a rainy day, so was the radiance around him.

This was the appearance of the likeness of the glory of the LORD. When I saw it, I fell facedown, and I heard the voice of one speaking (Ezek. 1:28).

---

[8] In Appendix 1 we give as a specimen a translation of one of the Mishnic Tractates; and in Appendix 2 translations of extracts from the Babylon Talmud.

Jesus replied, "And why do you break the command of God for the sake of your tradition? For God said, 'Honor your father and mother' and 'Anyone who curses his father or mother must be put to death.' But you say that if a man says to his father or mother, 'Whatever help you might otherwise have received from me is a gift devoted to God,' he is not to 'honor his father' with it. Thus you nullify the word of God for the sake of your tradition" (Matt. 15:3–6).

"receive," or "hand down") implies, represents the spiritual traditions handed down from earliest times, although mixed up, in course of time, with many foreign and spurious elements. The "Kabbalah" grouped itself chiefly around the history of the creation, and the mystery of God's Presence and Kingdom in the world, as symbolised in the vision of the chariot and of the wheels (Ezek. 1). Much that is found in Cabbalistic writings approximates so closely to the higher truths of Christianity, that, despite the errors, superstitions, and follies that mingle with it, we cannot fail to recognise the continuance and the remains of those deeper facts of Divine revelation, which must have formed the substance of prophetic teaching under the Old Testament, and have been understood, or at least hoped for, by those who were under the guidance of the Holy Spirit.

If now, at the close of these sketches of Jewish life, we ask ourselves, what might have been expected as to the relation between Christ and the men and the religion of His period, the answer will not be difficult. Assuredly, in one respect Christ could not have been a stranger to His period, or else His teaching would have found no response, and, indeed, have been wholly unintelligible to His contemporaries. Nor did He address them as strangers to the covenant, like the heathen. His was in every respect the continuation, the development, and the fulfilment of the Old Testament. Only, He removed the superincumbent load of traditionalism; He discarded the externalism, the formalism, and the work-righteousness, which had well-nigh obliterated the spiritual truths of the Old Testament, and substituted in their place the worship of the letter. The grand spiritual facts, which it embodied, He brought forward in all their brightness and meaning; the typical teaching of that dispensation He came to show forth and to fulfil; and its prophecies He accomplished, alike for Israel and the world. And so in Him all that was in the Old Testament—of truth, way, and life—became "Yea and Amen." Thus we can understand how, on the one hand, the Lord could avail Himself of every spiritual element around, and adopt the sayings, parables, ideas, and customs of that period—indeed, must have done so, in order to be a true man of the period,—and yet be so wholly not of that time as to be despised, rejected, and delivered up unto death by the blind guides of His blinded fellow-countrymen. Had He entirely discarded the period in which He lived, had He not availed Himself of all in it that was true or might be useful, He would not have been of it—not the true man Christ Jesus. Had He followed it, identified Himself with its views and hopes, or headed its movements, He would not have been the Christ, the Son of the living God, the promised Deliverer from sin and guilt.[9]

> *Through him all things were made; without him nothing was made that has been made. In him was life, and that life was the light of men. The light shines in the darkness, but the darkness has not understood it (John 1:3–5).*

And so we can also perceive the reason of the essential enmity to Christ on the part of the Pharisees and Scribes. It was not that He was a new and a strange Teacher; it was, that He came as the Christ. Theirs was not an opposition of teaching to His; it was a contrariety of fundamental life-principles. "Light came into the world, but men loved darkness rather than light." Closely related as the two were, the Pharisaical Judaism of that and of the present period is at the opposite pole from the religion of Christ— alike as regards the need of man, the purposes of God's love, and the privileges of His children. There was one truth which, we are reluctantly obliged to admit, found, alas! scarcely any parallel in the teaching of Rabbinism: it was that of a suffering Messiah. Hints indeed there were, as certain passages in the prophecies of Isaiah could not be wholly ignored or misrepresented, even by Rabbinical ingenuity, just as the doctrine of vicarious suffering and substitution could not be eliminated from the practical teaching of the confession of sins over the sacrifices, when the worshipper day by day laid his hands upon, and transferred to them his guilt. Yet Judaism, except in the case of the few, saw not in all this that to which alone it could point as its real meaning: "The Lamb of God, which taketh away the sin of the world."

---

[9] The full discussion of a subject of such unspeakable importance in all its bearings would require a separate work.

*The people walking in
darkness
have seen a great light;
on those living in the land
of the shadow of death
a light has dawned…
For to us a child is born,
to us a son is given,
and the government will
be on his shoulders.
And he will be called
Wonderful Counselor,
Mighty God,
Everlasting Father, Prince
of Peace
(Isa. 9:2, 6).*

And now, as century after century has passed, and the gladsome Gospel message has been carried from nation to nation, while Israel is still left in the darkness of its unbelief and the misery of its mistaken hope, we seem to realise with ever increasing force that "The people that walked in darkness have seen a great light: they that dwell in the land of the shadow of death, upon them hath the light shined." Yes: "unto us a Child is born, unto us a Son is given: and the government shall be upon His shoulder: and His Name shall be called Wonderful, Counsellor, The mighty God, The Everlasting Father, The Prince of Peace" (Isa. 9:2, 6). For assuredly, "God hath not cast away His people which He foreknew." But "all Israel shall be saved: as it is written, There shall come out of Sion the Deliverer, and shall turn away ungodliness from Jacob" (Rom. 11:2, 26). "Watchman, what of the night? Watchman, what of the night? The watchman said, The morning cometh, and also the night" (Isa. 21:11, 12).

MASSECHETH MIDDOTH

(BEING THE MISHNIC TRACTATE DESCRIPTIVE
OF THE MEASUREMENTS OF THE TEMPLE)

Middoth is the tenth Tractate of *Seder V. (Kodashim)* of the Mishnah. It has no *Gemara* either in the Jerusalem or the Babylon Talmud. In the former the whole of Seder 5 is awanting; in the latter only two and a-half Tractates (half *Tamid, Middoth,* and *Kinnim). Middoth* contains *Halachah* only in the following passages: i. 2, 3, 9; ii. 2, 4, 5, 6; iii. 3, 5, 8; iv. 2, 5; v. 3, 4. Throughout the Mishnah the names of 128 sages are introduced. Of those mentioned in this Tractate almost all witnessed the destruction of the Temple.

PEREK I.

1. The priests kept watch in the Temple in three places: in the house Avtinas, and in the house Nitsuts, and in the house of Moked; and the Levites in twenty-one places: 5 at the five gates leading into the Temple (the Mountain of the House), 4 in the four angles within, 5 at the five gates of the court, 4 in its four angles without, and 1 in the chamber of offering, and 1 in the chamber of the vail, and 1 behind the Most Holy Place (the House of Atonement).

2. The Captain of the Temple (the man of the Temple Mount) visited each guard, and burning torches *were carried* before him. And every guard which did not stand up (which was not standing), the Captain of the Temple said to him: "Peace be to thee." If he observed that he slept, he smote him with his stick, and he had authority to burn his dress. And they said, "What is the noise (voice) in

the court?" "It is the noise of a Levite who is beaten, and his clothes are set on fire, because he slept upon his watch." Rabbi Eliezer, the son of Jacob, said: "On one occasion they found the brother of my mother sleeping, and they burned his dress."

3. There were five gates to the Temple inclosure (Temple Mount): the two gates of Huldah from the south, which served for entrance and for exit; Kipponos from the west; Tadi from the north—it did not serve for anything; the eastern gate, upon which *was* a representation of the city of Shushan, and by it the high-priest who burned the Red Heifer, and all who assisted, went out upon the Mount of Olives.

4. There were seven gates in the court; three on the north, and three on the south, and one in the east. That in the south was the gate of burning; second to it, the gate of the firstborn;

third to it, the water gate. That in the east was the gate of Nicanor, and two chambers belonged to it, one on the right hand, and one on the left—the one the chamber of Phineas, the wardrobe keeper, and the other the chamber of those who made the pancake offering.[1]

5. And that on the north was the gate Nitsuts, and it was after the form of an Exhedra, and an *Alijah* was built on the top of it; and the priests kept guard above, and the Levites below, and it had a door to the *Chel.* Second to it was the gate of offering; third to it the *Beth Moked.*

6. And four rooms were in the Beth Moked, like small bed chambers[2] opening on a dining apartment; two in *the place that was* holy, and two in *that which was* not holy, and the heads of the beams[3] separated between *that which was* holy and *that which was* not holy. And for what did they serve? That on the south-west was the chamber of offering; that on the south-east the chamber of the shew-bread; on the north-east, there the Asmoneans deposited the stones of the altar which the King of Javan had defiled; on the north-west, there they went down to the bath-house.

7. There were two gates to the Beth Moked—one opened upon the Chel, the other upon the court. Rabbi Jehudah says: "That which opened upon the court had a small wicket by which they went in to explore the court."

8. The Beth Moked was arched, and was a great house surrounded by extensions (perhaps terraces) of stone, and the elders of the house of their fathers slept there, and the keys of the court in their hand; and the young priests, every one with his pillow on the ground (perhaps his dress).

9. And there was a place there, a cubit by a cubit, and a slab of marble, and a ring was fastened on it, and the chain with the keys were hung thereon. When the time came for closing, he lifted the slab by the ring, and took the keys from the chain, and the priest closed the gates from within, and the Levite had to sleep without. When he had finished closing, he returned the keys to the chain, and the slab to its place; he placed his pillow upon it and slept there. If an accident befell one of them, he went out and had to go by the winding stair[4] which went under the house, and lights were burning on either side, till he came to the bath-house. Rabbi Eliezer, the son of Jacob, said: "By the winding stairs he passed under the Chel, and went out and had to go through Tadi."

PEREK II.

1. The Temple inclosure (the Temple Mount) *was* 500 cubits by 500 cubits; *it was* largest on the south; next *largest* on the east; then on the north; smallest on the west. The place where there was most measurement there was also most service.

2. All who entered the Temple inclosure entered by the right, and turned and went out by the left, except those whom something[5] had befallen, who turned to the left. "What *ails* thee

---

[1] For the daily offering of the high-priest.

[2] In the original: Kaitunoth (evidently the Greek *koitan*) opening upon a *Teraklin,* evidently the *Triclinium.*

[3] *Roshe Paspassin.*

[4] *Mesibbah,* literally, that which goes round about.

[5] So literally *(Davar).* Of course, not the same expression as in i. 9.

that thou turnest to the left?" "Because I am a mourner." "He that dwelleth in this house comfort thee!" "Because I am under the bann." "He that dwelleth in this house put it in their hearts, that they restore thee!" So Rabbi Meir. Rabbi Jose says to him, "This would make it, as if they had transgressed against him in judgment; but *rather:* 'He that dwelleth in this house put it in thy heart, that thou hearken to the words of thy brethren, and they restore thee.' "

3. Farther on *was* the Sorag, ten handbreadths high. And thirteen breaches were in it, which the Kings of Javan had made. They restored and strengthened it, and they decreed towards them thirteen obeisances [*in remembrance*]. *Again* farther on the Chel, ten cubits; and twelve steps were there; the step half a cubit high, and half a cubit in extension. All the steps which were there, *each* step *was* half a cubit high, and the extension half a cubit, except those which were at the porch. All the doorways and gates which were there, were twenty cubits high, and ten cubits wide, except that in the porch. All the doorways which were there, had doors, except that in the porch. All the gates which were there, had lintels, except that in the gate Tadi, which had two stones resting, this on the back of that. All the gates which were there, were renewed to be with gold, except the gate of Nicanor, because there was wrought upon them a miracle, and some say, because the brass sparkled.

4. All the walls which were there were high, except the wall in the east, so that the priest who burned the heifer, standing on the top of the Mount of Olives, and directing himself to look,

saw through the gateway of the sanctuary, at the time when he sprinkled the blood.

5. The Court of the Women was 135 cubits long by 135 cubits broad, and four chambers were in the four angles, each 40 cubits square, and they were not roofed in. And so they are intended to be, as it is said: "And he brought me forth into the outer court, and caused me to pass by the four corners of the court, and behold, in every corner of the court a court. In the four corners of the court courts smoking"[6] ...*It is said*, they were "smoking," and that because they were not roofed. And for what did they serve? That on the south-east was the chamber of the Nazarites, where the Nazarites washed their peace-offerings, and polled their hair, and threw it under the pot. That on the north-east was the wood chamber, where the priests who were disqualified picked the wood, and every stick in which a worm was found, it was unfitted for the altar. That on the north-west was the chamber of the lepers. That on the south-west Rabbi Eliezer, the son of Jacob, said: "I have forgotten for what it served." Abba Shaul said: "There they put the wine and the oil; it was called the chamber of the house of Schamanyah." And it [the wall] was at first flush, and they surrounded it with a gallery, so that the women looked from above and the men from beneath, for the purpose that they might not be mixed together. And fifteen steps went up from there to the Court of Israel, like the fifteen degrees in the Psalms [Songs of Degrees in the Psalms]. Upon these the Levites stood singing the songs. They were not rectangular but rounded, like the arc of a rounded substance.

[6] Ezek. 46:21, 22.

6. And there were chambers beneath the Court of Israel, and they opened upon the Court of the Women. There the Levites placed their harps, and their psalteries, and their cymbals, and all the musical instruments. The Court of Israel was 135 cubits long by 11 broad, and similarly, the Court of the Priests was 135 long by 11 broad, and the heads of the beams divided between the Court of Israel and the Court of the Priests. Rabbi Eliezer, the son of Jacob, said: "There was a step, a cubit high, and upon it the *Duchan* was placed, and on it were three steps, each half a cubit. It results, that the Court of the Priests was 2¹/₂ cubits higher than that of Israel. The entire court was 187 cubits long and 135 cubits broad. Thirteen obeisances took place there. Abba José, the son of Chanan, said: "Towards the thirteen gates." The southern *were:* nearest to the west, the upper gate, *then* the gate of burning, the gate of the first-born, and the water-gate. And why was its name called the water-gate? Because through it they brought the pitcher of water for pouring out for the "Feast of Tabernacles." Rabbi Eliezer, the son of Jacob, said: "And by it the waters were flowing down, with the direction of coming out below the threshold of the Temple." And opposite to them to the north were: (nearest to the west) the gate of Jeconiah, the gate of offering, the gate of the women, and the gate of the song. And why was it called the gate of Jeconiah? Because by it Jeconiah went out into captivity. That on the east *was* the gate of Nicanor, and it had two wickets, one on its right and the other on its left. And *there were* two [gates] to the west; they had no name.

PEREK III.

1. The altar was 32 by 32 [cubits]. Upwards 1 cubit, and contract 1 cubit: that was the base. Remain 30 by 30. Upwards 5, and contract 1 cubit: that was the circuit. Remain 28 by 28. The place of the horns, a cubit on this side and a cubit on that side. Remain 26 by 26. The place for the tread of the priests, a cubit on this side and a cubit on that side. Remain 24 by 24: the place where the sacrifice was laid out. Rabbi José said: "At the first it was only 28 by 28; *though* it contracted and went up, according to this measurement, until there remained the place for laying the sacrifices: 20 by 20. But when the children of the Captivity came up, they added to it 4 cubits on the south and 4 on the west like a *gamma,* because it is said, 'And Ariel shall be 12 cubits long by 12 broad, square.'[7] That does not mean that it was only 12 by 12, since it is added: 'In the four corners thereof, to teach that it measured from the middle 12 cubits in every direction." And a scarlet line girdled it in the middle to separate between the upper and the lower blood-sprinklings. And the base ran round all the north and all the west side, but was shortened a cubit on the south and on the east.

2. In the south-western angle were two apertures, like small nostrils, and the blood, poured on the base to the west, and on the base to the south, descended through them, and co-mingled in the canal, and flowed out into the brook Kedron.

3. Below in the pavement, in that angle, there was a place, a cubit by a cubit, *with* a tablet of marble, and a ring

---

[7] Ezek. 43:16, "Ariel" = the lion of God = the altar.

was fastened in it, and here they went down into the sewer to cleanse it. And there was a sloping ascent to the south of the altar, 32 cubits long by 16 broad, and it had a pit at its west side, into which they put sin-offerings of birds that were defiled.

4. Both the stones of the sloping ascent and those of the altar were from the valley of Beth Cherem. And they dug beneath the virgin soil, and brought out from it undamaged (whole) stones, upon which iron had not been lifted, because iron defiles everything by contact, and by scratching. One of the stones was scratched: it was defiled; but the rest were lawful for use. And they whitened them twice in the year, once at the Passover, and once at the Feast of Tabernacles; and the Sanctuary once at the Passover. Rabbi[8] says: "On the eve of every Sabbath they whitened it with a cloth, on account of the blood-sprinklings." They did not plaster it with an iron trowel, lest it might touch, and defile. For the iron is created to shorten the days of man, and the altar is created to lengthen the days of man, therefore it is not right that that which shortens should be lifted upon that which lengthens.

5. And rings were to the north of the altar: six rows, each of four; but some say, four rows, each of six; and in these they slaughtered the holy sacrifices. The house (place) of slaughtering was to the north of the altar. And there were eight short pillars[9] and squares of cedar upon the top of them, and hooks of iron were fastened in them, and three rows were upon each of them, upon which they hung up, and they skinned upon marble tables which were between the pillars.

6. And the laver was between the porch and the altar, and inclined nearer towards the south. Between the porch and the altar were 22 cubits, and 12 steps were there, each step half a cubit high, and its extension a cubit—a cubit, a cubit, and then an extension of three (cubits); and a cubit, a cubit, and an extension of three; and the topmost, a cubit, a cubit, and an extension of four (cubits). Rabbi Jehudah said: "The topmost a cubit, a cubit, and an extension of five (cubits)."

7. The doorway to the porch was 40 cubits high and 20 broad, and five beams of ash were upon the top of it; the lowest protruded over the doorway a cubit on this and a cubit on that side; that above it protruded over it a cubit on this and a cubit on that side; it results, that the topmost [was] 30 cubits, and a buttress of stones was between each one of them.

8. And supports of cedar were fixed from the wall of the Sanctuary to the wall of the porch, lest they should bulge; and chains of gold were fixed in the roof of the porch, and by them the young priests mounted, to look at the crowns, as it is written:[10] "And crowns shall be to Helem, and to Tobijah, and to Jedaiah, and to Hen the son of Zephaniah, for a memorial in the temple of the Lord."[11] A vine of gold was standing over the entrance to the Sanctuary, and was suspended on the top of beams.

---

[8] *The* Rabbi, *i.e.* R. Jehudah the Holy.

[9] *Nannasin,* evidently the Greek *nanos.*

[10] *Malteraoth shel Milah*—Malterah or Ammaltera, from the Greek *melathron;* Milah, the Greek *melia.*

[11] Zech. 6:14.

Every one who vowed a leaf, or a berry, or a bunch, brought it, and hung it up there. Rabbi Eliezer, the son of Rabbi Zadok, said: "It happened (that they had to remove it) and there were numbered for it 300 priests."[12]

PEREK IV.

1. The entrance to the Sanctuary was 20 cubits high, and 10 cubits broad; and it had four doors [two folding-doors]: two within and two without, as it is said: "And the Sanctuary and the Holy Place had two doors."[13] The outer doors opened *to the* inside of the doorway, to cover the thickness of the wall, and the inner doors opened inwards into the house, to cover behind the doors. For, the whole house was covered with gold, except behind the doors. Rabbi Jehudah said: "They [both pairs of doors] stood within the entrance, and were like *Azteramita*,[14] and they folded backwards—these 2^1/$_2$ cubits, and those 2^1/$_2$ cubits. Half a cubit the door-post from this [corner], and half a cubit the door-post from that, and so it is said: 'And the doors had two leaves alike, two turning-leaves; two for the one door, and two leaves for the other.' "[15]

2. And the great gate had two wickets, one to the north and one to the south. That to the south, no man ever passed through it; and to this clearly refers what is said in Ezekiel, as it is written: "Then the Lord said unto me, This gate shall be shut, it shall not be opened,

and no man shall enter in by it; because the Lord, the God of Israel, hath entered in by it, therefore it shall be shut."[16] He took the key, and opened the wicket, and entered the little chamber (atrium), and from the little chamber into the Sanctuary. Rabbi Jehudah said: "Along the thickness of the wall he walked,[17] until he found himself standing between the two gates, and he opened the outer one from within and the inner one from without."

3. And thirty-eight little chambers were there—fifteen on the north, fifteen on the south, and eight on the west. On the north and on the south, five on the top of five, and five on their top; and on the west three on the top of three, and two on the top of them. And each one of them had three entrances, one to the little chamber on the right, and one to the little chamber on the left, and one to the little chamber on the top. And at the north-western corner were five entrances, one to the little chamber at the right, and the other to the little chamber on the top, and another to the winding-stair, and another to the wicket, and another to the Sanctuary.

4. And the lowermost (chamber) *was* 5 cubits, and the roofing (extension, platitude) 6; the middle (chamber) 6, and the roofing 7; and the uppermost 7, as it is said: "The nethermost chamber was 5 cubits broad, and the middle 6 cubits broad, and the third 7 cubits broad, for he made rebatements in the 'house'

---

[12] To remove or to cleanse it.

[13] Ezek. 41:23.

[14] The term, which seems not to have been quite understood even in Talmudical times, is rendered by Jost: twisted leaf, and derived from *strephō*.

[15] Ezek. 41:24.

[16] Ezek. 44:2.

[17] It is, however, supposed by some to refer to a kind of passage through the wall.

round about without, that [the beams] should not be fastened within the walls of the house."[18]

5. And a winding-stair went up from the north-eastern angle to the north-western angle, by which they went up to the roofs of the chambers. One went up the winding-stair with his face to the west, and went all along the north side, until he came to the west. He came to the west, and turned his face to the south, and went all along the west side till he came to the south. He came to the south, and turned his face eastwards, and went along the south side, till he came to the entrance of the Alijah; for the entrance to the Alijah opened to the south, and in the entrance to the Alijah were two beams of cedar, by which they went up to the roof of the Alijah, and the heads of the beams[19] divided in the Alijah between the Holy Place and the Most Holy Place. And trap-doors opened in the Alijah into the Most Holy Place, by which they let down the workmen in chests, that they might not feast their eyes in the Most Holy Place.

6. And the Sanctuary was 100 by 100, by 100 high; the solid foundation 6 cubits, and the height upon it 40 cubits; 1 cubit, decorated scroll; 2 cubits, the place for the water-droppings; 1 cubit covering, and 1 cubit pavement, and the height of the Alijah 40 cubits, and 1 cubit scroll-work, and 2 cubits the place for the dropping, and 1 cubit covering, and 1 cubit pavement, and 3 cubits balustrade, and 1 cubit scare-raven. Rabbi Jehudah said: "The scare-raven was not counted from the measurement, but the balustrade was 4 cubits."

7. From the east to the west 100 cubits—the wall of the porch 5, and the porch 11; the wall of the Sanctuary 6, and its interior space 40 cubits, 1 cubit intermediate wall, and 20 cubits the Most Holy Place, the wall of the Sanctuary 6, and the little chamber 6, and the wall of the little chamber 5. From the north to the south 70 cubits— the wall of the winding-stair 5, and the winding-stair 3, the wall of the little chamber 5, and the little chamber 6, the wall of the Sanctuary 6, and its interior space 20 cubits, the wall of the Sanctuary 6, and the little chamber 6, and the wall of the little chamber 5, and the place for the going down of the water 3 cubits, and the wall 5 cubits. The porch protruded beyond it, 15 cubits from the north and 15 cubits from the south, and it was called the house of the sacrificial knives, because there they deposited the knives. And the Sanctuary was narrow behind and wide in front, and like to a lion, as it is said: "O Ariel, the lion of God, the city where David dwelt."[20] As the lion is narrow behind and wide in front, so is the Sanctuary narrow behind and wide in its front.

PEREK V.

1. The whole court was 187 cubits long by 135 cubits broad. From the east to the west 187: the place for the tread of Israel 11 cubits; the place for the tread of the priests 11 cubits; the altar 32; between the porch and the altar 22 cubits; the Sanctuary 100 cubits; and 11 cubits behind the house of Atonement.

2. From the north to the south 135 cubits: the altar and the circuit 62;

---

[18] 1 Kings 6:6.
[19] *Roshe Paspassin.*
[20] Isa. 29:1.

from the altar to the rings 8 cubits; the place of the rings 24 cubits; from the rings to the tables 4; from the tables to the pillars 4; from the pillars to the wall of the court 8 cubits; and the rest between the circuit and the wall, and the place of the pillars.

3. There were six rooms in the court—three to the north, and three to the south. Those on the north: the salt-chamber, the chamber *Parvah*, the chamber of those who washed out. The salt-chamber: there they put salt to the offering. The chamber of *Parvah*: there they salted the skins of the holy sacrifices, and on the roof was the bath-house of the high-priest on the Day of Atonement. The chamber of those who washed out, where they washed the inwards of the holy things, and thence a winding- stair went up to the roof of the house of Parvah.

4. Those on the south: the wood-chamber, the chamber of the captivity, the chamber of "hewn stones." The wood-chamber—said Rabbi Eliezer, the son of Jacob: "I have forgotten for what it served." Abba Shaul said: "It was the chamber of the high-priest, and it lay behind the other two, and a roof was extended over the three (they had one common roof). The chamber of the captivity: a well was there which they of the captivity had digged, and a wheel was placed upon it, and thence they provided water for the whole court. The chamber of "hewn stones:" there the great Sanhedrim of Israel sat, and judged the priesthood. And the priest in whom was found disqualification was clothed in black, and veiled in black, and went out, and had to go. And if there was not found in him disqualification, he was dressed in white, and veiled in white; he went in and served with his brethren the priests. And they made a feast-day, because there was not found disqualification in the seed of Aaron the priest, and thus spake they: "Blessed be God,[21] blessed be He, that there has not been found disqualification in the seed of Aaron, and blessed be He Who has chosen Aaron and his sons, to stand to serve before the face of the Lord in the Most Holy House."

---

[21] The expression here is *Makom*, literally "the place," in the same sense in which *topos* is used by Philo.

EXTRACTS FROM THE BABYLON TALMUD

Berachoth is the first Tractate of the first *Seder* (*Seraim*, which consists of eleven Tractates). It contains nine *Perakim*, which successively explain the duty, the exceptions, the posture, the formulas, and the controversies in regard to prayer. The Tractate exists both in the Jerusalem and in the Babylon Talmud. The great Maimonides has prefaced the *Seder Seraim* by a General Introduction, which presents a general view of Talmudism, and explains what is of greatest importance to the student. Notwithstanding his vast learning and authority, incompleteness and inaccuracies have, however, been pointed out in his Introduction.

Mishnah.—From what time is the "Shema"[1] said in the evening? From the hour that the priests entered to eat of their therumah[2] until the end of the first night watch.[3] These are the words of Rabbi Eliezer. But the sages say: Till midnight. Rabban Gamaliel says: Until the column of the morning (the dawn) rises. It happened, that his sons came back from a banquet. They said to him: "We have not said the 'Shema.' " He said to them, "If the column of the morning has not come up, you are bound to say it." And not only this have they said, but, wherever the sages have said "till midnight," their command applies till the morning column rises. The burning of the fat and of the members (of sacrifices) is lawful till the morning column rise;[4] and so everything which is to be eaten on the same day (on which it has been offered) is allowed to be eaten till the rise of the morning column. If so, why do the sages say, "till midnight?" In order to keep a man far from transgressing.

Gemara—Fol. 3 a. *To the end of the night watch.*—How does Rabbi Eliezer mean this? If he means that the night has three watches, he should say till four hours; and if he means that the night has four watches, he should say till three hours. Indeed, he means that the night has three watches, but he indicates by the expression that there are night

---

[1] The well-known prayer, beginning "Hear, O Israel."

[2] The heave-offering given to the priests, which they ate within the Temple.

[3] The Jews divided the night into three watches.

[4] That is, they may be left to consume on the altar from the time of evening sacrifice till then.

watches in heaven, as there are night watches upon earth. For we have this doctrine: Rabbi Eliezer says, There are three night watches in the night, and in every one of these night watches the Holy One, blessed be His Name, sits and roars like a lion. For it is written (Jeremiah 25:30), "Jehovah shall roar from on high, from the habitation of His holiness shall He give out His voice; roaring shall He roar on account of His habitation."[5] The signs of this thing are as follows: In the first night watch the ass brays, in the second the dogs bark, in the third the suckling sucks his mother, and the wife speaks to her husband. How does Rabbi Eliezer indicate them? Does he thus indicate the commencement of the night watch? The commencement of the first night watch, what need is there for a sign of it, seeing it is night? Or does he refer to the end of the night watch? For the end of the last night watch, why does he give me a sign, seeing it is day? But he indicates the end of the first night watch and the commencement of the last night watch, and the middle of the middle night watch. And if thou wilt, I will say that he refers in all to the end of the night watches. And if thou sayest, the last does not require it, what is attained by it? The reading of the "Shema" for him who sleeps in a dark house, and does not know the time for saying the "Shema" when it is, so that, when the woman speaks with her husband and the babe sucks its mother, he may rise up and say the prayer.

Rabbi Isaac, the son of Samuel, says, in the name of Rab, "The night has three watches, and in each one of these watches does the Holy One, blessed be His Name, sit and roar like a lion, and say, 'Woe to the children, because on account of their sins I have laid desolate My house, and burned My temple, and have driven them forth among the nations of the world.' "

We have this doctrine: Rabbi Jose said, "On one occasion I was travelling, and I entered into one of the ruins of Jerusalem to pray. Then came Elijah—his memory be for good—and waited for me at the door till I had finished my prayer. After that I had finished my prayer, he said to me, 'Peace be to thee, Rabbi;' and I said to him, 'Peace be to thee, Rabbi, and my teacher.' And he said to me, 'My son, why didst thou enter into this ruin?' I said to him, 'In order to pray.' And he said to me, 'Thou mightest have prayed on the road.' And I said to him, 'I was afraid that those who passed on the road might perhaps interrupt me.' He said to me, 'Thou shouldest have prayed a short prayer.' In that hour I learned from him three things. I learned that one may not enter into a ruin, and I learned that one may pray on the road, and I learned that he that prays on the road should pray a short prayer. He also said to me, 'My son, what voice hast thou heard in that ruin?' And I said to him, 'I have heard the "Bath Kol,"[6] which cooed like a dove, and said, "Woe to the children, because on account of their sins I have laid waste My House, and I have burned My Sanctuary, and I have driven them forth among the nations." ' And he said to me, 'By thy life, and by the life of thy head, not only at that time did the voice say so, but every day three times does it say so; and not only this, but also at the time when

---

[5] So literally in the Hebrew.
[6] Literally "Daughter Voice"—the voice from heaven.

Israel enters the house of prayer and the house of study, and when they say, "Blessed be His great Name;" then the Holy One, blessed be His Name, moves His head, and says, "Happy is the king whom they thus praise in His house." What remains to the father who has driven his children into captivity? and woe to the children who have been driven forth from the table of their father.' "

The Rabbis teach: On account of three things a ruin is not to be entered. On account of suspicion,[7] and on account of falling in (of the wall), and on account of evil spirits. On account of suspicion— does it not suffice on account of falling in? (Would that not have been alone a sufficient ground?) Fol. 3 *b.* Not if it is recent.[8] But would it not suffice: On account of evil spirits? Not when there are two.[9] If there are two, does not the ground of suspicion cease? Not if the two are impudent...

The Rabbis taught: The night has four watches. These are the words of Rabbi (Jehudah the Holy). Rabbi Nathan says: Three. What is the reason of Rabbi Nathan? Because it is written (Judges 7:19), "So Gideon came, and the hundred men that were with him, unto the outside of the camp, in the beginning of the middle watch." He taught: 'There is no middle, unless there is one before and one after it. And Rabbi,[10] What is the meaning of the "middle?" ' (He replied) 'One of the middle ones among the middle ones.' And Rabbi Nathan, 'Is it written: "The middle of the middle

ones?" It is only written the middle one.' But what ground has Rabbi? Rabbi Serika said, that Rabbi Ami said, that Rabbi Joshua, the son of Levi, said: In one place it is said (Psalm 119:62), "At midnight I will rise to give thanks unto Thee, because of Thy righteous judgments." And in another place it is said (verse 148), "Mine eyes prevent the night watches." How is this? Because the night has four watches. And Rabbi Nathan? He interprets it just as Rabbi Joshua. For we have this teaching: Rabbi Joshua says, "To three hours (into the day the 'Shema' may be said); for this is the way of kings, to rise at three hours (after daybreak). Six hours of the night (from midnight to dawn are six hours) and two by day make together two night watches" (each of four hours). Rabbi Ashi says: "A night watch and a half might also be called night watches."[11]

Rabbi Serika also said, that Rabbi Ami said, that Rabbi Joshua, the son of Levi, said: "You must not speak before the dead anything but the words of the dead." Rabbi Aba, the son of Cahana, said: "They do not say this except in reference to the words of the law (because every one is bound to take part in such conversation); but as to ordinary conversation it does not matter." And some say, Rabbi Aba, the son of Cahana, said, "They do not say this merely concerning the words of Scripture, but much more also concerning ordinary conversation."

And David rose at midnight (as before quoted). Did he not rise in the

---

[7] Of secret sin.

[8] If it has only lately become a ruin, since then there would be no immediate danger.

[9] Because where there are two, they need not fear evil spirits.

[10] This is Rabbi Nathan's challenge to R. Jehudah.

[11] All this is intended to establish Rabbi Nathan's view, that there are only three watches in the night.

evening? since it is written (verse 147),
"I prevented the gloaming, and cried."
And how do we know that this gloaming
was that of the evening? Because it is
written (Prov. 7:9): "In the gloaming, in
the evening of the day, in the denseness
of the night and of darkness." Rabbi
Oshja said, that Rabbi Acha said, So
spake David: "Never has the middle of
the night passed over me in sleep." Rabbi
Seira said, "To the middle of the night he
was sleeping like a horse; from that time
and afterwards he strengthened himself
like a lion." Rabbi Ashi said, "To the
middle of the night he occupied himself
with the words of the law; from that and
afterwards with psalms and hymns."
And the gloaming is that of the evening.
Is there not also a gloaming of the morning? As it is written (1 Sam. 30:17): "And
David smote them from the gloaming
even to the evening of the next day." Is it
not so, from that of the morning to that
of the evening? No, from the evening
again to the evening. If this were so, it
would have been written, "From the
gloaming to the gloaming," or else,
"From the evening to the evening." Also
Raba said: "There are two gloamings, the
gloaming of the night, and then comes
the morning, and the gloaming of the
day, and then comes the night." And
David, How did he know the middle of
the night when it was, since Moses our
teacher did not know it? For it is written
(Exod. 11:4), "About midnight will I go
out into the midst of Egypt." What is it
"about midnight?" If it should be said
that the Holy One, blessed be His Name,
said to him "about the middle"—can
there be any doubting in heaven? But he
said to him "at midnight." Then came he
and said "about midnight" (that is,

Moses said so, because he did not know
exactly when midnight was). Accordingly he was in doubt; and David, should
he have known? David had a sign, for
Rabbi Acha, the son of Bisna, said that
Rabbi Simeon, the pious, said: "A harp
was hung up above the bed of David,
and when the middle of the night came,
the north wind arose and blew over it,
and it sounded of itself. Immediately he
rose up and studied in the Thorah till
the morning column arose. As soon as
the morning column arose, the sages of
Israel went to him. They said to him:
'Our Lord, O King! thy people Israel
require to be supported.' He said to them,
'Support yourselves one of the other.'
They said to him, 'A handful does not
satisfy a lion, and a pit is not filled with
its own sand.' He said to them, 'Go and
spread your hands in the army (make
wars of conquest).' Immediately they
took counsel with Ahithophel and
thought over it in the Sanhedrim, and
inquired at the Urim and Thummim."
Rabbi Joseph said: "What else should
this Scripture be (1 Chron. 27:34): 'And
after Ahithophel was Benajahu, the son
of Jehoiada (the reading is here different
from that of our text), and Abiathar; and
the general of the king's army was Joab.'
Ahithophel, he was the counsellor, and
so it is said (2 Sam. 16:23), 'And the
counsel of Ahithophel, which he coun-
selled in those days, was as if a man had
inquired at the oracle of God.' Benajahu,
the son of Jehoiada, that is the
Sanhedrim,[12] and Abiathar; these are the
Urim and Thummim. And so it is said (2
Sam. 20:23), 'And Benaiah, the son of
Jehoiada, was over the Cherethites, and
over the Pelethites.' And why was their
name called Cherethites and Pelethites?

---

[12]Whose chief he is supposed to have been.

Cherethites, because they cut short their words, and Pelethites, because they were wonderful in their words.[13] And after these was Joab, the general of the king." Rabbi Isaac, the son of Idi, said, "Some say, what else14 means the Scripture (Ps. 57:8), 'Awake up, my glory; awake, psaltery and harp; I myself will wake the morning?' " Rabbi Seria said, "Moses knew it (the midnight hour), and so also did David know it. But if David knew it, for what was the harp? To awaken him from sleep. And if Moses knew it, why did he require to say, 'about midnight?' Moses thought, perhaps, the astronomers of Pharaoh may err, and then say, 'Moses is a liar.' For the Master says, 'Teach thy tongue to say, I do not know; perhaps thou mayest be regarded as inventing, and be seized.' " Rabbi Ashi said, "It was in the middle of the night of the thirteenth, after which the fourteenth dawns;" and so Moses said to Israel, "The Holy One, blessed be His Name, says, 'To-morrow, about midnight, as now, I shall go out in the midst of Egypt.' "

Fol. 16 *b*. Rabbi Elazar said: "What is it that is written (Ps. 63:4), 'Thus will I bless Thee while I live; I will lift up my hands in Thy Name?' 'I will bless Thee while I live:' that is saying the 'Shema.' 'I will lift my hands in Thy Name:' that is prayer;—and if he does so, of him does the Scripture say, 'My soul shall be satisfied as with marrow and fatness.' And not only this, but he inherits two worlds—this world and the world to come, as it is written, 'And my mouth shall praise Thee with lips of joys.' "[15]

Rabbi Elazar, after he had finished his prayer, said thus: "May it please Thee, O Lord our God, that Thou wouldest cause to dwell in our lot love and brotherhood, peace and friendship, and increase our possession with disciples, and gladden our end with a happy end, and with hope, and place our portion in Paradise. Order us in good fellowship, and with the inclination for good in this world, that we may rise and find our hearts in the fear of Thy Name, and that the desire of our souls may come before Thee for good."[16]

Rabbi Jochanan, after he had finished his prayer, said thus: "May it please Thee, O Lord our God, that Thou mayest look upon our shame and see our sorrows, and that Thou clothe Thyself with mercy, and that Thou cover Thyself with Thy might, and that Thou robe Thyself with Thy grace, and that Thou gird Thyself with favour, that there come before Thee the measurement of Thy goodness and of Thy condescension."

Rabbi Seira, after he had finished his prayers, said thus: "May it please Thee, O Lord our God, that we may not sin, and not be put to shame, and not be confounded before our fathers."

Rabbi Chija, after he had finished his prayers, said thus: "May it please Thee, O Lord our God, that Thy Thorah be our labour, and that our hearts be not faint, and that our eyes be not darkened."

Rab, after he had finished his prayers, said thus: "May it please Thee, O Lord our God, to give us prolonged life, a life of peace, a life of good, a life of blessing, a life of nourishment, a life of

---

[13] There is here a play on the words.

[14] Referring again to the saying of Rabbi Simeon, the pious, mentioned earlier.

[15] The plural indicating the two worlds.

[16] This and the following are prayers at night.

vigorous strength, a life in which there shall be the fear of sin, a life in which there shall be neither shame nor confusion, a life of riches and honour, a life in which there shall be among us love of the Thorah and the fear of heaven, a life in which Thou fulfil in us all the desires of our hearts for good."

Rabbi, after he had finished his prayers, said thus: "May it please Thee, O Lord our God, and the God of our fathers, to preserve us from the daring sinner and from daring sin, from an evil man and an evil accident, from the evil impulse, from an evil companion, from an evil neighbour, from Satan the destroyer, from a severe judgment, and from a severe opponent, whether he be a son of the covenant or not." And this, although the officers stood around Rabbi.[17]

Rabbi Saphra, after he had finished his prayers, said thus: "May it please Thee, O Lord our God, that Thou wilt put peace among the family above (the angels) and in the family below, and between the students who busy themselves with Thy Thorah, whether they busy themselves with it for its own sake or not for its own sake; and with reference to all who busy themselves with it not for its own sake, may it please Thee, that they may busy themselves with it for its own sake."

Rabbi Alexander, after he had finished his prayer, said thus: "May it please Thee, O Lord our God, to place us in a corner of light, and not in a corner of darkness, and let not our heart become faint, nor our eyes become darkened." But some say, it was Rab who prayed this prayer, and that Rabbi Alexander, after he had prayed, said thus: "Lord of the

worlds, it is manifest and known before Thee that our pleasure is to do Thy pleasure, and who hinders it? The leaven in the bake-meat and the service of foreign domination. May it please Thee to deliver us from their hands, that we may return to do the laws of Thy good pleasure with a perfect heart."

Raba, when he had finished his prayer, said thus: "Lord, until I was created I was nothing, and now that I am created, I am as if I were not created. Dust I am in life, and how much more when I am dead? Behold I am before Thee like a vessel filled with shame and confusion. May it please Thee, O Lord our God, that I may no more sin, and what I have sinned before Thee, blot out in Thy great mercy, but not through chastisements and evil diseases." And the same was the confession of Rab Hamnuna the Less on the Day of Atonement.

Mar, the son of Rabina, when he had ended his prayer, said as follows: "Lord, keep our tongue from evil, and our lips from speaking guile. And towards those who curse my soul, let me be silent, and let my soul be like the dust towards all. Open my heart in Thy law, and let my soul follow after Thy commandments, and deliver me from an evil accident, from the evil disposition, and from an evil woman, and from all evil which lifts itself up to come into the world. And all who think evil against me, speedily destroy their counsel, and render vain their thoughts. May it please Thee, that the words of my mouth and the meditation of my heart be acceptable before Thee, O Lord, my strength and my Redeemer."

Rabbi Sheisheth, when he had fasted, said, after he had finished his

---

[17] He was not deterred by their presence from so praying.

prayer: "Lord of the world, it is evident before Thee, that at the time that the Sanctuary stood, a man sinned, and he brought an offering, nor did they offer of it anything but its fat and its blood, and he was forgiven. And now I have remained in fasting, and my fat and my blood have been diminished, may it please Thee, that my fat and my blood which have been diminished be as if I had offered them upon the altar, and be merciful to me."

Rabbi Jochanan, when he had finished the book of Job, said thus: "The end of a man is to die, and the end of an animal is to be slaughtered, and all are appointed to death. Blessed is he who has grown up in the Thorah, and busied himself with the Thorah, and labours to have a quiet spirit towards his Creator, and who has grown big with a good name, and who has departed from this world with a good name. And of him, says Solomon (Eccles. 7:1): 'A good name is better than precious ointment; and the day of death than the day of one's birth.'"

It was customary in the mouth of Rabbi Meir: "Learn with all thy heart and with all thy soul, in order to know My ways, and to grow up by the gates of My Thorah. Keep My Thorah in thy heart, and let My fear be before thine eyes. Keep thy mouth from all sin, and cleanse and sanctify thyself from all transgression and sin, and I shall be with thee in every place."

Fol. 55 *a*. Rabbi Chisda said: "Every dream is without a meaning, but not if one has fasted (on account of it)." Also Rabbi Chisda said: "A dream which is not interpreted is like a letter which is not read." Also Rabbi Chisda said: "Neither is there a good dream in which everything comes to pass, nor yet a bad dream in which everything comes to pass." Also Rabbi Chisda said: "An evil dream is better than a good dream." Also Rabbi Chisda said: "An evil dream, its sorrow is sufficient; a good dream, its pleasure is sufficient." Rabbi Joseph said: "A good dream even the joy with me annuls it."[18] Rabbi Chisda also said: "An evil dream is heavier than a chastisement, for it is written (Eccles. 3:14), 'And God doeth it, that men should fear before Him.'" And Rabbah, the grandson of Chanah, said, Rabbi Jochanan said: "This refers to an evil dream. (Jer. 23:28), 'The prophet that hath a dream, let him tell a dream; and he that hath My Word, let him speak My Word faithfully. What is the chaff to the wheat? saith the Lord.' But what have the wheat and the chaff to do with a dream?" But, says Rabbi Jochanan, in name of Rabbi Simeon, the son of Joche, "As wheat alone is not possible without straw, so also is a dream not possible without false things." Rabbi Berachiah said: "A dream, even if a part of it is fulfilled, the whole of it is not fulfilled. Whence have we this? From Joseph, for it is written (Gen. 37:9), 'And behold the sun and the moon,' etc. And at that time his mother was no more." Rabbi Levi said: "Let a man always look forward in regard to a good dream, even as long as twenty-two years. Whence have we that? From Joseph, for it is written (Gen. 37:2), 'These are the generations of Jacob. Joseph was seventeen years old,' and so on. And it is written (Gen. 41:46), 'And Joseph was thirty years old when he stood before Pharaoh,' and so on. From seventeen to thirty, how much is it? Thirteen. And seven of plenty, and two of famine, that makes twenty-two."

[18] This Rabbi was blind.

Rabbi Huna said: "To a good man a good dream is not shown, and to an evil man an evil dream is not shown. We have this doctrine: All the years of David he did not see a good dream, and all the years of Ahithophel he did not see an evil dream. But yet it is written (Ps. 91:10), 'There shall no evil befall thee.' "...

Rabbi Huna, the son of Ami, said, Rabbi Pedath said, Rabbi Jochanan said: "He that seeth a dream, and his soul is distressed, let him go and interpret it before three." Let him interpret it? But Rabbi Chisda said: "A dream which is not interpreted is like a letter which is not read." But certainly (I mean), that he give a good interpretation before three. He summons three, and he says to them, "I have had a good dream." And they say to him, "Behold, it is good, and it will be good. The Merciful One turn it to good. Seven times let it be decreed upon thee from heaven that it be good, and it will be good." Then they say three turnings, and three deliverances, and three times "Peace." Three turnings (Ps. 30:11), "Thou hast turned for me my mourning into dancing: Thou hast put off my sackcloth, and girded me with gladness." *Again* (Jer. 31:13), "Then shall the virgin rejoice in the dance, both young men and old together: for I will turn their mourning into joy," and so on. *Again* (Deut. 23:5), "Nevertheless the Lord thy God would not hearken unto Balaam; but He turned," and so on. "Three deliverances," as it is written (Ps. 55:18), "He hath delivered my soul in peace from the battle that was against me," and so on; (Isa. 35:10), "And the ransomed of the Lord shall return," and so on; (1 Sam. 14:45), "And the people said unto Saul, Shall Jonathan die, who hath wrought this salvation in Israel?" "Three times peace," as it is written (Isa. 57:19), "I

create the fruit of the lips; Peace, peace to him that is far off, and to him that is near, saith the Lord," etc.; (1 Chron. 12:18), "Then the spirit clothed Amasai," and so on; (1 Sam. 25:6), "Thus shall ye say to him that liveth, Peace be both to thee, and peace be to thine house," and so on.

Ameimer, and Mar Sutra, and Rabbi Ashi were sitting all together. They said: "Would that each one might say something which had not been heard by his companion." Then began one among them, and said: "If any one has seen a dream, and does not know what he has seen, let him place himself before the priests of his time, while they spread their hands (in blessing), and let him say thus: 'Lord of the world, I am Thine, and my dreams are Thine. I have dreamt a dream, and I know not what it is, whether I have dreamed for myself, or whether my companions have dreamt of me, or whether I have dreamt of others. If they be good (dreams) confirm them, and strengthen them, like the dreams of Joseph; and if they need healing, heal them, as the waters of Marah by the hands of Moses, our teacher, and as Miriam from her leprosy, and as Hezekiah from his sickness, and as the waters of Jericho by the hands of Elisha. And as Thou hast turned into blessing the curse of Balaam, the wicked one, so turn all my dreams for me to good.' And let him finish with the priests, that the congregation may say, 'Amen.' And if not, let him say thus: 'Mighty One in the heights, Who dwellest in strength, Thou art peace, and Thy name is peace. May it please Thee to dispense to us peace.' " The next one began, and said: "If any one enters into a city, and is afraid of the evil eye, let him take the thumb of his right hand into his left, and the thumb of his left hand into his right hand, and let him say thus:

'I, such an one, the son of such an one, descend from the seed of Joseph, over whom an evil eye can have no power, as it is written (Gen. 49:22), "Joseph is a fruitful bough, even a fruitful bough by a well," and so on.' " Read not: "by a well" but "transcending the eye."[19] Rabbi Jose, the son of Rabbi Chaninah, said: "From this (Gen. 48:16), 'And let them grow' (like fishes).[20] As fishes, which inhabit the waters, are covered by them, and no evil eye has power over them, so also the seed of Joseph, no evil eye has power over it. But if he is afraid of his own evil eye, let him look on his left nostril." And the third commenced and said: "If any one is sick, let him not make it known the first day, lest he make his fate worse. But after that and onwards let him make it known. So it was with Raba when he was ill, the first day he did not make it known. From that and onwards he said to his servant: 'Go outside, and cry, Raba is sick; he that pitieth me, let him ask for me pity, and he that hateth me, let him rejoice over me.' " And it is written (Prov. 24:17, 18), "Rejoice not when thine enemy falleth, and let not thine heart be glad when he stumbleth: lest the Lord see it, and it displease Him, and He turn away His wrath from him."

Samuel, when he had seen an evil dream, said (Zech. 10:2): "For the idols have spoken vanity, and the diviners have seen a lie, and the dreams speak false things." And when he saw a good dream he said: "And should dreams indeed speak falsehood seeing it is written (Num. 12:6), 'I will speak in a dream to him?' " Raba asked: "It is written, 'In a dream I will speak to him;' and it is written, 'And dreams speak falsehood.' "

That is no question—for the one is by an angel and the other by an evil spirit.

Rabbi Bisna, the son of Sabda, said, Rabbi Akiba said, Rabbi Panda said, Rabbi Nahum said, Rabbi Birim said in the name of an aged man—and who is he? Rabbi Banah: "There were four-and-twenty interpreters of dreams in Jerusalem. Once I dreamed a dream, and I went before them all, and what the one interpreted to me the other did not interpret to me, and yet all were fulfilled to me, in order to fulfil what is written, 'All dreams go after the mouth.' But is this Scripture, 'All dreams go after the mouth?' " Yes, and according to Rabbi Elasar. For Rabbi Elasar said, "Whence this, that all dreams go after the mouth?" Because it is said (Gen. 41:13), "And it came to pass, as he interpreted to us, so it was." Raba said: "But this only, if he interpret to be according to the contents of the dream, as it is written (Gen. 41:12), 'To each man according to his dream he did interpret;' (Gen. 40:16), 'And the chief baker saw that the interpretation was good.' " Whence did he know it? Rabbi Elasar said: "This teaches, that each one of them saw the dream and the interpretation of the dream of his companion."

Rabbi Jochanan said: "If one rises, and a verse comes into his mouth, behold this is like a little prophecy." And Rabbi Jochanan said: "Three dreams are fulfilled—a morning dream, a dream which one's companion has dreamed, and a dream which is interpreted in the middle of the dream" (or by a dream). And some say also, a dream which is repeated, as it is said (Gen. 41:32), "And for that the dream was doubled," and so

---

[19] There is a play here upon the words.
[20] Another play upon the words.

on. Rabbi Samuel, the son of Nachmeni, said, Rabbi Jonathan said: "Nothing else is shown to a man but what is in the thoughts of his heart." For it is said (Dan. 2:29), "As for thee, O king, thy thoughts came into thy mind upon thy bed." And if thou wilt, I shall say: from this (Dan. 2:30), "That thou mightest know the thoughts of thy heart." Raba said: "Thou canst know it, for there is not shown to a man either a golden palm tree, nor an elephant going through the eye of a needle."…

Folio 56 a.—The son of Hedja was an interpreter of dreams. If any one gave him a reward, he interpreted his dreams for good; if any one did not give him a reward, he interpreted for evil. Abaje and Raba saw a dream. Abaje gave him a *susa,* and Raba gave him nothing. They said to him: "We read in the dreams (Deut. 28:31), 'Thine ox shall be slain before thine eyes,' etc." To Raba he said: "Thy business will be ruined, and thou shalt have no desire to eat from sorrow of thy heart." To Abaje he said: "Thy business will be extended, and thou shalt have no desire to eat from the joy of thy heart." They said to him: "We read (ver. 41), 'Thou shalt beget sons and daughters,' and so on." To Raba he said: "They will be taken captive." To Abaje he said: "Thy sons and thy daughters shall be many, and hence thy daughters shall be married outside the land, so that they will seem to thee as if they had been led captive." "We read (ver. 32): 'Thy sons and thy daughters shall be given unto another people.'" To Abaje he said: "Thy sons and thy daughters shall be many. Thou shalt say, to thy relatives (thou wilt wed them), but she (thy wife) shall say: to her relatives, and she will induce thee, that thou wilt give them to her relatives; which are like another

nation." To Raba he said: "Thy wife shall die, and her sons and her daughters shall come under the hands of another wife." For Raba said, Rabbi Jeremiah, the son of Aba, said, Rav said: "What is it that is written: 'Thy sons and thy daughters shall I give to another nation.' That is, the wife of the father (step-mother)." "We read in the dreams (Eccles. 9:7): 'Go, eat thy bread with joy.' " To Abaje he said: "Thy business shall be extended, and thou shalt eat and drink, and read the verse in the joy of thy heart." To Raba he said: "Thy business shall be ruined, thou shalt kill, but shalt not eat nor drink, and shalt read for the sake of comforting thyself."…

In the end Raba went alone to him. He said to him: "I have seen that the inner house-door has fallen." He said to him: "Thy wife shall die." He said to him: "I saw that my molar teeth and my teeth fell out." He said to him: "Thy sons and thy daughters shall die." He said to him: "I saw that two doves flew away." He said to him: "Two wives shalt thou divorce." He said to him: "I saw two heads of cabbage." He said to him: "Two boxes on the ears shalt thou swallow." Raba went on that day and sat in the academy all the day. Then he found two blind men who quarrelled with one another. Then Raba went to separate them, and they struck Raba twice; they lifted up to strike another time, and he said, "Hold, I have seen only two."

In the end Raba came and gave him a reward. He said to him: "I saw that the wall fell." He said to him: "Property without limits shalt thou obtain." He said to him: "I saw the Palace of Abaje that it fell, and its dust covered me." He said to him: "Abaje shall die, and his chair shall come to thee." He said to him: "I saw my own palace that it fell, and then the whole world came and took brick by brick." He said to him: "Thy teaching shall spread through the world." He said to him: "I saw that my head was split and my brain came out." He said to him: "The wool of thy pillow shall come out." He said to him: "I read the Egyptian Hallel in the dream." He said to him: "Miracles shall be done for thee." He went with him upon a ship. He said: "To a man for whom miracles shall be done, what is the use of this?" As he ascended, a book fell from him. Raba found it, and saw that there was written in it: "All dreams go after the mouth." He said to him: "Wicked One, upon thee it depended, and thou hast much afflicted me. Everything I forgive thee, except about the daughter of Rabbi Chisda (who was his wife). May it be the will (of God), that this man be given over into the hands of the government, who have no pity upon him." He said: "What shall I do? for it is ordered, that the curse of a sage, even if it come causeless, shall happen. How much more is this the case with Raba, who has judged me with justice." He said: "I will go and emigrate, for the master said, 'Banishment expiates sin.' " He arose and emigrated to the Romans. He went and sat down at the door of the head treasurer of the king. The head treasurer saw a dream. He said to him: "I saw a dream, that a needle went into my finger." He said to him:

"Give me a *susa*;" but he gave him nothing, and hence he said nothing at all to him. He said to him: "I saw that a worm fell upon two of my fingers." He said to him: "Give me a *susa*;" but he gave him nothing, and he did not say anything at all to him. He said to him: "I saw that a worm fell upon my whole hand." He said to him: "A worm has come into all the garments" (of the king). They heard this in the house of the king, and they brought the head treasurer in order that they might kill him. He said to him: "Why I? let him be brought who knew it and did not say." They brought the son of Hedja. He said to him: "On account of thy *susa* have been spoiled the garments of the king." They bound two cedars with rope, and tied one foot to one cedar, and the other foot to the other cedar, and let go the ropes, so that his head was split; for each cedar went back and stood in its place, and he was split and fell in two.

[And so the interpretation of dreams goes on for other two and a half folio pages. These three specimen extracts may suffice to give examples of the indifferent, the good, and the absurd, which constitute the Talmud. They will show the necessity of discrimination, and how readily the Talmud, as a whole, may be either decried by enemies or unduly exalted by a judicious selection of passages.]

ANALYSIS OF CONTENTS

INDEX

INDEX TO SCRIPTURE REFERENCES